"When reformers talk about multicult[...] mention religion. For the last four cent[...] dered quite as much controversy as gend[...] contention shows no sign of diminishin[...] approaches. In this wide-ranging, even-handed, and vivid [...] clears away myths, analyzes episodes of accommodation and conflict in the past, and illuminates how public education can incorporate religion as part of cultural democracy."

—David Tyack, Vida Jacks Professor of Education
and Professor of History,
Stanford University

"Between Church and State is a bold and courageous book that speaks the truth by placing religion in its appropriate historical and cultural spaces in our multicultural society. Fraser's well researched work tells the stories of how different generations of diverse Americans have struggled with the controversial principle of separation of church and state. No longer resigned to let religion be the tool of the conservative right, he has given us permission to include religion in the expression of our cultural identity. Most importantly, he has challenged our democratic society to become more inclusive, respectful, and tolerant of our increasingly diverse citizenry. This book is a must read for all teachers, teacher educators, and policy leaders."

—Jacqueline Jordan Irvine,
Candler Professor of Urban Education,
Emory University

"Fraser's voice speaks with understanding and compassion. This book explores ways in which a democratic society deals with issues of religion in the public schools. Fraser makes the claim that these institutions must be places where tolerance is built and diversity is respected. These values are particularly relevant to all citizens who are willing to engage the social reality of pluralism and who also respect the convictions of religious faith practice."

—Joseph C. Williamson,
Dean of Religious Life and Dean of the Chapel,
Princeton University

"At the core of Fraser's argument is the need for embracing diversity—a position that is reflected in the most progressive versions of multicultural education. Fraser speaks eloquently against the forces of balkanization, separatism, triumphalism, and absolutism that are on the rise throughout the United States. Instead he calls for an ecumenical and democratic culture that is able to move beyond mere tolerance to informed dialogue. This book will do more than touch a partisan nerve, it will force us to sit down and reflect deeply on the most urgent issues that both divide us as a nation and offer us a way to rethink and reunite our communities."

—Peter McLaren, Author of *Schooling as Ritual Performance*,
and Professor, Graduate School of Education
and Information Studies,
University of California at Los Angeles

BETWEEN CHURCH AND STATE

Religion and Public Education in a
Multicultural America

James W. Fraser

St. Martin's Griffin
New York

ISBN 0–312–23339-6

Library of Congress Cataloging-in-Publication Data

Fraser, James W.
Between church and state : religion and public education in a
multicultural America / James W. Fraser.
    p. cm.
  Includes bibliographical references (p.) and index.
  ISBN 0–312–21636–X (cloth) 0–312–23339-6 (pbk)
  1. Religion in the public schools—United States—History.
2. Church and state—United States—History. 3. Pluralism (Social
sciences United States—History. I. Title.
LC111.F68 1999
379.2'8'0973—dc21   98–55303
                                                            CIP

First published in hardcover in the United States of America in 1999
First St. Martin's Griffin edition: August 2000
10 9 8 7 6 5 4 3 2 1

In memory of three great educators:

Lawrence A. Cremin
Paulo Freire
Kenneth Haskins

CONTENTS

ACKNOWLEDGMENTS

THIS BOOK OWES ITS EXISTENCE to two friends who insisted I write it. My longtime friend and former colleague, Nancy Richardson, associate dean at Harvard Divinity School, extended an invitation for me to discuss this topic at Harvard. After some reluctance I agreed, and the result was a seminar on religion and public education, which I taught at the Divinity School in the fall of 1997. In the midst of my teaching that seminar, a new friend, Michael Flamini, senior editor at St. Martin's Press, responded to my enthusiasm for the conversations taking place in my class with a proposal that I publish a book on the same topic. *Between Church and State* is a result of the support and persistence of these two friends.

I am deeply grateful to the faculty and staff of Harvard's Divinity School for their welcome while I taught there. Most of all I am grateful to all of those students from the Divinity School, the Graduate School of Education, the Kennedy School of Government, and the Law School who participated so enthusiastically in our mutual efforts to understand this complex and difficult issue. Our conversations and their research are reflected throughout this volume. For fourteen weeks that fall we were able to model the kind of thoughtful, engaged, and respectful society that is essential if more light and less heat is to be brought to this difficult topic. I want to acknowledge the crucial role that each of them played in this work. They are: Michele Bagby, Kristin Barstow, Christopher Burr, Nell Carlson, Albert Chevez, Lorraine Claassen, Lucy Conroy, Brendan Cullen, Cathleen Dennison, Jeremy Dutchman, Mark Farha, Valerie Forti, Leslie Gelsleichter, Delia Gerraughty, Richard Grenell, Joshua Howard, Asbury Jones, Angela Lee, James Oliver Lee, Patricia Lyons, Jacob Montwieler, Peter Niemeyer, Sandra Platt, Tonya Robinson, Deborah Sabin, Christine Sandoval, Elizabeth Sclater,

Regis Shields, Bethany Shull, Margaret Sommerfeld, Carrie Stambaugh, and Gail Tatum.

Every book takes a toll on all of life's other activities. I appreciate the support of many friends and colleagues who have put up with missed deadlines and unreturned telephone calls. At Northeastern University presidents John A. Curry and Richard M. Freeland and deans Robert P. Lowndes and James Stellar supported my need to take time away as did my many colleagues in the Center for Innovation in Urban Education, especially the assistant director, Angela Irving. As with previous publications, Elizabeth Wallace's research and editorial assistance has been indispensable. This is our third book together and I am very grateful for her commitment. Eliza Garfield of the Harvard Graduate School of Education has been a thoughtful and engaged critic throughout the development of this book. My friends at Grace Church in East Boston have been a constant source of encouragement, friendship, and sanity. No book can be written without family support, and I have been richly blessed by Britney, by my daughters Madison, Kaitlin, Rebecca, and Megan, my son-in-law Robert, and by my beloved wife, Katherine.

Finally, research and writing on the topic of religion and education has returned me to my own earliest roots as a scholar. In writing this book I have been reminded of my deep intellectual debt to my extraordinary teachers at Columbia University, Lawrence A. Cremin, Robert T. Handy, Robert W. Lynn, and Douglas M. Sloan. All four are cited in this book, but all four shaped me and my thinking about these issues far more deeply than the limited citations in the text imply.

INTRODUCTION

IN THE LAST HALF DECADE OF THE TWENTIETH CENTURY, students in DeKalb County, Alabama, with the support of the state's governor, boycotted classes while demanding the right to have prayers in their schools. A school board in Fort Myers, Florida, fired the superintendent and the board's own lawyer because both seemed to be dragging their feet in implementing a program to study the Bible in the schools. The Wisconsin state Supreme Court approved a program in which families in Milwaukee could use state-funded vouchers to attend private religious schools. The National Academy of Sciences bemoaned the fact that, because of political pressure, many high school science classes skip over the study of evolution. And, tragically, in the fall of 1997, a high school student in Kentucky killed three of his classmates while shooting into a crowd of praying students. At about the same time, the U.S. Supreme Court overturned a congressional action called the Religious Freedom Restoration Act as well as one of its own decisions so that teachers supported by federal funds could again offer their services inside parochial and other private religious schools. A majority of members of the U.S. House of Representatives voted in favor of the Religious Freedom Amendment to the Constitution. Clearly the proper relationship between religion and the public schools of the nation is a pressing issue to many of the nation's citizens.

Those who thought that the issues of religion in the schools had been solved some time after the battles over evolution in the 1920s, or after the Supreme Court's decisions in the 1960s banning formalized prayer and Bible reading, have clearly turned out to be mistaken. The United States enters a new century with its citizens deeply divided, sometimes confused, and often angry about their differing opinions about the proper place of religion in the public schools of the nation and the current legal mandates regarding the relationship of religion and public education. Different citizens often are unhappy in different ways. But one thing is very clear: a consensus does not exist. And a thoughtful observer can be relatively certain that battles about church and state, and more specifically about religion in the schools, are going to be characteristic of the first decades of the new millennium as they have been for the last two centuries.

Americans have always disagreed about the proper relationship of religion and the public schools, but they have disagreed differently at different points in the nation's history. The European colonial settlers generally believed that the schools should teach the faith of the established church, but they argued passionately and violently over which religion should be established. After the American Revolution, with the question of a formal religious establishment for the United States generally resolved in the negative, a new split emerged between those who saw the need for a civic religion that could hold a diverse citizenry together, and who argued that the school was the perfect means to secure this civic religion, and those many others who feared that the new establishment would trample on their unique faith as much as a formal state church might have in the past. By the end of the nineteenth century, these splits had shifted so that much of the nation's elite was in agreement regarding the broad terms of a "civic religion"—although they might not use that term—and growing minorities, including most Roman Catholics, many Jews, and an emerging group of Protestant fundamentalists, who felt themselves to be clearly excluded from the consensus. The end of the twentieth century has seen yet another new development as the consensus that served for so long has itself become unglued in the tensions of a diverse nation attempting to come to terms with its new diversity—diversity of race, faith, and worldview. This volume seeks to place the contemporary crisis in the nation's approach to church-state or religion and public education debates in a historical and cultural context in order to shed more light and less heat on the debates that are sure to follow.

It has become popular in some communities in the United States to say that, somewhere between the Supreme Court decisions banning prayer and Bible reading in 1962 and 1963 and the political and cultural turmoil of the latter part of that decade, "God was kicked out of the public schools in the 1960s." In response, in other communities, there is an equally popular charge that the Christian right is engaged in a campaign to impose God on public schools whose purposes have always been secular. Both charges show an amazing lack of historical understanding. And both charges are unhelpful if the United States is to function as a tolerant, intellectually informed, and dynamic democracy in the twenty-first century. The purpose of this volume is to make a small contribution toward the kind of understanding that will make the latter a reality.

God's place within the public schools of the United States has been debatable, and subject to controversy, for as long as there have been public schools. In colonial America, religion played a central role in the schools of every colony, but the understanding of religion differed substantially from colony to colony. With the coming of nationhood and the separation of church and state on the federal level, the public school was pressed into service as a new kind of national church, commissioned to create and carry the common culture and morality of the nation. Since citizens differed dramatically in their definitions of this culture and morality, and especially since newly arrived Catholics, newly freed African Americans, and newly conquered Native Americans all had still other ideas, the content of the nation's common creed—and especially the appropriateness of its more overtly religious dimensions—was a subject of fierce debate and continuing change throughout the nineteenth century.

By the end of that century, due as much to exhaustion as any thoughtful will, schools had dropped the more obviously religious— and generally Protestant Christian—trappings of the school faith, replacing them with a generic commitment to democracy reinforced by a set of patriotic symbols, including flags and flag salutes and the omnipresent pictures of George Washington and Abraham Lincoln. Some religious symbols—Bible reading and prayer in a minority of states, Christmas carols and pious references in most communities— continued well into the twentieth century. Moments of crisis developed from time to time over the teaching of evolution—most dramatically in the 1920s but continuing in future decades, over federal aid to religious schools in the 1940s, 1950s, and 1960s, and over the deeply symbolic issues of prayer and Bible reading in much of the latter half of the century. By century's end, most public schools are pretty secular places, but the debates about what is appropriate in these most public of institutions are as heated as ever.

At the end of the twentieth century, the United States is a much more diverse place, ethically and culturally as well as ethnically and religiously, than at any previous time. The mid-twentieth-century description of the nation's people as Protestant, Catholic, Jew has been expanded to include practitioners of ancient Native American traditions, immigrant and native Hindus, Muslims, Taoists, and Buddhists, and a new generation, many of whom include a rich amalgam of many creeds in their personal worldview. And of course, many Americans in every generation carry on their social and personal lives with no association with any religion of any kind and are quite content to remain that way. To say that the nation is more secular or more religious misses the point. At the dawn of the new millennium the peoples of the United States are more secular, especially in their public culture, more religious, in many different private forms, and more diverse than ever before in the nation's history.

All of this leads, of course, to the central question of this book: How should a diverse and democratic society deal with issues of religion in the public schools? This volume begins to answer that incredibly complex question with two strong assertions. First, the discussion of the ways to deal with religion in the schools is not served by nostalgia for a simpler past that never was or by a historical amnesia that often assumes that the solutions "when we were in school" worked then or can work now. Only a careful and thoughtful historical analysis of the many different ways that different generations and different citizens have approached these questions in the past can inform a current debate that must be rich, nuanced, and filled with intellectual curiosity and compassion.

Second, if the United States is to survive and thrive in the twenty-first century, the nation's schools must be places for embracing and building tolerance and a love of diversity. Tolerance alone is not enough if it means a single dominant culture that allows certain forms of dissent as long as they stay within bounds. The American revolutionary hero Thomas Paine was right when he said: "Toleration is not the opposite of intolerance, but it is the counterfeit of it. Both are despotism, the one assumes to itself the right of withholding liberty of conscience, the other of granting it."[1] That was the tolerance of most eighteenth-century schooling, and it was not sufficient then or now for a democratic society. But there is another kind of tolerance, one that enthusiastically embraces diversity, is truly based on the beliefs that all of us are smarter than any of us and that all citizens have much to teach each other and much to learn from each other. This is the tolerance that is celebrated in multicultural education at its best.

Multiculturalism too can degenerate into a kind of exotic study of many different cultures. But a commitment to multicultural education, and a multicultural nation is a commitment to a society in which many different cultures survive and thrive and are encouraged, and in which representatives of these different groups each make their own contribution to a larger common culture that is more vibrant for what all of them bring. Such an approach has allowed schools to attend well to issues of race, culture, class, and gender. It is by far the best way for schools to attend to issues of religion also. If religion can be added to the multicultural agenda, along with race, class, gender, then there is hope of transcending some of the nation's longest-running and most bitter school wars. And there is hope that schools can truly be what John Dewey envisioned, a microcosm and an incubator of a larger democratic society which is "worthy, lovely, and harmonious."[2]

Framing the discussion of religion in the schools in the context of multiculturalism enriches our understanding of multiculturalism and provides a framework for discussing religion—and religious differences—that is both informed and respectful. Religion is a fundamental part of most cultures. Efforts to understand different cultural traditions without attention to their religious roots invites a shallowness unhelpful to true cultural understanding. At the same time, far more than with race or gender, individual people make individual decisions about their own faith and their ways of understanding the sacred. This dimension of choice adds important complexity to the larger discussion of multiculturalism. Using the lens of multiculturalism to approach the teaching of religion in the schools provides an extraordinarily helpful means of approaching religion. During the last two decades, advocates of multicultural education have found ways to approach some of our society's most divisive issues with new levels of respect and tolerance while also insisting that the sometimes hidden dimensions of power and control are understood and dealt with properly. This same approach is exactly what is needed in our approach to religion. Religious symbols— whether prayers, Christmas carols, or readings from sacred texts—can be a means of asserting the power of a dominant culture over others when used inappropriately in school. On the other hand, the very same symbols, when approached by students seeking to understand difference with respect and insight, can be a means of vastly enriching the school's curriculum.

Too often school people, especially liberals and progressives, have responded to the issue of religion in schools by hoping for absolute silence. Acting more like Victorian prudes in the face of a reference to sex than true progressives, they have not embraced the potential of religious difference and discourse. Prior to the 1960s, many school leaders took this same approach to issues of race and sex. They seemed to say, "Maybe if we never mention the subject we will be okay." This continues to be the approach to religion in far too many schools at the end of the twentieth century. Yet this approach is not helpful. The child who is militantly secular or an atheist, or who is a Protestant fundamentalist, or who is Unitarian, a conservative Catholic, Muslim, Janist, Buddhist, Adventist, Presbyterian, or Jew, or any one of so very many other traditions; each must be welcomed not only as a person with an equal right to respect and a public education but as a citizen who has his or her own unique contribution to make to the school and to the society, a contribution which every other child will be poorer if they fail to understand.

This multicultural approach to religion is very different from the lowest-common-denominator Christianity sought by school leaders of the nineteenth century. It is also very different from the deafening silence on issues of religion that many school officials of the late twentieth century have sought, avoiding religious references one by one when there was any chance of offending anyone, creating a situation that the Catholic school historian Neil McCluskey has rightly described as a religious vacuum in which, "only the child from a secularist family can feel perfectly at home in the common public school."[3] While religion should never again be introduced into the common public school in a way that will make a secular child one bit less welcome, it should be vigorously welcomed in ways in which children of all faith traditions will be equally at home and in which all will be wiser for what they have learned.

Taking a multicultural approach to the issue of religion in the schools will not be easy. It will certainly not always be comfortable for students or especially for teachers and parents. Differences can be disquieting and frightening. This approach also makes certain theological assumptions. For practitioners of a creed that demands absolute and unquestioning obedience to authority, the notion that there is something to learn from others—even while holding fast to one's own faith—is anathema. If people believe they are right and everyone else is wrong, what do they have to learn from others? But such absolutism is the basis of all inquisitions—whether of the Spanish Catholic type, Stalinist atheist type, or Iranian Islamicist type. No religious tradition has been without its militant fanatics. But a democratic society must reject militant fanaticism. At the same time, it must not reject strongly held beliefs. The point of a school approach to religion in which everyone learns from everyone else is not a dilution of belief or a slow movement toward a common faith. The goal is rather a common democratic culture in which a diversity of citizens, each holding their own creed with passion and wisdom, respects other citizens who hold other creeds, or no creed, with equal passion and—it is hoped—equal wisdom. The goal is an American democracy that is both religiously tolerant and religiously informed. What higher goal could the public schools of a society that aspires to democracy have regarding the topic of religion?

ONE

From Holy Commonwealth
to the Strange Compromise of 1789

FOR THE MOST PART, COLONIAL EUROPEAN SETTLERS did not
come to England's North American colonies seeking religious freedom writ large. The majority who came for religious reasons came for
the freedom to practice their own form of religion and to impose it on
all other residents of their colony. And when they founded schools,
which most of them did rather quickly, they expected the schools to
raise up the next generation in the faith of the established church,
whether it was the Congregationalism of Puritan Massachusetts or
the Anglicanism of Virginia or the Dutch Reformed tradition of New
Netherlands. This situation is not surprising. In the Europe from
which these settlers came, the notion of anything more than a
grudging tolerance for other forms of faith, or the notion that either
church or state could survive a separation, existed only among a few
radicals on the very margins of society. In the early 1600s, when
serious North American colonization began, no state had actually
tried separating religion and government or conducting schools in
any way separate from religious authority; none would do so for
another two hundred years.

Of course, Europeans were not the only people in the colonial
mix in the 1600s. The European immigrants arrived on a continent
whose indigenous residents had highly developed forms of both faith
and government. Soon after their arrival, the Europeans also began
importing African slaves, adding yet another set of cultural and
religious traditions to the North American mix. In time, as later
chapters will show, the Native American and African forms of

spirituality interacted with European traditions in a multitude of ways. The American religious scene cannot be understood without paying serious attention to the contribution of indigenous American, African, and more recently Asian traditions as well as those of European Christianity, Judaism, and Enlightenment secularism. And these diverse contributions had powerful implications for the relationship of religion and education. The conflicts between the traditions and the understanding of the contributions of each one generally came later. From the beginning, the Europeans brought not only Christianity but also gunpowder and leg irons. They meant to dominate the culture and they had the power to do so. When schools first began in the colonies, European concerns about shaping the culture, ways of passing that culture to a new generation, and the best institutions for doing so were clearly dominant. This institutional domination continues to the present.

If people do not believe in the separation of church and state, if people have as a goal a homogeneous society united in faith, morals, and forms of government, then the relationship of religion and public education is quite simple—for the notion of religion and the notion of the public are one. And so it was in most of the colonies of British North America for most of the 1600 and 1700s. Thus the earliest schools in Massachusetts taught youth to read using *The New-England Primer*, which taught the alphabet from "In Adam's Fall, We sinned all" right through to "Zacheus he did climb the Tree, Our Lord to see." As with any good text, the subsequent reading lessons grew in complexity from The Lord's Prayer, to stories of Puritan martyrs in England, to the Westminster Catechism.[1]

For the New England Puritans, education was essential to faith. Rejecting, as they did, any intermediary of church, bishop, or priest, each believer needed to make his or her own peace with God, and he or she needed intelligence and therefore education to do so. Thus it should not be surprising that the famous 1647 law requiring a school for every town in Massachusetts began: "It being one chief project of that old deluder, Satan, to keep men from the knowledge of the Scriptures. . . ." Being practical, the authors of the law also moved quickly to counter Satan. The next sentence read, "It is therefore ordered, that every township in this jurisdiction, after the Lord hath increased them to the number of fifty householders, shall then forthwith appoint one within their town to teach all such children as shall resort to him to write and read."[2] Five years earlier the colony's legislature passed another law also requiring that every parent and master of indentured servants ensure that all children in the household were taught "to read and understand the principles of religion and the capital laws of the country."[3] The Puritans of Governor John Winthrop's holy City on a Hill clearly intended to include schools in their city. And the curriculum of these schools, equally clearly, included Puritan piety as surely as it did reading, writing, and arithmetic.

In the 1600s Massachusetts, more than the other colonies, had a significantly structured civil society, including churches and schools—what one of its leading ministers, Cotton Mather, called "the evangelical church-state."[4] The Massachusetts Puritans were never as intolerant as their latter-day detractors have portrayed them, but they were single-minded in their commitment to pursue their own form of church and state—religion and school—and their tolerance never extended to any who might challenge that polity.

Even before the first Puritan migration to New England, the first General Assembly in Virginia in 1619 ordered all ministers to "read divine service, and exercise their ministerial function according to the ecclesiastical laws and orders of the Church of England," setting the stage for an Anglican/Episcopal state church that would continue in Virginia up to the time of the Revolution. Anglican clergy had arrived with others settlers in Virginia as early as 1610, although the continued efforts of the local gentry to ensure that no bishop was ever appointed meant that the ecclesiastical system always remained incomplete. And Virginia's dispersed settlements meant that education would always be less structured than in Massachusetts. Nevertheless there were requirements that parents and masters send their children to religious instruction and that church officials present "such masters and mistresses as shall be delinquents in the catechizing the youth and ignorant persons" with substantial fines. The law seems to have been honored as often in the breach as not, but the legislature's concern for rudimentary education was clear.[5]

The separate colonies of Connecticut and New Haven adopted laws patterned on the Massachusetts model in 1650 and 1655 respectively. With the English takeover of New York from the Dutch in 1674, the new laws included similar requirements that parents ensure the literacy of all children and servants in their households.

Finally, Pennsylvania adopted an ordinance in 1683 providing that all parents and guardians of children "shall cause such to be instructed in reading and writing, so that they may be able to read the Scriptures and to write by the time they attain to twelve years of age; and that when they be taught some useful trade or skill, that the poor may work to live, and the rich, if they become poor, may not want." Enforcement of the laws varied, and the focus shifted between the practical and the scriptural. The different colonies clearly empha-sized different elements of scripture that tended to prove the correctness of their particular interpretation of Christianity. But all of these heirs of the English reformation continued a significant part of their inheritance, the clear belief that it was their responsibility to raise youth in the correct—read their own—interpretation of the one true faith and guard them against the errors that might be taught in the other colonies.[6]

Throughout the colonial era, the different colonies carried on their own versions of church, state, and school. Distance from England and from each other allowed them to continue their differ-ent ways. However, with the Declaration of Independence from England and the creation of the new nation, a new crisis was also created. While Massachusetts and Connecticut could have their well-established and state-supported Congregational churches, while Pennsylvania could work out its own complex relationship between Quakers and non-Quakers, while the Church of Virginia could comfortably be the Church of England—with the nearest bishop carefully kept a safe 3,000 miles away across the Atlantic—none of these models quite worked for the new nation created by the rebellion and union of these thirteen quite different colonies.

At the time of the Constitutional Convention in 1789, no nation known to the framers had separated religion from the state's respon-sibilities. At the same time, the notion of adopting any one of the churches from the various colonies was fraught with problems, not the least of which was the degree to which such a move would alienate the other colonies and their churches. While there were at least some among the Congregationalists, Presbyterians, and Episco-palians who believed that their church would make an ideal state church for the new nation, not enough representatives of any one party could carry the day. And everyone's second choice—far prefer-able to the selection of someone else's sect—was a far stronger separation of church and state than the world had yet known. Thus there was relatively little objection in 1789 when the framers of the Constitution included Article VI stipulating that "no religious test shall ever be required as a qualification to any office or public trust under the United States," or two years later when Congress included in the First Amendment to the new Constitution a fairly hard line on the church-state issue with the sentence: "Congress shall make no law respecting an establishment of religion, or prohibiting the free exercise thereof."[7]

In the framer's minds there were few options. During the debates surrounding the adoption of the Constitution and the Bill of Rights, there was almost no opposition to the radical disestablishment included in the final documents. Of course, individual states could maintain their state church, as Massachusetts did until 1833. Only with the Fourteenth Amendment in 1868 were the protections of the Bill of Rights applied to the states, and not until *Everson v. Board of Education* in 1947 did the U.S. Supreme Court specifically apply the establishment clause to state legislatures. Ironically, only in the last half century has the debate about the meaning of the First Amendment been fought out at the level of the U.S. Supreme Court. But that is getting far ahead.

Generations of Americans have grown up with a simpler story line. For a century school children have learned that the earliest European immigrants came to these shores for religious freedom. A sampling of most Americans today, regardless of region, gender, race, or class, would give similar answers; religious freedom is seen as a significant part of the bedrock on which this country was founded. But reality is not nearly so simple.

A COLLECTION OF HOLY COMMONWEALTHS

The great mid-twentieth century religious historian, Sidney Mead, has provided a convincing if significantly more complex view of the emergence of religious freedom in North America. For most of Christianity's 2,000-year history, certainly from the time of the Roman emperor Constantine's conversion in the fourth century A.D. until the Protestant Reformation in the sixteenth, church and state were seen as one entity living out God's preordained order for the temporal world. The Reformation broke Europe's religious unity forever, but not before almost two centuries of warfare, as Catholics and Protestants of various persuasions—Lutheran, Calvinist, and others—fought to return the continent to what they saw as God's unifying design. While issues of a growing nationalism, cultural and territorial differences, and nascent capitalism all played into Europe's post-Reformation wars, the right to determine the religion of the state was dominant and few voices spoke for tolerance of other religious traditions. If there was a one true faith—however much people differed about the contents of that faith—then alternatives to that faith must, by definition, be wrong—and why tolerate error?

By the mid-1600s, not long after the first permanent European settlements in North America, Europe arrived at an exhausted peace. The Peace of Westphalia in 1648 and a number of similar treaties and concessions created a new model for the continent in which different nations and territories would each define the one true faith within their boundaries. Within each realm a single faith would dominate, chosen for the most part by the secular leader of the land. So Germany's different duchies and small kingdoms were divided up, some Protestant and some Catholic. Lutheranism reigned in Scandinavia; Calvinism in Switzerland, Scotland and the Netherlands; while Roman Catholicism was the faith of Spain, France, and the different parts of Italy. As Mead correctly described the arrangement: "Each of these groups claimed within its territory religious absolutism. All the dominant groups believed in and demanded religious uniformity within their civil commonwealth enforced by the civil power. In this situation religious fervor combined with patriotism to tinge the relationships between rival groups and individuals with suspicion, fear, and hatred."[8] And rivalry, suspicion, fear, and hatred were all transported to the European colonies in the Americas, especially in North America, where a far greater variety of Europeans arrived than in South America, which was dominated by Catholic Spain and Portugal.

Thus the colonists, whom generations of schoolchildren have learned came for religious freedom, came for a very narrow kind of freedom. With rare exceptions, such as the Baptist followers of Roger Williams in Rhode Island, the colonists came seeking religious freedom for themselves and the right to persecute—or at least banish—anyone who did not share the colony's faith. The compromise of the Peace of Westphalia was thus transported to the new world. Different colonies could have different faiths, but within any one colony a single faith was as obvious a necessity as a single set of laws and form of government. But this arrangement was not to last.

In their early years, most colonies enforced a uniformity at least as strict as had occurred in their homelands. Early Puritan intolerance in Massachusetts and Connecticut has been legendary, but it was also real. Those on the other side of the English civil wars, the Anglican Royalists, who settled in Virginia were only marginally more tolerant. The Virginia Charter of 1606 required that "the true word and service of God and Christian faith be preached, planted, and used . . . according to the doctrine, rights, and religion now professed and established within our realm of England," which meant state support for Episcopal priests and the Episcopal liturgy of the *Book of Common Prayer.*[9]

The non-English colonies of North America had similar policies. French Canada was Catholic. Dutch New Netherlands, later New York, included in its 1640 charter a proviso that "no other religion shall be publicly admitted in New Netherlands except the Reformed, as it is at present preached and practiced by public authority." The governor of Sweden's short-lived colony came with instructions to "take good measures that the divine service is performed according to the true confession of Augsburg, the Council of Upsala, and the ceremonies of the Swedish church."[10]

These instructions were not idle words. Massachusetts banished Anne Hutchinson and many others over the years when they differed with the established faith. Governor Peter Stuyvesant moved forcefully against Lutherans, Jews, and Quakers when he discovered them in New Netherlands, sending the Quakers back to Holland as quickly as possible.

Exceptions have been important in building the mythic self-image of the United States. Lord Baltimore did establish religious tolerance in his Maryland colony as a means of protecting his own beleaguered fellow English Catholics. William Penn and his Quakers were far more tolerant than the Presbyterians who shared the land of Pennsylvania with them. And Roger Williams and the Baptists who founded Rhode Island actually spoke as if they believed in religious freedom for all, although for this they were widely distrusted by most of the other colonists who shared what fast became British North

America with them.[11] Yet within little more than a century and a half of Rhode Island's founding, the polity of this small colony became the national model. Again, Mead's analysis is correct:

> What had been accepted as an axiom by all respectable Christian thinkers for about fourteen hundred years and transplanted to America as the guiding intention of the dominant groups was almost completely overthrown in the short span of one hundred and eighty years. The great experiment of religious freedom on a national scale, which Protestants in America now sometimes defend as the traditional way of doing things, has actually been tried for less than two hundred years.[12]

And, nice as the story line would be, the experiment did not come from a growing embrace of the kind of tolerance advocated by the founders of Rhode Island, Pennsylvania, or Maryland. Rather, its roots were far more prosaic.

Seventeenth- and eighteenth-century Europe was dominated by many issues besides religion. And when the struggle for empire or new and emerging forms of nationalism collided with religious absolutism, absolutism often lost. Thus, in spite of Peter Stuyvesant's efforts to cleanse New Netherlands of all but Dutch Calvinists, the authorities in Holland would not support him. Their instructions to him were clear: Stop banishing others lest "you intend to check and destroy your population." The new colony needed people if it was to survive. So Stuyvesant was ordered to "let everyone be unmolested, as long as he is modest; as long as his conduct in a political sense is irreproachable; as long as he does not disturb others, or oppose the government."[13] The last clause was clearly the most important. And so, in spite of its intolerant governor, the settlement at the base of the Hudson became a haven for a wide assortment of Christians and Jews.

The end of the English civil wars and the restoration of the monarchy under Charles II in 1660 meant that the Anglican polity was triumphant in the homeland of the British colonies, but it was a more tolerant Anglicanism than had existed before the wars. If Charles could keep his head and his throne by tolerating Presbyterians, Congregationalists, Baptists, and other assorted Protestants, he certainly meant to do so. And the newly restored king lost little time in ordering his Congregationalist colony in Massachusetts Bay to end its persecution of Quakers or in giving the Baptists of Rhode Island full freedom despite objections from their northern neighbors. Well before 1700, then, the intolerance with which most of the colonies had begun was over. Not all sects were embraced, not all were equal in the eyes of the law or their neighbors, but punishments and legal disabilities were at an end. Religious toleration, sometimes grudging and sometimes more open, was the rule of eighteenth-century Britain in both the old and new worlds. Still, it was a long way from tolerance of dissenters to equality of all religions in the eyes of the law. Although tolerance continued to expand gradually in Britain in the nineteenth century, with the last disabilities for Catholics ended in midcentury, England still has a state church, and the monarch still receives the crown—the ultimate symbol of authority—at the hands of an Episcopal bishop.

RELIGIOUS FREEDOM BY ACCIDENT

The United States took a different route from the moment of the nation's beginning. As we have seen, full religious freedom and equality came to the new nation because it was everyone's second choice. While the heirs of the Massachusetts Puritans still hung on tightly to their Congregational polity at the time of the Revolution, they met in the Continental Congress with representatives of New York who were heirs of both the Reformed Dutch and of later English settlers, Presbyterians from the middle colonies, and Anglicans from the South. Since it was clear from the beginning that no one group could get a majority vote for its own faith as the established church of the new and already diverse nation, all factions reluctantly agreed that religious toleration was preferable to the establishment of someone else's church. Everyone wanted religious freedom for themselves, and the only way they saw to get it was to grant it, however grudgingly, to others. Thus religious freedom came to the new United States not by ideology or design but by compromise and accident.

While the various religious communities that dominated the political landscape never formulated a clear rationale for the religious freedom that they embraced as a necessary expedient, they were not the only voices on the political scene in the late 1700s. Although they had only limited numbers of followers for their religious—as opposed to their political—views, secular disciples of John Locke and the Enlightenment philosophy, such as Thomas Jefferson and James Madison, did have a carefully worked out rationale for religious disestablishment. And as Mead also argues, the First Amendment to the U.S. Constitution is a product of a temporary alliance of the many religious minorities in the new nation with these representatives of the Enlightenment deist intellectual classes. It was an alliance that did not last. The religious groups quickly turned their attention to the new enterprise of building their competing denominations and battling with each other, with their former Enlightenment allies, and in most of the nineteenth century with new Roman Catholic immigrants, for the souls of the nation's citizens. As a result of all these shifting alliances, the only group to have worked out a careful rationale for religious freedom, the Jeffersonian deists, were quickly outnumbered and overwhelmed by many competing voices for the nature of American religiosity. Yet the deists' rationale remains the primary one, however few defenders it has had in subsequent generations.[14] The major builders of religious freedom as it actually has been practiced in the United States for the last 200 years, the representatives of the different religious groups that became America's nineteenth-century denominations, have never worked out their own clear rationale for the polity on which so much of the nation's religious, political, and educational life is based.

The ideological, as opposed to the political, battles over religious freedom in the revolutionary era were centered in Virginia. At the time of the Revolution, Virginia had the same Episcopalian establishment as it had when it was first chartered in 1607, although there was widespread tolerance of other sects. But tolerance was not sufficient for Virginia's most articulate revolutionary leaders.

In 1783, in the midst of the American Revolution, James Madison authored his Memorial and Remonstrance, arguing that the legislature of the Commonwealth of Virginia, if it was serious about its support of independence and freedom, needed to apply the ideology of freedom to its own religious institutions. Madison's ally, Thomas Jefferson had already introduced legislation in Virginia's legislature calling for religious freedom. He wrote:

> Well aware that the opinions and belief of men depend not on their own will, but follow involuntarily the evidence proposed to their

minds; that Almighty God hath created the mind free, and manifested his supreme will that free it shall remain by making it altogether insusceptible of restraining; that all attempts to influence it by temporal punishments, or burthens, or by civil incapacitations, tend only to beget habits of hypocrisy and meanness, and are a departure from the plan of the holy author of our religion, who being lord both of body and mind, yet chose not to propagate it by coercions on either, as was in his Almighty power to do, but to extend it by its influence on reason alone.[15]

The legislation separating religion from government includes some significant theological assumptions with which many in Jefferson's day or today might disagree. Individual reason alone has hardly been the major carrier of faith for many. Nevertheless, after years of debate, the bill for establishing religious freedom passed the Virginia Assembly in 1786, ending the colony's 180 year Anglican religious establishment and placing all religious bodies of the state on an equal footing—free of state influence and wholly dependent on the resources they could raise from the voluntary contributions of their members and friends rather than state government tax dollars. It was an extraordinary step in the experiment of separating the worlds of sacred and secular authority, and the full implications of the change would continue to be explored long after Jefferson and Madison had passed from the scene.

As president, Jefferson continued to voice similar views. Thus in 1802, after one year in the White House, he wrote to the Danbury Baptist Association of Connecticut:

Believing with you that religion is a matter which lies solely between man and his God, that he owes account to none other for his faith or his worship, that the legislative powers of government reach actions only, and not opinions, I contemplate with sovereign reverence that act of the whole American people which declared that their legislature should "make no law respecting an establishment of religion, or prohibiting the free exercise thereof," thus building a wall of separation between Church and State.[16]

Few lines of presidential correspondence have entered the nation's language as firmly as Jefferson's description of the First Amendment to the Constitution as "a wall of separation between Church and State." Debates about how seriously to take this one letter, which have become numerous, miss the point. Jefferson, perhaps the nation's most truly secular president, always represented a minority view on questions of religion.

During his last year in office, Jefferson again noted the clear line he drew between the civil government and the various religious groups of the nation. Differing from his predecessors—and successors—he declined to call for a national day of fasting and prayer. For him that was a matter for religious groups: "I consider the government of the US. as interdicted by the Constitution from intermeddling with religious institutions, their doctrines, discipline, or exercises. . . . Every religious society has a right to determine for itself the times for these exercises, & the objects proper for them, according to their own particular tenants; and this right can never be safer than in their own hands, where the constitution has deposited it."[17] For the nation's third president, the line was very clear indeed.

However much the careful logic of Jefferson, Madison, and their allies provided ideological cover for one of the nation's great accidental decisions, the separation of church and state has served both churches and the rest of the nation well. Separation of church and state has been adopted by many other nations around the world and has moved in 200 years from a radical experiment to being seen as one of humanity's most basic rights. But in part because of its origins in compromise, in part because it came about in a unique historic moment, many of the deepest implications of America's lively experiment have never been fully explored. And most basic among these implications are those related to education. So again Mead is right: "Perhaps the most striking power that the churches surrendered under religious freedom was control over public education which traditionally had been considered an essential aspect of the work of an established church if it was to perform its proper function of disseminating and inculcating the necessary foundational religious beliefs."[18]

For most of Europe's history, the state conducted education as an arm of the church, ensuring that the young were brought up with a knowledge of both proper doctrine and proper behavior as defined by those doctrines. But what would happen in the new nation? Were elements of a common faith similar enough that the state could conduct schools to teach them without offending the differing religious bodies? Was there a common secular or democratic faith on which all could agree? And who would define it? These questions have never been fully answered. Indeed they have been a source of struggle in almost every succeeding generation. And at no time were the debates more intense than in the early years of the Republic when Horace Mann and his many allies and opponents created the public schools as we know them.

Creating an American Common School and a Common Faith: Horace Mann and the Protestant Public Schools, 1789–1860

IN THE MIDST OF THE AMERICAN REVOLUTION, when future president John Adams wrote a new Constitution his home state of Massachusetts, he included a provision for requiring the cities and towns to provide for "the public worship of God and the support and maintenance of public Protestant teachers of piety, religion, and morality" in the schools. He further elaborated the need for schools to inculcate all citizens in "Public and private charity," "industry and frugality," "honesty and punctuality." For Adams, the Revolution did not mean the fall of the Congregational Standing Order in his home state and it certainly did not mean that Massachusetts would cease to be a Christian commonwealth. In this arena, Adams was not unique in his views. In 1787 the federal Congress, working under the Articles of Confederation, adopted the Northwest Ordinance which stated "religion, morality, and knowledge being necessary to good government and the happiness of mankind, schools and the means of education shall forever be encouraged." For most in the revolutionary generation, religion, schools, and good government were inextricably linked. The adoption of the First Amendment to the U.S. Constitution four years later hardly ended the debates about the proper relationship of religion and the public schools of the new nation.[1]

Until the Civil War the constitutional separation of church and state clearly applied only to the federal government. The First

Amendment was clear: *"Congress* shall make no law." The individual states were free to make laws respecting an establishment of religion, and while Madison, Jefferson, and their allies had been successful in securing a state-level separation of church and state in Virginia in 1786, New England remained a holdout well into the nineteenth century.

The most sustained post-revolutionary fight over the separation of church and state took place in Connecticut early in the nineteenth century. An alliance of Baptists, Methodists, Anglicans, Jeffersonian Democrats, and others began to challenge that state's Congregational establishment. Although Connecticut had long since stopped any form of legal discrimination against other religious groups, the Congregational clergy and lay leaders fought back, seeking to maintain their state financial subsidies and their recognized rank as the "official" religion of the state. Finally, in 1818, they lost and the Congregational Church in Connecticut was officially disestablished, joining the other denominations as an equal partner, dependent as the others were on the voluntary contributions of its own members rather than state tax revenue. It took more than a decade for the two remaining holdouts, Massachusetts and New Hampshire, to follow the Connecticut model, but once Connecticut had fallen, the fight went out of the Congregational leadership and it was only a matter of time before they all gave in.[2]

Ironically, New England was not only the last bastion of a state religious establishment in the United States, it was also the national seedbed of schools. In his home state, Jefferson was wonderfully successful in getting the legislature to enact his Enlightenment notions of the proper relationship of religion and the state into law, just as he was successful in gaining at least modest support for his University at Charlottesville. But the wide dispersion of Virginia's population on rural plantations and the racial divide between its population, white and black, free and slave, meant that no meaningful support for public schooling would take place there until after the Civil War. The North was different and it is important to turn to New England to understand the post-disestablishment relationship of religion and public education in the new United States. It was left to a generation after the founding fathers to work out what sort of education might be appropriate in a newly secular society.

HORACE MANN AND THE NEW COMMON FAITH

Horace Mann's name remains inextricably linked with public schools throughout the United States. This is not inappropriate. In his twelve years, from 1836 to 1848, as secretary of the Massachusetts state Board of Education, Mann did more to define the role and purpose of public schools (or common schools, as he called them) in the new nation than any other American. Mann clearly understood the tensions that had been created for educational institutions once the church and state had been firmly separated. In his valedictory report as secretary of the board in 1848, Mann described the tensions which the new school system faced. He recognized, first, that the United States was embarked on a new experiment; that most nations with which he and his fellow citizens were familiar had agreed on a system of government in which "the regulation and control of the religious belief of the people [are seen] to be one of the functions of government, like the command of the army or the navy, or the establishment of courts, or the collection of revenues," and that this system "with very few exceptions, has prevailed throughout Christendom, for fifteen hundred years." But the United States had chosen a different route. "Our own government is almost solitary example among the nations of the earth, where freedom of opinion and the inviolability of conscience, have been theoretically recognized by law." Writing in 1848, five decades after the French Revolution had offered another more militantly secular option, which he chose to ignore, Mann was nonetheless correct regarding most of the history of the western world for the last millennium and a half. In this arena, the United States truly was a *novus ordo seclorum.* The meaning of this new order for the schools was yet to be clarified when Mann began his work in 1836, three years after Massachusetts became one of the last states in the union to end its own religious establishment. Mann's role was to give definition to the new order.[3]

Mann believed he knew exactly how this should be done. He felt that common schools should provide "religious education" of a general and tolerant nature. The goal of this religious education was a deeply democratic "free agent." The school's role was to lead the individual child to an informed and free choice regarding which form of religion, if any, might be appropriate later in life. So Mann argued:

The elements of a political education are not best owned upon any school child for the purpose of making him vote with this or that political party, when he becomes of age; but for the purpose of enabling him to choose for himself, with which party he will vote. So the religious education which a child receives at school, is not imparted to him for the purpose of making him join this or that denomination, when he arrives at years of discretion, but for the purpose of enabling him to judge for himself, according to the dictates of his own reason and conscience, what his religious obligations are, and whither they lead.[4]

A more democratic approach, Mann believed, was impossible to imagine.

During his twelve year tenure as the first secretary of the new Massachusetts state Board of Education, Mann was also a very active evangelist for his vision of schooling and of the proper relationship of religion to the schools. Mann's office had virtually no real authority. The board, and its full-time secretary, could collect information and write reports about the schools, but it had no policymaking role. All authority continued to reside with the individual city and town school committees, or in some cases with the state legislature. But Mann made brilliant use of his reporting authority. In his careful annual reports, which were publicized throughout the United States and Europe, in continuing visits and speeches around the state and the world, he used his bully pulpit to instruct and to convert.

In spite of the risks and uncertainty associated with the new venture of religious freedom in education, Mann knew just what he wanted to have. If the schools of Massachusetts assured that every student heard the Bible read, "without note or comment," if all interpretation was left to "the pulpits, the Sunday schools, the bible classes, the catechisms, of all the denominations, to be employed according to the preferences of individual parents," then a solution to the problem of appropriate religious instruction was at hand. The details of the different sects would be left to those sects and their members. But the core of religion, the heart of Christianity, would be alive and well in the schools. And who could complain? Certainly this did not mean that the schools were irreligious or unchristian. Mann insisted, "The bible is the acknowledged expositor of Christianity. In strictness, Christianity has no other authoritative expounder." The problem was solved:

> If the bible, then, is the exponent of Christianity; if the Bible contains the communications precepts, and doctrines, which make up the religious system, called and known as Christianity; if the Bible makes known those truths, which according to the faith of Christians, are able to make men wise unto salvation; and if this Bible is in the schools, how can it be said that Christianity is excluded from the schools; or how can it be said that the school system, which adopts and uses the bible, is an anti-Christian, or an un-Christian system?[5]

From Mann's perspective, everyone should be pleased.

Of course, happy as Mann was with the solution, not everyone else agreed. Mann tended to ignore criticism, and when he did attend to it, he dismissed his critics quickly. They did not appreciate, "our noble system of Free Schools for the whole people," and instead favored, "that rival system of 'Parochial' or 'Sectarian Schools'" which a few in Massachusetts and far too many in other states were proposing as an alternative to Mann's vision of a single system of schools common to all. To his critics, Mann's easy solution to the vexing problem of what religion, if any, to teach in the schools was embedded in his failure to understand the degree to which he was really proposing to make the public schools of Massachusetts a kind of Unitarian parochial school system that would mirror his own deeply held Unitarian beliefs.

Mann's own conversion to Unitarianism was hard won. He had grown up in the small town of Franklin, Massachusetts, under the strict Orthodox Calvinism of Nathaniel Emmons. Emmons, whose influence was spread far in New England because of the large number of the next generation of clergy who had "read divinity" with him in the years before the first theological seminaries were established, was a proponent of the strictest forms of Calvinism, including strict predestinationism and a heavy emphasis on original sin. For the young Horace Mann, growing up attending a meeting house where these creeds were the regular fare, there were important times of soul-searching. But the soul-searching did not result in the conversion for which Emmons longed in all his parishioners. As Mann recalled years later, "I remember the day, the hour, the place and the circumstances, as well as though the event had happened but yesterday, when in an agony of despair, I broke the spell that bound me." Mann's words have the ring of conversion, but it was a conversion that rejected what Mann saw as Emmons' angry faith. In its place, "I began to construct the theory of Christian ethics and doctrine respecting virtue and vice . . . I still retain."[6] Mann moved from Franklin to a college career at Brown University followed by study at Tapping Reeve's famous law school in Litchfield, Connecticut, and then a move to a far more cosmopolitan part of the state in Dedham. From Dedham, the young lawyer followed a not unusual career path when, in 1827, he was elected to represent the town in the Massachusetts legislature. His political career was checkered but highly successful, and it was as president of the State Senate in 1836 that Mann first supported the bill to create a state board of education and then resigned from the Senate to become its first secretary.

Not everyone in Massachusetts agreed with Mann's vision of the kinds of schools needed for Massachusetts and the nation, especially what seemed to be Mann's commitment to using the schools to establish a kind of genial Unitarian faith. Disagreement took many forms. While Mann himself tended to see his opponents as either anti-education or narrow-minded bigots, they were, in fact, a much more diverse group. Some who were troubled by the faith which Mann wanted in the schools were heirs of Mann's old nemesis, Nathaniel Emmons. Trinitarian Calvinism, in more or less orthodox forms, was alive and well in Massachusetts. The disestablishment of the Congregational churches in 1833 had finalized the internal split within the old Puritan churches between the Unitarians and the more orthodox Trinitarians. While most churches in the greater Boston area were taken over by Unitarian majorities, leaving the more orthodox to form new assemblies, the opposite occurred in the more rural parts of the state. The Trinitarians were the majority and the Unitarians were left to found their own new meeting houses. To staunch Trinitarians the thought of the Unitarians taking over the schools was not pleasant.

However, by the 1830s, Massachusetts was much more diverse than a focus on the internal battles of the old establishment would imply. The Episcopal church was growing rapidly. Many people were joining with what had once been solely southern and western denominations such as Methodist and Baptist. Roman Catholics, traditionally a tiny minority in this Puritan stronghold, were just getting the first infusion of Irish immigrants that would make them the majority in Boston, if not in the state, by the Civil War. And plenty of Massachusetts residents wanted none of any of the traditions. Free thinking and antireligious sentiment was alive and well in many parts of the state. While Mann preferred to blame all opposition on the rigidly orthodox, his opponents were much more diverse. In fact, one of the most careful studies of Mann's opponents concludes that "representatives from towns whose schools used bibles or whose school committees included members of the clergy were less hostile to the board of education than legislators from communities whose schools did not use bibles or did not have ministers on their school boards."[7] Not everyone, it seems, agreed that reading the Bible in the schools, even without note or comment, was a good idea.

Mann's opponents came closest to success during his third year as secretary. In 1840 the Committee on Education of the Massachusetts House of Representatives recommended abolishing the state board and the office of secretary. The recommendation was framed with a clear statement that the committee did not want to be seen as anti-education (a charge Mann made over and over again). The report insisted: "But, since our system of public schools did not owe its origin to the Board of Education, but was in existence for two centuries before that Board was established, a proposal to dispense with its further services cannot be reasonably considered as indicating any feelings of hostility or of indifference towards our system of Common Schools."[8] But there were other reasons for abolishing the board. The Democratic majority in the 1840 legislature (Mann was a Whig) distrusted most efforts to centralize what were traditionally local issues. They warned, "In France or Prussia [two models which Mann cited often], the smallest bridge cannot be built, or any village road repaired, until a central Board has been consulted."[9] Who wanted that sort of bureaucracy in Massachusetts' education?

Bureaucracy and cost were not the only problems with the board, however. Mann's opponents were worried about what he saw as his central mission: creating moral citizens. So they warned:

> Your Committee [has] already stated, that the French and Prussian system of public schools appears to have been devised, more for the

purpose of modifying sentiments and opinions of the rising generation, according to a certain government standard, than as a mere
means of diffusing elementary knowledge. Undoubtedly, Common
Schools may be used as a potent means of engrafting into the minds
of children, political, religious, and moral opinions;—but, in a
country like this, where such diversity of sentiments exists, especially upon theological subjects, and where morality is considered a
part of religion, and is, to some extent, modified by sectarian views,
the difficulty and danger of attempting to introduce these subjects
into our schools, according to one fixed and settled plan, to be
devised by a central Board, must be obvious. The right to mold the
political, moral, and religious, opinions of children, is a right
exclusively and jealously reserved by our laws to every parent; and
for the government to attempt, directly or indirectly, as to these
matters, to stand in the parent's place, is an undertaking of very
questionable policy.[10]

Mann's grand design clearly offended these Democrats.

One thing that most bothered this group of Mann's critics was his
effort to have the state board create a library in every school in the
state. The critics did not object to the support for books per se, but
to the centralized board's selection of a certain list of books. They
understood, as Mann and his allies never seemed to, that a board
dominated by Unitarians could not avoid using the book selection
process to impose their creed on others.

It is professed, indeed, that the matter selected for this library will
be free both from sectarian and political objections. Unquestion-
ably, the Board will endeavor to render it so. Since, however,
religion and politics, in this free country, are so intimately con-
nected with every other subject, the accomplishment of that object
is utterly impossible, nor would it be desirable, if possible. That
must, indeed, be an uninteresting course of reading, which would
leave untouched either of these subjects; and he must be a
heartless writer, who can treat religious or political subjects, without affording any indication of his political or religious opinions.
Books, which confine themselves to the mere statement of undis-
puted propositions, whether in politics, religion, or morals, must be
meager, indeed.[11]

The authors of this now long forgotten report stated mo[re?]
than many in later generations the real tensions that mak[e]
resolution of the proper relationship of religion and the schools
impossible. Mann's sunny resolution of the issue simply does not
work. Generations of students have been subjected to boring textbooks that have tried for a neutrality which is "meager indeed."

The committee's recommendations failed when they came to a
vote in the legislature. Mann served for another nine years until
being elected to Congress as an abolitionist to fill the seat left open
by the death of John Quincy Adams. The Massachusetts state Board
of Education continues to the present. The debates of the 1830s and
1840s are with us still. Horace Mann understood better than most of
his contemporaries that in a nation without a single established
church, some new institution needed to step in to fill the void. Some
force had to continue the process of shaping and carrying the
common culture and morality if there was to be a unified people. And
what better to fill the role than an institution that had long been an
arm of the church, the common school? But if the school was to teach
the elements of a common faith, who would decide what those
elements would be? The legislature's fight with Mann in the 1840s
was really a struggle between those who wanted a state agency to
make the determination and those who argued that it should be left
to localities and their individual school committees. There is little in
the history of this nation to indicate that local institutions are more
protective of individual rights than state or federal institutions. But
schools will not work if every individual parent selects the curriculum
for her or his child. And all higher levels of authority have the
potential to be oppressive. There is, indeed, no easy solution.

GROWING UP TOGETHER:
COMMON SCHOOLS AND MIDWESTERN CULTURE

While, much to Horace Mann's frustration, the struggle about the
relationship of religion and the schools was a major issue during his
tenure, there was far less controversy about the topic once one moved
West. And it was in the west of the great Mississippi Valley, in the
settlement of what is now known as the Midwest, that the common
school took hold most firmly as an instrument of education and as a
means of creating a civic religion for the new nation.

In 1832, four years before the creation of the Massachusetts Board of Education and Mann's election as its first secretary, another Massachusetts resident, fifty-seven-year-old Lyman Beecher, resigned as pastor of Boston's Hanover Street Trinitarian Congregational Church, left behind his long struggle with New England Unitarians, and moved to a position as president of the newly created Lane Theological Seminary in Cincinnati, Ohio. Beecher took with him his daughters Catharine and the more famous Harriet and his son-in-law Calvin Stowe (Harriet's husband). These leaders provided much of the nucleus of the campaign to build public schools in Ohio. Others with similar goals labored in Michigan, Wisconsin, Illinois, and the rest of the Midwest to create a system of public schools that ensured that the rising generation of the nation's youth would be well versed in reading, writing, arithmetic, and an evangelical Protestant version of civic religion.[12]

For Lyman Beecher the public schools as they developed in the American midwest were an essential element in his larger campaign to Christianize the nation in the tenents of his ecumenical and evangelical Protestantism.[13] Many of those who worked to make public schools a reality were collaborators or students of Beecher's. And when they needed a spokesperson for their cause, these school leaders often drew on the doughty old Yankee who had traveled west to save the nation's soul. In an important sense, the schools were a part of his agenda.

Of course, many channels led to the creation of the public schools in the nation's heartland. There were few Unitarians west of the Hudson, and Beecher's battles with the followers of Horace Mann's religion were not repeated in the West. More conservative and doctrinaire Protestants, who often battled with Beecher on theological grounds, joined forces with him when it came to the schools. While Congregationalists and Presbyterians—liberals and conservatives—Methodists, Baptists, and Episcopalians all had significant differences when it came to church issues, for the vast majority, support of the public schools was a unifying feature.

In the 1960s American historians, led by Timothy Smith and David Tyack, rediscovered the role of evangelical Protestantism in the founding of public schools.[14] Protestant missionaries provided the major energy behind the creation of the school system in many states. And they did so sure in the conviction that the schools would help spread their notion of the right form of civil religion for the nation. Correcting a view developed by an earlier generation of school historians, David Tyack has pointed out that the assumptions that "secularization meant progress" and that "schooling should be secular, public in support and control, and managed by professionals" were more a result of polemical view of a much later generation of educational professionals than of careful historical analysis of the development of schools, especially on the western frontier.[15] The professional historians could also have been corrected, as another historian Robert Lynn has noted, by many Americans who every morning sent their children to the public school, and who believed, "in the inherent and inevitable harmony of public education and the Protestant cause."[16]

Timothy Smith has also shown that Protestant support for the public schools as they were developing in the 1830s and 1840s was based on "a new religious synthesis, one which would give members of the diverse sects a common Faith."[17] And this religious synthesis was being built by the evangelicals themselves. Thus as the frontier opened in Ohio and farther west, "Missionaries attempted to provide a Protestant paidea for settlers on the frontier: a total education through the common school, sectarian academies and colleges, Sunday Schools, the pulpit, religious reading, and a number of formal and informal associations."[18]

Ministers and their lay allies in the evangelical movement enthusiastically worked for the development of public schools, especially west of the Alleghenies, because of their confidence in the Protestant nature of the public school movement. They did not intend these schools to be secular in any twentieth-century meaning of that word. Rather, they believed that evangelical Protestants could work together across a limited range of denominational lines to create a national culture in which they would all be comfortable. As Timothy Smith noted, they represented "an evangelical consensus of faith and ethics [which] had come so to dominate the national culture that a majority of Protestants were now willing to entrust the state with the task of educating children, confident that education would be 'religious' still."[19] Or as Calvin Stowe put it: "These are facts which show plainly, that notwithstanding the diversity of sects, there is common ground, on which the sincerely pious of all sects substantially agree."[20] Of course, the "sincerely pious" did not include

Catholics, more creedal Protestants such as Lutherans, many of the Baptists and Methodists, or the considerable numbers of free thinkers and atheists. For Stowe and most of his allies, including in many ways Horace Mann, all of these people were beyond the national consensus and more in need of conversion than serious consideration. Understanding the roots of the public schools in this evangelical consensus is essential in order to comprehend the hurt and anger of many in the late twentieth century who feel that they have lost "their" schools. While schools gradually became much more secular in the decades between Stowe's era and the end of the twentieth century, for many the confidence that, as Timothy Smith has argued, there was an "inherent and inevitable harmony of public education and the Protestant cause," has been hard to surrender.[21]

When the public schools were being created in the nineteenth century, most of those doing the institution building were confident that "Schools and churches were allies in the quest to create the Kingdom of God in America."[22] In this effort "from the Alleghenies to the Pacific . . . evangelical clergymen spread the gospel of the common school in their united battle against Romanism, barbarism, and skepticism."[23] The key to rescuing people from the grasp of these evils, the preachers believed, was moral education and assimilation into the American, Protestant consensus. So Lyman Beecher wrote: "Let the Catholics mingle with us as Americans and come with their children under the full action of our common schools and republican institutions, and the various powers of assimilation, and we are prepared cheerfully to abide the consequences."[24] Beecher also had a fairly good sense of what the consequences would be. A commitment to a diversity in which each learned from each and each respected the other was not at the heart of his agenda. For him, and for many who followed him, Americanism and Protestantism were inseparable.

In one of his many speeches on schooling, Calvin Stowe, who was professor of Bible at Beecher's Lane Seminary, voiced his fear of native "barbarians" and immigrant Catholics—that is, almost anyone who disagreed with the Beechers and Stowes of this world. Such fear helped fuel the commitment to schooling in Protestant morality. "It is not merely from the ignorant and vicious foreigner that danger is to be apprehended. To sustain an extended republic like our own, there must be a national feeling, a national assimilation; and nothing could be more fatal to our prospects of future national prosperity than to have our population become congeries of clans, congregating without coalescing, and condemned to contiguity without sympathy."[25] Thus modern critics of multiculturalism and diversity are clearly not the first to voice such fears.

With his colorful language, Stowe was pointing beyond mere moral education to the need for schools to be institutions for building community. The evangelicals and their allies in the school-founding business were never concerned merely with individual morality and rectitude. "Whether building a church or a school, the clergy led those who chose community rather than individualism."[26] Their ultimate concern, after all, was not merely law and order but a community of people united by a common memory and a common hope in the new nation. Morality was a first step, but assimilation was the goal. Timothy Smith has noted that their goal was "the emergence of a national identity that was not simply religious, but distinctively Protestant. Its vision of the future was not the heavenly city of the eighteenth-century enlightenment, but the New Jerusalem of the Christian millennium."[27] Jefferson, Madison, and other seekers of the enlightenment's heavenly city might have been the first to give voice to a new polity in which the churches did not control any state function, especially education, but Smith is right. Those who actually built most of the nation's school systems were far more focused on the New Jerusalem of the Christian millennium. No wonder that this nation has had such difficulty resolving the proper relationship between schools and matters of faith. Different people, with radically different goals, were involved in building the institutions from the beginning.

Many Americans, east and west, shared Stowe's fear of increased immigration. He often spoke of this concern: "It is altogether essential to our national strength and peace, if not even to our national existence, that the foreigners who settle on our soil, should cease to be Europeans and become Americans."[28] Few asked whether the immigrants wanted this sort of assimilation. In Stowe's view, it was not for Germans, whether Protestant or Roman Catholic, or for Catholics from any country to consider holding to the traditions that had supported them in the past. The school leaders were sure that such traditions would lead only to the nation's becoming "an unconsolidated mass."[29] The goal was to make them Americans in the image of such people as Beecher, Stowe, and their allies. And the common schools would induct all into the common culture. Through his speeches, Stowe quickly became known as something of an authority on immigration and assimilation.[30]

In addition to assimilation, of course, this seminary professor was always focused on the place of religion in education. In a brief pamphlet, "The Religious Element in Education," Stowe expanded on his ideas that religious instruction "without violating any of the rights of conscience" was possible in the schools so long as they contained the common elements of all Christian faiths and excluded only that which was unique to each. Sounding very similar to Mann, Stowe insisted that moral education in the schools was to be religious but undenominational. As for those who objected to even this much religion in the schools, Stowe dismissed them with the comment, "A man who has no conscience, certainly has no right of conscience to be violated."[31]

The text for religious instruction in the schools which all people of good will could agree upon was the Bible. In words that anticipated Horace Mann by several years Stowe wrote: "The Bible, the whole Bible, and nothing but the Bible, without note or comment, must be taken as the text-book of religious instruction. Instruction in those points which divide the sects from each other must be confined to the family and the Sunday school."[32] Here was a common faith around which middle-class Protestant America could rally.

By far the best known of Stowe's writings on public schooling was his *Report on Elementary Public Instruction in Europe*, based on his travels there in the summer and fall of 1836.[33] Stowe returned in January 1837 and made his report to the Ohio legislature. Regarding the moral nature of education in Prussia he reported: "Every teacher whom I consulted, repelled with indignation the idea that moral instruction is not proper for schools; and spurned with contempt the allegation, that the Bible cannot be introduced into common schools without encouraging a sectarian bias in the matter of teaching; an indignation and contempt which I believe will be fully participated in by every high minded teacher in christendom."[34] Stowe also saw other advantages in Prussian educational theory. Like Mann, who had also traveled there, and had based his ideal educational system for Massachusetts on schools he had visited there, Stowe saw his German counterparts as allies in the effort to use the schools as the primary incubator of a common Christian culture.

Catharine Beecher was an equal participant with her father and brother-in-law in the issue of school reform. Fresh from her work at the Hartford Female Seminary, Catharine traveled west with her father in 1832, intending to share with him the task of rearing educational institutions there.[35] She attended meetings of the Western Literary Institute with the rest of her family.[36] She also began the Western Female Institute, "a school dedicated not merely to the 'technical acquisition of knowledge,' but to 'mental and moral development.'"[37]

Catharine Beecher's most significant contribution to the common school movement was her leadership in encouraging the belief that elementary teachers should be women and that teaching was a uniquely acceptable profession for women.[38] In 1835 she wrote "An Essay on the Education of Female Teachers" in which she asked: "What is the most important and peculiar duty of the female sex? It is the physical, intellectual, and moral education of children. It is the care of the health, and the formation of the character, of the future citizen of this great nation."[39] Combining the traditional belief in women's mothering and domestic role with recognition of the need for people to staff the new schools, Catharine Beecher was creating a new image for women and for the teaching profession. For her, opening teaching to women would provide an important new level of freedom for many women like herself whose lives were highly constrained by the social mores of the early nineteenth century. At the same time, by offering the services of her sisters at lower salaries than those paid to male teachers, she made the expansion of schooling popular because it was cheap. In her own generation, the teaching profession in the United States shifted from being predominantly male to overwhelmingly female.[40]

During the next decade, Catharine Beecher worked to implement her ideas through the National Board of Popular Education, an agency she founded in 1843. Like the benevolent societies in which her father had played such an important role, the National Board would use money and recruits from the East to exert an educational and moral influence on the West. Young women recruited from the Atlantic seaboard would be trained by qualified educators and sent to assigned posts in the western frontier. There they would open schools and at the same time exert moral leadership in building a Christian, Protestant civilization.

A letter from one woman who had been sent out through a parallel Baptist society illustrates the task undertaken by these teacher-missionaries. "For nearly a year I was the only professor of Christianity in town. The weight of responsibility resting upon me has at times pressed sorely . . . I sometimes felt all the anxieties of minister, sabbath-school teacher, superintendent, and teacher of day school combined."[41] In time, others would follow. But in many frontier communities the first professional was the teacher sent out by the National Board or one of its successor or parallel societies.

Many people besides the Beecher clan were involved in building Ohio's common schools. One was Samuel Lewis, a Methodist minister and school reformer. Through the efforts of many like him, the Ohio legislature was convinced to create the office of state Superintendent of Common Schools in 1837, only a year after Mann's secretaryship was created in Massachusetts. As Mann had been the obvious choice for Massachusetts, once the office was created in Ohio, the next logical step was to appoint Lewis to the post.[42] He served for only three years until ill health forced him to retire. In the three annual reports he wrote, Lewis' words reflected the feelings of an era when faith in the common school was being formed.

Like most of his contemporaries, Lewis began his work with the presupposition that the school was first of all a moral influence. In a statement that could have come from any one of a number of his contemporary school builders he wrote: "It can not be too deeply impressed on all minds, that we are a Christian, as well as a republican people; and the utmost care should be taken to inculcate sound principles of Christian morality. No creed or catechism of any sect should be introduced into our schools; there is a broad, common ground, where all Christians and lovers of virtue meet."[43] Like Mann or Beecher or Stowe, Lewis never seemed to realize the degree to which the school was being used to re-create a Protestant religious establishment.

Ohio's Methodist superintendent also defined the common school in ways remarkably similar to Mann. In his third report Lewis wrote: "Unless the Common Schools can be made to educate the whole people, the poor as well as the rich, they are not worthy the support of the patriot or the philanthropist."[44] The common schools were not merely for the common people, they were to be common to all of the people, rich as well as poor, for only in that way could a united nation be created out of the diverse people in the land. The support of the rich had to be cultivated so that they too would use the common schools. But little attention was given to cultivating the good will of the poor or people of color. Non-white residents were never considered, while white immigrants were considered to be essential to the process, whether they wanted to be or not. The school was to bring them into a common culture, one that was defined by others.

Ohio was not unique in the rapid development of a statewide system of common schools in the 1830s and 1840s. Samuel Lewis and Calvin Stowe in Ohio had their counterparts in John Pierce in Michigan and Caleb Mills in Indiana. In the iconography of American schooling, these westerners took their places only a slight notch below Horace Mann from Massachusetts and Henry Barnard in Connecticut in the public school's hall of fame. The fact that all of the westerners were evangelical ministers was missed by most of the early twentieth-century propagandists who sought to describe the heroic efforts to build a secular school system. But for all of their differences about theological details, the midwestern preachers and their political counterparts on the East Coast were all engaged in a very similar effort. They sought to build a generally Protestant Christian America that could function without an established church because its educational institutions were so effective in building and transmitting a common culture that only the minor details had to be left to the different denominational educational efforts.[45]

The common school movement was spectacularly successful in the Midwest. In 1832 Cincinnati had 2,252 students in attendance in the common schools. By 1875 the number had risen to 27,822.[46] The story was duplicated throughout the land for many reasons. However, some recent historians are in danger of implying that evangelical Protestants were the only ones working for public schools when in fact there were many others. The whole system did not emerge full blown from the mind of Horace Mann. But Mann, and many other nonevangelicals, did play an important part in developing popular acceptance of the common school idea. Most school founders were Whigs and Protestants. Democrats distrusted state institutions and taxes. Many Methodists and Baptists and members of smaller religious groups were not sure that they were included in the emerging consensus. And after 1830, the growing numbers of Catholics were quite sure that they were not included, except as subjects ripe for conversion to generalized Protestantism. Too often historians have accepted Beecher's image of the "frontiersmen . . . prey to Satan's wiles,"[47] unless rescued by eastern evangelical aid. People who had been residents of the West a bit longer were constantly correcting him on that point.[48]

Fears about immigration and the general agreement about the need for moral education and assimilation encouraged broad-based cooperation on public school issues. Horace Mann, in no way an evangelical, still believed in the necessity of assimilation through schools which "the children of the entire community may attend."[49] Enough common ground existed among all school proponents to build a broad-based movement.

MCGUFFEY'S READERS:
TEXTBOOK FOR THE COMMON CREED

Perhaps the most consistent element in the mid- to late-nineteenth century common school classroom were the omnipresent *McGuffey's Readers*. According to Timothy Smith those who seek to understand the reader's popularity must examine it in the context of the widespread Protestant embrace of schooling. "Only against this background can one understand the immense popularity of such moralistic schoolbooks as William H. McGuffey's readers. The author knew his buyers well. What men who had established schools and who must approve the textbooks required, and what McGuffey produced, were handbooks of the common morality, testaments to the Protestant virtues."[50]

Tradition has it that when the Cincinnati publisher Winthrop B. Smith was looking for an author for a new series of elementary school texts, he first asked Catharine Beecher.[51] Because she was then heavily involved in her campaign for women's education, she declined, recommending instead William Holmes McGuffey.

If the story is true, it shows perception on Catharine Beecher's part. Representing the small Cincinnati publishing house of Truman & Smith, Winthrop Smith offered McGuffey $1,000 for a primer, a speller, and four readers. The first readers were published in 1836.

McGuffey received his $1,000 and some modest additional royalties. Winthrop Smith became a millionaire.[52]

The *Readers* were an immediate success. Through several revisions and a series of publishers, they sold an estimated 122 million copies between 1836 and 1920.[53] As the historian Henry Steele Commager has pointed out, "part of the greatness of the McGuffey Readers was that they were *there* at the right time—they were *there* to be read by millions of children from all parts of the country."[54] Just as the common school movement was exploding throughout the trans-Allegheny West, and the population was increasing to support the movement, a Cincinnati publisher brought out a textbook ideally fitted to the needs of these schools. Its success should not be a surprise.

McGuffey's Readers reflected American white middle-class Protestant morality as it was circa 1836. They also became one of the major shapers of American morality in the decades ahead. Naturally, they reflected "the notion that education itself was primarily moral." This was something about which the Beechers, father and daughter, Stowe, Horace Mann, and their counterparts across the country clearly agreed. McGuffey seems to have had this notion clearly in mind when he began to write of "The Grateful Indian" or "The Good-Natured Boy," who "took care of his faithful dog as long as he lived, and never forgot that we must do good to others, if we wish them to do the same to us."[55]

Yet it is a mistake to see McGuffey's morality as merely one of individualistic goodness. Robert W. Lynn stated: "Individual rectitude, sound literary taste, the capacity for hard work and success— these goals (so often attributed to McGuffey by latter day observers) constituted an intermediate way station on the road to the *summum bonum* of education. To educate the 'mind and heart of the nation' meant, above all, to form a public, one people out of many."[56] And McGuffey offered the text to accomplish this task.

McGuffey developed this goal of forming a public in many ways. For example in selections from ancient Greek and Roman classics, and modern European and English writers, the students were introduced to a heritage that was reflected more currently in the *Readers'* praise of the Puritans and the Revolutionary heroes. All (even the most recent immigrant from Ireland or Germany) could look to a past when: "Every settler's hearth was a school of independence; the scholars were apt, and the lessons sunk deeply; and thus it came that our country was always free; it could not be other than free."[57] All could share in the common morality and history and faith the books inculcated, one that fit well with a common evangelical and Whig morality.[58] All could learn their place and "take care of the faithful dog." The children also learned to recite the Psalms, "Oh, that men would praise the Lord for his goodness, and for his wonderful works to the children of men!"[59] Citizens were not only to be good; they were to praise a common (Protestant, Christian) Lord. This latter characteristic made Beecher express his pleasure in knowing "that our youth have access to so perfect a series of Reading Books. They are excellent for educational purposes—their religion is unsectarian, true religion—their morality, the morality of the Gospel."[60] McGuffey reciprocated Beecher's enthusiasm.

Given the moral style which McGuffey chose to use, it is not at all surprising that he also should have chosen selections by his fellow Presbyterian minister, Lyman Beecher. In the twentieth century it might seem strange to place Beecher with Shakespeare and Longfellow or Noah Webster or Henry Clay. Yet in his own day it made perfect sense.

The readers began with a very simple morality. In the *First Reader* children read:

Shall birds, and bees, and ants, be wise
While I my moments waste?
O let me with the morning rise,
And to my duty haste.[61]

While greater ability was needed to read Beecher, the selections of his work that McGuffey chose to incorporate into his readers provided equally simple moral lessons. Thus McGuffey used a Beecher temperance sermon in the *New Fifth Reader* to show the dangers of drink. In the sermon, a happy household is led to destitution because of the father's drinking. "And is this, beloved youth, the history of your course? In this scene of desolation, do you see the image of your future selves?"[62]

Questions of individual direction were naturally not the end of the matter for either McGuffey or Beecher. Soon the student moved on to the larger questions presented in Beecher's widely publicized sermon, *A Plea for the West:*

But what will become of the West, if her prosperity rushes up to such a majesty of power, while those great institutions linger which are necessary to form the mind and the conscience, and the heart of the vast world? It must not be permitted. . . . The great experiment is now making, and from its extent and rapid filling up, is making in the West, whether the perpetuity of our republican institutions can be reconciled with universal suffrage. Without education of the head and the heart of the nation, they can not be.[63]

It was neither simple reading nor simple morality. Beecher was issuing a call to make a commitment to the "great experiment" of building a new society in the American land.

As a modern expert on McGuffey's work, John Westerhoff, has shown, the nature of the morality in the *McGuffey's Readers* changed over the years. Comparing the early 1836-37 editions with those published in 1879, Westerhoff concluded, "Calvinistic theology and ethics have been replaced by American middle-class civil religion, morality, and values." Nevertheless, for much of the nineteenth and early twentieth centuries, the *Readers* taught a clearly religious outlook and became objects of almost religious veneration.[64]

CONFIRMING A PROTESTANT CULTURE

For a wide range of white Protestants, the new religious establishment that was created through the common schools in most of the North and West in the 1830s and 1840s served their purposes amazingly well. Different denominations could maintain their unique features. More important, churches and Sunday schools could focus their efforts on the conversion of individual sinners into believing Christians, an enterprise that they did not hand over to the schools.[65] But the vast majority of nineteenth-century American Protestants could happily and safely assign the larger enterprise of building and transmitting an American culture to the common schools, confident that the students were being enculturated in a religious world that was comfortably familiar.

Confirmation of the success of the common school in serving a wide range of Protestant Americans can be found in the failure of one alternative movement. Throughout the 1830s and 1840s, the Presbyterian Church was split between members who adhered to the New

School party, who tended to be at least moderate abolitionists and who favored cooperation with others in a range of enterprises, and those of the Old School, who maintained a glacial silence on the issue of slavery and saw inter-denominational ventures as a serious neglect of their uniquely Presbyterian heritage. In 1844 the Old School Presbyterian General Assembly began considering "the expediency of establishing Presbyterian Parochial Schools" as an alternative to participation in the common school consensus.[66] It was a consistent course for them to take. The Old School had always criticized the New School for the latter's willingness to modify doctrine for the sake of unity with other Protestant groups. They saw that such modifications would only be extended in the public school movement. Naturally they were wary of Horace Mann's advice that they participate in the common schools and then use adjunct schools for teaching their own creed, for they sensed which articles of faith the children would take as primary.[67] Thus they opened their own separate Presbyterian day schools, reminding their churches that "Education is incomplete without instruction in the Scripture and the 'doctrines of grace.' The Assembly desired as near an approach as possible to the method of mingling 'the doctrines of our church with the daily teachings of the school.'"[68] Separating a generalized Christianity and the unique aspects of their own tradition into two different educational institutions did not sit well with these conservative Presbyterians.

In his *Presbyterian Parochial Schools,* Lewis J. Sherrill has provided an excellent study of the experiment. For over twenty years the independent Presbyterian school system persisted. Not all Old School Presbyterians joined in. For example, Cincinnati's Old School leader, Joshua Wilson, who had railed at Lyman Beecher on church issues, joined with his nemesis in support of common schools. But enough did join the parochial school movement to keep the system going for a time. Ultimately, however, the Presbyterian school system failed. Sherrill has given many reasons for the failure, including curriculum and administrative problems. The most important reason, however, was the success of the public school movement in convincing people that it truly represented the public. Most Presbyterians did not want to be set apart. They saw themselves as primarily a part of the American public, with differences small enough to be taken care of in the adjunct institutions of church and Sunday school. The common school worked for them.[69]

Well before the Civil War, a very large number of white Protestant Americans in the North and West had come to see the common school as their educational institution. Historian of religion Winthrop Hudson is right in calling it a new Protestant establishment, for the schools fulfilled many of the roles that had previously been assigned to the established church.[70]

Of course, for this establishment to succeed, it required ignoring significant numbers of people who did not agree. While the Old School Presbyterians could not find enough differences with the public schools to maintain a separate system, more creedal denominations, especially Lutherans, and religious groups for whom the primary language was not English did maintain their own separate religious schools. As will be seen in the next chapter, Roman Catholics were the great exception to the public school consensus. Lyman Beecher invited Catholics into the public schools, on the school's terms, but with no accommodation to their own concerns.[71] Horace Mann disparaged that "rival system of 'Parochial' or 'Sectarian schools.'"[72] Generally antebellum school reformers chose to ignore Catholic concerns. This was not sufficient for these new immigrants.

People of color were even more thoroughly excluded from the notion of the public being developed in the common school movement. Chapters Four and Five explore their responses. Lyman Beecher spoke positively of missions to the Indians, but they were to be under the direction of the Board of *Foreign* Missions. African Americans, the vast majority of whom were still slaves, were generally not considered. A few northern cities, notably Boston, did develop separate systems of racially segregated schools. A few free blacks and abolitionists challenged these arrangements and demanded integrated educational opportunities. As will be seen, schools were embraced in the African American community, free and slave. But as far as the school reform leaders were concerned, the needs of these communities were far from the center of their field of vision.

While other groups were ignored or consciously excluded from the common school enterprise, one must also ask if the evangelical Protestants themselves may have lost something by their decision to participate so fully in it. William Kennedy has described the problem. "By assuming a major part of the moral and religious instruction of the American public, the schools took on a responsibility which they could not easily fulfill. . . . Hence also the emergence of Americanized religion in which a national morality and a 'lowest-common denominator' theology were mixed."[73] While "Protestantizing" the culture, the evangelicals were also secularizing their own faith. The schools would take on a dynamism of their own, their leaders confident that "the idea of universal, free education, is fast becoming the grand central idea of the age."[74] In far too many places, Protestant Christianity, certain of its primary role in this "grand central idea," lost its unique edge and vision.

The great religious historian Robert T. Handy has described the experience of many who were part of this new educational system. According to Handy, Protestants failed to understand the cost of their new loyalties.

> Their religion was becoming more and more patterned after the culture. . . . The evangelicals of that period did not see—perhaps they could not see—what seems obvious to us, looking back, that they were often expressing quite understandable class and economic interests in their speeches and actions, but always interpreting their aims and deeds almost wholly in a religious frame of reference. They found a sense of unity in a concept of civilization which had socio-economic and racial aspects, yet they interpreted their position in simple evangelical terms.[75]

The resulting link, in the minds of many Americans in the nineteenth and twentieth centuries, among their religion, their country, and especially their schools led to times of considerable self-confidence and comfort. But as the country changed—and it began to do so very dramatically by the middle of the nineteenth century and even more throughout the next hundred years—this self-confidence turned to discomfort and fear. There seemed to have been a golden age when all agreed on faith, morals, and the right institutions to carry them out. Now more and more people disagreed. More and more of those who had been left out joined new immigrants with their own faiths and concerns to demand change. For many in Protestant America, the result has been more than a century of uncertainty about their place in the culture and the role of their religion in its educational enterprises.

Beginning with such confidence in the fundamental religious soundness of the schools, lacking a clear rationale of their own (as opposed to that borrowed from their Enlightenment forebears) for a separation of church and state, uncertain about the full meaning of the nation's growing diversity, white Protestant Americans have suffered a long-term sense of loss and uncertainty. It has emerged loudly at certain moments—during the Scopes trial in the 1920s, in the response to the Supreme Court's ban on official prayers in schools in the 1960s, in the Reagan revolution in the 1980s—and it has been quiet at others. But the heart of the problem, the public school system's founders' failure to understand the need to respect the faith of a wide diversity of citizens or to actively maintain their own religious identity has never really been addressed. The results are with us still.

THREE

Who Defines What Is Common?
Roman Catholics and the Common School Movement, 1801–1892

IF THE PUBLIC SCHOOLS of the first half of the nineteenth century were really a new form of Protestant religious establishment, what happened to those who did not agree with the establishment? To the constant surprise and annoyance of Horace Mann and his many allies many people asked this question. But no group asked more persistently or acted more decisively when they did not like the answers than the nation's rapidly growing Roman Catholic population.

In 1800 the Catholic population of the United States was tiny, and virtually non- existent outside of the state of Maryland, which had been founded as a haven for persecuted Catholics from England over a century earlier. By 1850 Catholics were the largest single religious denomination in the nation. This rapid and dramatic change had implications for all of the nation's institutions, but none more than the public schools.

Catholic schools date from the earliest colonial years. The oldest recorded Catholic school was established in St. Mary's City, Maryland, around 1640; and New York, always a haven for a wide range of religious persuasions, had a Catholic school by the 1680s. But these schools were a standard, if small, part of the colonial mix in which church-sponsored, private, and quasi-governmental schools all existed in rich profusion. The abdication of England's Catholic King James II and the Glorious Revolution of 1689 led to a rise of anti-Catholicism in England and the colonies; even tolerant Maryland passed the "Act to Prevent the Growth of Popery," in 1704 which included a provision for deporting any Catholic who kept a school or attempted to instruct children.[1]

The later years of the eighteenth century leading up to the American Revolution saw greater and greater tolerance for the small Catholic minority in the colonies. Nevertheless, deep distrust of "Papists" remained. As the Jesuit historian Neil McCluskey notes, at the time of the Revolution, in only four of the original thirteen states were Catholics free of some legal disabilities in terms of the right to vote and hold office.[2]

The Vatican responded quickly to the creation of the new nation. In 1789, even before the passage of the First Amendment, guaranteeing an end to governmental interference in church affairs, John Carroll was appointed the first Catholic bishop in the United States. Based in Baltimore, Carroll's diocese included all of the new nation and its approximately 30,000 Catholics. In his first pastoral letter to his new flock, Carroll devoted significant attention to education, addressing both his concern for recruiting and training priests and nuns and for the general Catholic population. Regarding the latter, he reminded, "Knowing, therefore, that the principles instilled in the course of a Christian education, are generally preserved throughout life . . . I have considered the virtuous and Christian instruction of youth as a principal object of pastoral solicitude."[3] It was a theme that would continue among Carroll's successors, but in a remarkably different context.

Carroll's concern for providing a Christian Catholic education continued throughout his episcopate, but with two very important changes. First, after an initially slow start, the Catholic population of the nation mushroomed. And the change was more than in numbers. Whereas colonial Catholics had been primarily English dissidents, descendants of the minority who had rejected the Protestant Reformation in their homeland, joined by a small number of German immigrants, the Catholic immigrants of the 1830s, 1840s, and 1850s, were predominantly Irish or German, drawn from the poorest of Europe's poor who came to the United States to avoid starvation in their homelands. Added to the religious differences, there were now huge class and economic differences between the more established Protestants and the newly arrived Catholics. McCluskey notes that, from the Protestant perspective, "These people were not just Catholics, but foreigners with a different look and a strange accent to them. Their cheap labor flooding the market posed an economic threat. They were people of the ghetto, the slum, and the saloon."[4] From the Catholic perspective, especially for Irish Catholics fleeing the potato famine, the English- speaking Protestant majority looked, spoke, and acted an awful lot like the Protestant establishment that had starved them out of their homeland.

At the same time as these new Catholic immigrants were arriving, and in large part in response to their arrival, the schools of the nation were being organized into a much tighter system. Where once many different kinds of arrangements for schooling had existed side by side, by the 1830s the North and West had a public school system in which the state-supported common school was supposed to serve, and mold, all citizens. And as the last chapter has shown, in the antebellum era, this system was quite clearly a Protestant system, designed to instill Protestant values, especially in those who might not otherwise share them. Catholics were tolerated, even welcomed, but only on Protestant terms. It was not an arrangement designed to make the new immigrants or their religious leaders happy.

THE CATHOLIC SCHOOLS SEEK EQUAL FUNDING

Nowhere did the fight between immigrant Catholic and nativist Protestant notions about the kind of schooling that should be offered to the nation's children become more bitter than in New York City. In the often-told story of the efforts to create a public school system and a tax-supported Catholic school system in New York, the basic arguments about the appropriate relationship of religion, public education, and democracy were drawn with great clarity.[5]

In 1800, out of a total population of approximately 60,000, New York City had an estimated Catholic population of 1,300, almost all of whom worshipped at St. Peter's Church, which had been built in 1785. In 1801 a day school was opened there. The parish applied for and in 1806 began to receive its share of the state school fund. At the beginning of the nineteenth century, a wide array of schools, spon- sored by different Protestant denominations and other private groups, organized their own schools and received state aid. New York state's postrevolutionary approach to schooling was initially based on the provision of state funds to many different kinds of schools. And the New York City Common Council chose not to establish any schools of its own but rather to pass its share of the state subsidy on to local charity schools. In this context Catholics applied for, and received, their share.[6]

By 1815 New York City's Catholic population had grown to around 15,000 out of a total city population approaching 100,000. A second school was opened at St. Patrick's Church and it too began to receive state funds in 1816. Together these two schools enrolled approximately 500 students. New York seemed well on its way to a pluralistic approach to the funding of public education in which different groups, religious or secular, would form their own schools, apply for state aid, and serve their constituency. It was not to last.[7]

Among the others also operating schools in the city was the Free School Society, founded in 1806 by a group of New York's business elite and including several different Protestant groups, although dominated by Quakers. The Free School Society's goal was to provide schools for the city's poor on a nonsectarian basis. Initially the society's schools coexisted comfortably with various denominational schools, but by 1825 the Free School Society's leaders began to aspire to being *the* common school society of the city. Concerned that funding for denominational schools was draining away resources they could use, they wrote in their annual report: "Our free schools have conferred the blessings of education upon a large number of the children of the poor, but still it is to be lamented that a description of public school is wanting amongst us, where the rich and the poor meet together."[8] The words sounded like those of Horace Mann or any other advocate for common schools. But in New York's very different context they also indicated a shift from a society offering charity schools as one among many of the city's educational options to a society interested in creating a single system under its control. Other New Yorkers would not cede their position easily.[9]

The trustees of the Free School Society did more than write about their desire for a unified school system. And being well-connected civic leaders, they were able to move quickly. Having already, in 1824, persuaded the state legislature to allow the New York City Common Council resolve any disputes about the use of school funds in the city, the society quickly persuaded the council to take the radical step of making the society's schools the only ones to receive public education funds. In 1825, the society's trustees returned to the legislature for permission to change their name to the Public School Society with a goal of attracting all citizens, not just the poor, to their set of common schools. By year's end, New York City had a single publicly funded school system, although its administration remained in the hands of the trustees of a private society for almost two more decades.

The trustees of the Free School Society acted as they did for a number of reasons. Their most immediate cause of concern in the 1820s was not Catholic schools but the rapidly growing school system of the Bethel Baptist Church, which had established its first school in 1820 and had added two more by 1824, in direct competition with the Free School Society. In response to this competition, the society began to lobby for an end to any state funds flowing to sectarian schools.

The society's trustees were also looking to other parts of the nation and to Europe for new models for the New York City schools. They were especially impressed that in New England, even before Horace Mann's arrival, "the child of the poorest citizen feels on a perfect equality with his richer classmate . . . and where all feel the dignity of receiving their instruction as a right."[10] They wanted to create the same kind of common school experience in New York.

Finally, as the education historian Lawrence Cremin has noted, educators in the United States in the 1820s and 1830s became increasingly focused on the need for a system of education. The chaotic colonial approach did not seem appropriate for a rapidly developing society. And members of New York's elite wondered who but themselves should control the system? So DeWitt Clinton wrote to his friend Isaac Collins, "The obtrusion of Charity Schools on our System has done much evil. I was opposed to it from the start—but how to get ride of it, is difficult."[11] Within two years Clinton and his friends had done the "difficult" thing, and they were in charge.

While the creation of the Public School Society as the only publicly funded school system in New York cut off resources for all denominational schools, the impact on Catholic schools was especially severe. In general, recent Catholic immigrants were among the poorest of New Yorkers, with the least expendable funds for maintaining their own schools. And, perhaps more important, the schools of the Public School Society, like their counterparts in New England and the Midwest, were clearly Protestant schools, although they avoided anything unique to any one denomination of Protestants. Through the use of the King James version of the Bible, and through the clear morality of their textbooks, these schools taught the superiority of Protestant values to Protestant and Catholic alike.

In spite of the difficulties, New York's Catholics generally suffered in silence for fifteen years. Schools continued to open in new parishes; by 1840 eight Catholic parochial schools served an estimated 5,000 students out of an estimated 12,000 to 16,000 Catholic school-age children. By that year New York's total Catholic population had grown to somewhere in the range of 60,000 to 80,000, or approximately one-fifth to one-fourth of the city's population of 312,710. Now under the leadership of a new young bishop John Hughes, and with the support of New York's Whig governor, William Seward, New York's Catholics were ready to challenge the dominance of the Public School Society and to demand their fair share of school funds.

Early in 1840 Governor Seward proposed reconsideration of the 1825 arrangements for New York City and urged that funds be made available to schools that shared the students' language and religion. Understanding a clear signal, the trustees of the eight Catholic schools petitioned the Common Council for a share of the school funds. The Public School Society fought back, initially seeking some compromise with the Catholics, including an offer to remove any textbook especially offensive to Catholic views. However, in April 1840 the trustees issued a hard line document accusing their opponents of "Religious zeal, degenerating into fanaticism and bigotry." They appealed to the constitutional provisions that "there should be no establishment of religion by law; that the affairs of the State should be kept entirely distinct from, and unconnected with, those of the Church." And most of all, they rejected the notion that Catholics had a right to a share of the school funds since they were taxed for support of the schools. "[I]t should be borne in mind that they are taxed not as members of the Roman Catholic Church, but as citizens of the State of New York; and not for the purposes of religion, but for the support of civil government." And civil government, in the form of an appropriation for the Public School Society, was thus the only appropriate means of spending school funds, its advocates argued.[12]

For Bishop Hughes and his coreligionists, the fight had just begun. In September, 1840, at a meeting chaired by the bishop, they wrote a formal petition to the Board of Aldermen for a portion of the common school fund. This petition makes the case as effectively as any that have followed for the right of a religious minority to its own separate share of public school funds. As citizens who "bear, and are willing to bear, their portion of every common burden; and feel themselves entitled to a participation in every common benefit." They also felt compelled to outline the reasons why the schools of the Public School Society did not serve their needs. The issue, from a Catholic perspective, was clear. Either the Public School Society was sectarian (and sectarianly Protestant and anti-Catholic) or it was nonreligious and therefore antireligious and anti-Christian. There were simply no other options. "But they [the Public School Society] profess to exclude all sectarianism, from their schools. If they do not exclude sectarianism, they are avowedly no more entitled to the school funds than your petitioners or any other denomination of professing Christians. If they do, as they profess, exclude sectarianism, then your petitioners contend that they exclude Christianity." The battle lines have not changed dramatically in the last century and a half.[13]

From the perspective of many Catholics, and many Protestants also, a common school in a religiously pluralistic society, by definition, fails one of two standards. Either it favors one religion over another or it is secular and anti-religious. The position of lowest-common-denominator faith in the schools, defended by the Horace Manns and trustees of the Public School Society, simply does not work for many people.[14]

In the case of the curriculum of the Public School Society schools, the point of failure was clear. The petitioners had many examples in the texts:

> The term "Popery" is repeatedly found in them. This term is known and employed as one of insult and contempt towards the Catholic religion, and it passes into the minds of children. . . . Both the historical and religious portions of the reading lessons are selected from Protestant writers, whose prejudices against the Catholic religion render them unworthy of confidence in the mind of your petitioners, at least so far as their own children are concerned.

While the Public School Society denied that there were texts with anything "reasonably objectionable to Catholics," these petitioners found plenty. For another specific example the petitioners noted a biographical reference for: "Huss, John, a zealous reformer from Popery, who lived in Bohemia, towards the close of the fourteenth, and beginning of the fifteenth centuries. He was bold and preserving; but at length, trusting himself to the deceitful Catholics he was by them brought to trial, condemned as a heretic, and burnt at the stake." With considerable sarcasm, the petitioners excused the society for historical inaccuracy in the statement but wondered if it really needed Catholic consultants to guess that the reference to "deceitful Catholics" might be offensive.[15]

Finally, of course, the petitioners turned to the heart of the matter. For good reason, they argued, they had lost all confidence in the schools of the Public School Society. For good reason, their only option was to establish schools of their own. "The expense necessary for this, was a second taxation, required not by the laws of the land, but by the no less imperious demands of their conscience." In this unfair situation, where they clearly could not use the tax-supported schools, the petitioners were left with an unfair choice: "They were reduced to the alternative of seeing their children growing up in entire ignorance, or else taxing themselves anew for private schools, whilst the funds provide for education, and contributed in part by themselves, were given over to the Public School Society." The solution was clear. They wanted to return to the pre-1825 arrangement and receive public funds for the eight schools of the diocese.[16]

The battle continued for another two years with a final compromise that pleased no one. The Common Council asked the Public School Society to make another effort to remove anti-Catholic bias in the schools. The state superintendent of Common Schools recommended a decentralized district plan for the city that would break the authority of the Public School Society. Finally, in April 1842, the state legislature passed and Governor Seward signed a bill that placed the schools under the control of public officials and a city Board of Education with an explicit prohibition on any sectarian teaching in the schools. From the Catholic perspective, "We have to consider more the evils from which it relieves us, than the positive benefits which it confers."[17] The private Public School Society had lost its power. But Bishop Hughes did not get any aid for his parochial schools. And, in fact, the Board of Education's first superintendent was the nativist William Stone, who immediately enforced Bible reading, "without note or comment," in the style of Horace Mann. New York City had joined most of the rest of the nation in having a public school system that was publicly funded and publicly controlled and that reflected a generic Protestantism at its core.

It is important to note that at the critical juncture of New York's 1840-1842 school wars, no major player was able to envision a common school in which mutual respect and the ability to learn from differences was at the core. The most tolerant of the players, Governor Seward and Secretary of State John Spencer, envisioned fair play and competition among different schools receiving funds. Certainly this was a more open- minded approach than that of the trustees of the Public School Society, or Bishop Hughes, for that matter. But, disappointingly, a dynamic democracy did not produce more. The final compromise became all too common for the future. While the schools of the new Board of Education were more secular than those of the Public School Society by only the barest of margins, the direction was set. More and more in the future, public and school officials would resolve controversy by simply dropping any discussion of the particular and the distinctive. The generic Protestantism of the 1840s had, in most of the more diverse urban centers of the North and Midwest, become a very generalized theism by the 1880s and 1890s and in the twentieth century a thoroughly secularized cult of democracy and American goodness. When "Washington brave his country did save" replaced the biblical story of Jonah and the Whale in the New England primer, a move toward secularization was begun that never ended. For many people, of many different faiths, the issues have been—and remain—troubling.

CREATING A CATHOLIC
PAROCHIAL SCHOOL SYSTEM

For Archbishop Hughes, as one of the nation's most outspoken mid-nineteenth century Catholic leaders, the issue was resolved. He continued to assert the Catholic schools' right to public funds, but he had given up on ever getting them. Instead, he became one of the leading advocates of Catholic parochial schools. While later historians have debated the degree to which Hughes was a defender of his faith or a builder of a fortress mentality among Catholics, or both, his role in the debates of the 1840s poses the great unresolved issues of public financing of education in a diverse society as clearly as any case study can. His resolution of the issue after 1842 also set the tone for Catholic education for the next century and more. Unfair as it was, the best option available to Catholics, Hughes argued, was to pay a double tax. First they had to support public schools they could not in conscience use. And then, with their own funds, it was their duty to develop a system of their own schools that would be funded and controlled by the Catholic faithful. It was the beginning of a spectacularly successful alternative.[18] For over a century Catholic parochial schools continued to grow as the dominant form of Catholic education. By the early 1960s, 120 years after Hughes' statements, 5.5 million young people, 14% of the nation's school-age population and approximately 60% of the Catholic elementary and 30% of the Catholic secondary population, were in Catholic parochial schools.[19]

The growth of Catholic parochial schools did not happen immediately. There was resistance and there was a simple shortage of resources. In New York, the parochial school population doubled in a decade in spite of the ban on public funds. While in 1840 there had been 5,000 students enrolled in the eight parochial schools seeking aid, by the early 1850s there were approximately 10,000 students in twenty-eight parochial schools our of a total estimated Catholic school age population of 20,000.[20]

Chicago provides an interesting parallel to New York. While there had been Catholics and Catholic schools in New York for almost 200 years before the school conflict of the 1840s, as far as anyone knows there were few, if any residents, let alone schoolchildren, in what became Chicago even a few decades before. Chicago was chartered as a city only in the early 1800s. In 1833 the city's small Catholic population, numbering around 100, petitioned the Bishop of St. Louis to send them a priest. A decade later one parish had grown to a diocese. By the death of the first bishop in 1848, Chicago had three parish schools in operation. By the early 1850s a handful of schools had 900 students. By 1870 fifteen schools served 10,000 students within the City of Chicago.[21]

Throughout the United States the same pattern developed in many other urban areas, the primary home to the continuing massive immigration of Roman Catholics from Ireland, Germany, and elsewhere. In Cincinnati, where Lyman Beecher and Calvin Stowe had held forth so vigorously on the virtues of a Protestant

America in the 1830s and 1840s, Catholics had become a majority by the end of the Civil War, and the great "Cincinnati Bible Wars" of the 1860s, which are described in chapter six, divided the city over the same issues of Protestant prayers and Bibles in the public schools and the question of public funding for Catholic schools that had divided New York in the 1840s.

There were also exceptions. Boston, long considered one of the nation's most Catholic of cities, and scene of some of the most violent Protestant-Catholic tensions, moved much more slowly to found Catholic schools. According to James Sanders, historian of Catholic education, there are several reasons for this. Boston's major nineteenth-century bishops, Benedict Fenwick (1825-1846), John Fitzpatrick (1846-1866), and John Williams (1866-1907), were all strong accommodationists. Fitzpatrick was himself a graduate of the city's Latin School, and he moved easily within Boston's social elite. All three bishops sought access and advancement in Yankee Boston for themselves and their flocks more than they sought a separationist approach to religion or society. And they saw the public schools as an important means of access.

At the same time all three bishops and many of their followers battled with the Protestant elite in a different way. They meant to show Protestant Boston that the Catholics were in the city to stay by building some of the grandest churches anywhere. The Mission Church in Roxbury, St. Peter's in Dorchester, and the cathedral in the South End tower over their neighbors, including the neighboring Protestant churches. It was not accidental that the spire of St. Francis de Sales Church in Charlestown reached the same height as the Yankee-built Bunker Hill Monument. And with funds flowing to these massive construction projects, little was left for schools. For all of the nineteenth century, in a city whose school-age population was mostly Catholic after 1850, no more than 10 percent of those children were in parochial schools at any time. Only with the coming of a new bishop in 1907 did that situation begin to change.[22]

On the national scene, American Catholics clearly committed themselves to parochial schools. The nation's Catholic bishops gathered for three major plenary councils during the nineteenth century. Each time they asserted their commitment to parochial schools in stronger language than the last. In 1852 the First Plenary Council of Baltimore urged Catholics to "encourage the establishment and support of Catholic schools, make every sacrifice which may be necessary for this object." The 1866 council reaffirmed the commitment to "the establishment and support of Parochial Schools," reminded Catholics that "religious teaching and religious training should form part of every system of school education," and admonished the bishops themselves to "see that schools be established in connection with all the churches of their dioceses." Finally, at the Third and final Plenary Council of Baltimore in 1884, the bishops gave their most definitive statement, which has guided Catholic schooling for more than a century. After considerable discussion, the council decreed: "That near every church a parish school, where one does not yet exist, is to be built and maintained in perpetuum within two years . . . [and] [t]hat all Catholic parents are bound to send their children to the parish school." While exceptions were allowed for unique circumstances, the decrees could not have been more clear.[23]

As McCluskey has noted, this commitment to build a separate church-controlled and church-funded school system came at the expense of any meaningful influence on the public schools and on the expansion of Catholic higher education. While there were exceptions on both counts, Catholic creative energy and Catholic dollars flowed primarily to the parochial schools. As in the case of race, so in the case of religion, the American pattern seemed to be one of separate and not really equal. For all the words to the contrary, especially from the advocates of the public schools, this kind of segregation was not designed to build understanding, trust, or unity.

RETHINKING THE COMMITMENT: ARCHBISHOP IRELAND AND THE SCHOOL QUESTION

For a time in the 1890s, there was an effort within the Catholic hierarchy to rethink the commitment to parochial schools as the approved approach to the spiritual and temporal education of the young. In 1890 the American Catholic church was rocked by a bitter debate over what came to be known as "the school question." John Ireland, archbishop of St. Paul, Minnesota, was at the heart of the controversy. Indeed, he began it with an address to the National Education Association, which was then dominated by university and school administrators who were overwhelmingly Protestant and deeply protective of the public schools. In his speech, Ireland made a number of surprising comments.

He began with considerable praise for public schools. America was blessed by a system of universal instruction "in which knowledge is to be had for the asking." "No tax is more legitimate than that which is levied in order to dispel mental darkness, and build up within the nation's bosom intelligent manhood and womanhood." He challenged the notion that Catholics were opposed to the public schools. "Never was accusation more unfounded." (Some of his fellow bishops quickly expressed surprise on that point!) But he did have a quarrel with the public schools. He had, he said, to defend the system of parochial schools for the time being, though "I wish that the need for it did not exist." But the reality was that state schools tended "to eliminate religion from the minds and hearts of the youth of the country."[24]

In fact Ireland was quite articulate on the growing secularism of the public schools and the problems it presented. He rejected the notion that schools could teach a vague "common Christianity," saying "This will not do. In loyalty to their principles, Catholics cannot and will not accept a common Christianity. To Catholics, what does not bear on its face the stamp of Catholicity is Protestant in form and in implication." It was a complaint of long standing among his co-religionists.[25]

But a vague common Christianity was no longer the greatest danger. The schools were excluding more and more religion of any kind. Ireland asked Protestants to join with him in responding to the danger:

> Let me be your ally in warding off from the county irreligion, the destroyer of Christian life and of Christian civilization. What we have to fear is the materialism that does not see beyond the universe a living personal God, and the agnosticism that reduces Him to an unknown perhaps. . . . Let us be on our guard. In our fear least Protestants gain some advantage over Catholics, or Catholics over Protestants, we play into the hands of unbelievers and secularists. We have given over to them the school the nursery of thought.

Many religious people the end of the twentieth century—Protestant and Catholic alike—would share almost the same complaint. In such a context, "brief and hurried lessons of the family fireside and the

Sunday school will be of slight avail. At best the time is too short . . ." and besides, how could a child be expected to take seriously a lesson when "the teacher, in whom he confides most trustingly has said nothing."[26]

In this context, Ireland warned, Protestants and Catholics had to find a different solution. And, he also noted, Catholics had extra reason for wanting change, burdened as they were by the added expense of running two school systems. In place of secular public schools and expensive parochial schools, Ireland proposed consideration of several alternatives: "I would, as is done in England, pay for the secular instruction given in denominational schools according to results; that is, every pupil passing the examination before state officials, and in full accordance with the state program, would secure to his school the cost of the tuition of a pupil in the state school." Under this option, surprisingly like the voucher proposals of a century later, the state simply would subsidize Catholic schools at the cost of public schools as long as the Catholic—or other Protestant parochial schools for that matter—provided an education so that the students met state standards.[27]

A second option, for which Ireland became much better known, was the so-called Poughkeepsie plan in which the state, or city or town, simply rented the parochial school building and paid the staff salaries between 9 a.m. and 3 p.m., during which hours the staff addressed only secular subjects. After these hours, with no state subsidy, the same teachers in the same parish building could turn their attention to the teaching of their faith. Protestants could do the same in their own buildings. Ireland noted that this plan was in effect not only in Poughkeepsie, New York, but also in Florissant, Missouri, Conewago, Pennsylvania, and parts of New Mexico. And shortly after the speech he put it into effect in his own diocese in the towns of Faribault and Stillwater.[28]

A storm of controversy immediately broke over Ireland's speech. Bishop Bernard McQuaid of Rochester and Archbishop Michael A. Corrigan of New York along with the so-called German bishops of the Midwest, such as Frederick F. X. Katzer of Green Bay, later archbishop of Milwaukee, attacked him in the press and appealed to Pope Leo XIII for a condemnation of Ireland and the speech. In his letter to the pope, McQuaid agreed with Ireland that "It is the indifferentism with regard to all religious belief we most of all fear," but to him

Ireland's proposals were a long-term concession of defeat to that "indifferentism" and worse. "The only arrangement that is now possible between the State and Church on this question is one that entirely surrenders our rights, and that puts our schools on a par with the State schools from which the inculcation of morals based on religious motives is altogether excluded." Besides the danger of yielding far too much control to the state, McQuaid feared that "Associations in schools, especially in State schools, where all classes, Protestants, Jews and infidels, meet promiscuously, present another danger" and could quickly lead to the evil of mixed marriages. For McQuaid American Catholicism really existed in two linked institutions, the church and its parish school, for "there is little likelihood that the Gospel reaching and abiding in the hearts of the children except through the instrumentality of the schoolhouse." And so, he urged, all the compromises embodied in Ireland's approach should be soundly rejected.[29]

Ireland, however, had very strong allies. His good friend Cardinal Gibbons had primacy in the American church. In fact Gibbons had approved the speech in advance, and when Leo XIII asked the cardinal for more information, Gibbons in turn asked Ireland, who staunchly defended the speech. "The Church is not established to teach writing and ciphering, but to teach morals and faith." Let others take care of the "writing and ciphering," Ireland insisted. "The true solution, in my judgment, is to make the State-School satisfactory to Catholic consciences, and to use it." And his proposals were a way to do that. He was not speaking of any lowest-common-denominator faith. "I demand positive Catholic dogmatic teaching—rejecting mere moral teaching, rejecting totally the so-called 'common Christianity' theory." His proposals allowed Catholics to teach Catholic Christianity but at the same time to receive public funds for the secular part of their school day.[30]

Ireland's support went even higher than the cardinal. The pope's legate to the United States, Archbishop Francis Satolli told an audience in St. Paul that, "while holding in veneration and love all the prelates of the American Church, yet he [Leo] has a special esteem and affection for your Archbishop." And when Satolli was asked to settle the school question, he was sufficiently vague so that both sides could claim victory, but he also left little doubt where his and the pope's favor fell. His statement affirmed the right of the state to conduct public schools and to compel attendance when parents made no other provision. He explicitly forbade any priest or bishop from excommunicating parents or children for attending public schools. He allowed, with diplomatic vagueness, for Ireland's arrangements in Faribault and Stillwater schools to continue and in fact said that "it is greatly to be desired and will be a most happy arrangement, if the bishop agree with the civil authorities, or with the members of the school board, to conduct the school with mutual attention and due consideration for their respective rights." He demanded highly qualified teachers in all Catholic schools. And he added a number of new options, including release time for Catholic children during school hours to learn their catechism, or classes outside of the school buildings at special times for teaching Christian doctrine. He called on all pastors to give equal attention to the education of all the children of their parish, whether those children attend the parish school, the public school, or were taught in other arrangements.[31]

If one considers only the documents of the case, Ireland's proposal seems to have won hands down. With the endorsements of Cardinal Gibbons, Archbishop Satolli, and Pope Leo XIII himself, what more could he want? The American press, still overwhelmingly in Protestant hands, endorsed Ireland and condemned his opponents. New York and midwestern conservatives grumbled, but it seemed that they had lost. But, in fact, the opposite happened. After 1892 almost nothing is heard of Ireland's proposals. For one thing, nativist and hostile Protestantism was still far too alive and well for many school boards to agree to the proposals. There might be isolated experiments, but they were not likely to be embraced in a country in which Protestants still outnumbered Catholics five to one. At the same time, the bishops who disagreed with Ireland were in the majority. And while some fought angrily and publicly with him, many others kept silent but carried on with their tasks of building their own school system.

Perhaps the epitaph for Ireland's vision was written not in McQuaid's urgent appeal to the pope but in dozens of dioceses like Chicago. In that city, and in many others, the momentum was in the hands of leaders like Archbishop Patrick A. Feehan, who had helped to draft the decrees of the Council of Baltimore in the 1884. As James Sanders has described the situation, in Chicago "Feehan characteristically took no part in a controversy over the possible phasing out of parochial education that agitated the Church nationally during the 1890's, apparently preferring to express his position simply by building schools." And that he did with a vengeance. In 1890 Chicago had sixty-two parish schools, out of a total of eighty-one parishes, with an enrollment of 31,000. And the numbers kept growing.[32]

Nationally, the decades after "the school controversy" were the time of fastest growth of parochial schools, with little if any attention given to alternatives. So McCluskey reports that in 1900 there were 854,523 pupils in Catholic schools, by 1920 there were 1.8 million, and in 1963 there were 5.5 million or 14 percent of the total school age population. At the elementary level, this figure amounted to a significant majority of Catholics.[33] It is true that the second half of the twentieth century has seen a dramatic decline in Catholic school enrollments, and higher levels of support for the Catholic public school students in Sunday schools and catechism classes. But there has yet to be a fundamental rethinking of the great divide established 150 years ago in which the choices for Catholics were a Catholic education at private expense in a segregated parochial school or attendance at an increasingly secular public school with religious instruction and formation squeezed in around the rapidly disappearing edges. In this sense, Ireland was right; the situation represents a lack of vision for educational possibilities that has served neither Catholics nor others well.

Literacy in the African American Community: Church and School in Slave and Free Communities, 1802–1902

IN 1935 W. E. B. DUBOIS WROTE, "Public education for all at public expense was, in the South, a Negro idea."[1] Most of the literature about the development of public schools in the United States prior to the Civil War focuses almost exclusively on the Northeast and Midwest or West. Public schools did not flourish in the South before the war. Class divisions among whites and the great divide of black and white, slave and free, meant that the notion of a common schooling for all simply did not find fertile soil in the antebellum American South. And DuBois is right: In the years immediately after the war, public schooling took off in the South under the leadership of newly freed slaves. Literacy and education had been nourished, often in secret, by both slave and free black communities prior to the war. With emancipation, these hidden springs quickly welled up into a powerful commitment to schooling. And as most histories of the African American community in the United States note, this movement was one of many that had strong roots in the black church.

African American schools have, in fact, existed in the United States as long as any other kind. A survey of schools in New York City when the Common Council sought to distribute the city's portion of the state school fund reported six charity schools, including the African Free School with an enrollment of fifty-one students, a figure only slightly below the citywide average of seventy-one students per charity school.[2] As early as 1787 African American parents in Boston petitioned the state legislature for a school since they received "no benefit from the free schools" of the city. Boston's free black community was small—766 out of a total population of 18,038 in the first census of 1790—but that community clearly sought schooling for their children. Some early records indicate that African American students attended both the public schools and private schools in Boston, but the petition of 1787 is the first sign of a long-term dissatisfaction with schools in which a white child was punished by being forced to sit in the "nigger-seat."[3]

A decade later Boston's African American community began a stronger drive for its own separate schools with a 1798 petition from black parents for their own school. The selectmen denied the request, not because they were opposed to segregation but because they feared petitions for the "privilege" of separate schools by French, Scots-Irish, and German parents. The petition was repeated in 1800 by sixty-six African Americans; the idea received strong support from some prominent white Bostonians, but was defeated in the School Committee. Finally, in 1802 a private African school was founded in the home of Primus Hall and in 1806 a permanent school for African American children opened in the basement of the African Meeting House on Beacon Hill, then the heart of Boston's black community. Over the next few years the school received private support from blacks and whites and eventually support from the School Committee, becoming in time a de facto public school under the committee's supervision.[4]

As can be seen, a small and discriminated against community of free blacks in the North consistently turned to the one institution under their control—the church—to support their educational efforts. In the early years of the nineteenth century, they were not acting particularly differently from others for whom the distinction between religious and secular, public and private institutions was a vague and changing one. However, while many of the church-based schools of the early decades of the nineteenth century were missionary schools for "other people's children," in the African American community far more of the church-based schools were run by and for the community.

In many cities throughout the United States, Sunday Schools served as the primary educational institution for blacks, children and adults. Indeed, the Sunday School movement as it began in England

and the United States in the early nineteenth century focused on basic literacy, albeit with a strongly religious flavor for all comers. At a time when many children worked six days a week, Sunday was *the* time when education was possible. In New York, where there were at least limited public school options for children of color, blacks still constituted 25% of the Sunday school pupils in the city by 1817. In Philadelphia, approximately two-thirds of the Philadelphia Sunday and Adult School Union students were black. Southern cities including Charleston, Nashville, and St. Louis also reported large black Sunday school attendance in the early 1800s. White-run schools for free and slave blacks declined in the 1830s, in large part due to the fears sparked by the Nat Turner slave revolt in 1831. Turner's literacy and familiarity with the Bible sparked fear in the hearts of many whites, most especially the slave owners themselves, who quickly pushed legislation that made it illegal to teach a slave to read or write in almost every state of the South by 1835.[5] Still, growing fear and prejudice did not mean the end of Sunday schools for blacks.

In Baltimore and Washington, D.C., when white parents objected to their churches offering even separate classes for free blacks, black churches picked up the slack. Baltimore's African Methodist Episcopal Church became a well-known educational center for the free blacks of that city. In Elizabeth, New Jersey, the formation of an African church in 1838 lead to a mass transfer of black Sunday school students from the white Presbyterian school to their own institution.

While most recorded African American Sunday schools were for free blacks, they were not the only ones in existence. In the 1820s, prior to Nat Turner's revolt, a growing movement arose in some border states to provide slaves with literacy and religion. Thus John Mason Peck, the well-known Baptist missionary, reported in 1825, "I am happy to find among the slave holders in Missouri a growing disposition to have blacks educated, and to patronize Sunday-schools for the purpose." After 1831 most white-sponsored Sunday schools in the South turned exclusively to oral instruction with a focus on loyalty and service. But there were exceptions. For example, one white woman ran a Sunday school for slaves on her Louisiana plantation in 1840. She reported that her efforts were "at that time not a very popular thing to do, " but the school "was always well attended." And a Presbyterian visitor reported in the

New York *Observer* that in one southern city, which he would not name, there were eight Sunday schools for slaves, and "In all of these schools the scholars are taught to read." Most important, and most difficult to document, slaves also ran their own Sunday schools just as they did their own preaching. Frederick Douglas taught Sunday school in Baltimore, and later he conducted a school for slaves on a rural Maryland plantation where he taught the Bible and literacy to "twenty or thirty young men." These underground Sunday schools did not report statistics to the American Sunday School Union, but they provide a powerful example of the thirst for literacy among African Americans reported by all observers in the years immediately after the Civil War.[6]

LITERACY IN THE
SLAVE COMMUNITY: FORBIDDEN AND PRECIOUS

Until the Civil War, the vast majority of African Americans were slaves. For slaves, the important church-state divide did not have to do with the teaching of religion in the schools. The primary role of the state for African American slaves was as the maintainer of slavery. As the great historian John Hope Franklin and his colleague Alfred A. Moss have written:

> The regulatory statues were frankly repressive, and whites made no apologies for them. The laws represented merely the reduction to legal phraseology of the philosophy of the South with regard to the institution of slavery. Slaves had no standing in the courts: they could not be a party to a law suit; they could not offer testimony, except against another slave or a free black; and their irresponsibility meant that their oaths were not binding. Thus, they could make no contracts.[7]

Punishment, from whipping to branding, imprisonment, or death, could be in the hands of the courts but more often was in the hands of the individual slave master. Slaves had no recourse to higher authority. And as the nineteenth century wore on, especially after 1831, slave state after slave state forbade teaching any slave to read or write. The story of the slave Scipio who was put to death for teaching his grandson

Jamie to read and spell from the Bible was the most famous only because the grandson attained the freedom to tell the story.[8]

In this context, forbidden literacy became precious indeed. For those who achieved it, literacy meant a powerful link to freedom. And many shared the opinion of one ex-slave who said after emancipation, "There is one sin that slavery committed against me, which I will never forgive. It robbed me of my education." So James Anderson has written: "Blacks emerged from slavery with a strong belief in the desirability of learning to read and write. This belief was expressed in the pride with which they talked of other ex-salves who learned to read or write in slavery and in the esteem in which they held literate blacks." For all of the increasingly stringent slave codes, some slaves did become literate. Some, like Frederick Douglas, were taught by compassionate white masters. Some were taught in white-run quasi-legal schools and Sunday schools. In every slave state, a few whites risked punishment to run schools—more or less formal—for slaves. And for many, slave-controlled religious communities were not just a source of succor in hard times but often the only source of instruction. In this role, the church took on a powerful link to liberation, whatever its initial intentions.[9]

In *Deep Like the Rivers*, Thomas Webber makes the important distinction between slave "religious instruction" as it was conducted by the white community and "true Christianity" as it was defined by slaves in opposition to "slaveholding priestcraft." As he notes, "Quarter people [slave residents of the slave quarter community] made a distinction between the word of God and the words preached by white masters or their ministers." It is an important distinction. Whites taught religion to slaves with one set of goals and theological ideas. Slaves learned religion with very different goals and ideas. So William Craft spoke for many ex-slaves when he said that the conduct of whites gave him a "thorough hatred, not for true Christianity, but for slave-holding piety." Another former slave, James Simler, remembered a white preacher who "used to tell us not to be disorderly on taking the sacrament [but] I thought he was disorderly himself, for he kept slaves." And, of course, there are Frederick Douglas' great words: "Without appeals to books, to laws, or to authorities of any kind, I knew to regard God as 'Our Father' condemned slavery as a crime."[10]

Very early in the development of American slavery, there were debates within the white community about the desirability of encouraging Christianity among the slaves. Some argued that once an African converted to Christianity he or she should be freed. Others, needing as much legitimacy for the institution of slavery as possible, argued that slaves were not human at all and therefore were not capable of conversion or salvation. Henry Box Brown, born a slave in Virginia in 1816, remembered one slaveholder who told his slaves that "Negroes have nothing to do with God." In time, especially after the planter class convinced themselves that conversion did not yield emancipation, most slaveholders came to believe that conversion to Christianity would have a positive effect on their slaves. Of course, the kind of Christianity to which the slaves were to convert was predictable. It offered salvation in the next life based on perfect obedience in this one. Thus William Meade, Episcopal bishop of Virginia, was not alone in preaching a Christianity to slaves that told them: "Take care that you do not fret, or murmur, or grumble at your condition, for this will not only make your life uneasy, but it will greatly offend Almighty God." St. Paul's line, "Slaves, be obedient to those who are your earthly masters" (Ephesians 6:5) may have been the single most popular text in white sermons preached to slaves.[11]

Early in the nineteenth century, there were many efforts to teach slaves to read the Bible as well as simply listen to devotional sermons. As has been noted, however, as the century wore on, fears of Bible reading, of any literacy, and of any black worship not under white supervision grew. Franklin and Moss have described this ambivalent white attitude toward religious knowledge well:

When the abolitionists began their crusade against slavery, planters became more cautious regarding religious activities among slaves and undertook to control them more effectively. In most states black preachers were outlawed between 1830 and 1835, and thereafter slave religious services were presided over by a white person. More and more, however, slaves were required to attend the churches of their masters. This ambivalent attitude toward autonomous religious activity reflected whites' fears that it would be difficult, if not impossible, to control and monitor the beliefs and practices of slaves who were devout Christians. Such fears proved accurate, for many of the most pious and influential slaves had a keen understanding of the difference between the gospel of proslavery preachers and the Christian scriptures' message of divine punishment for oppressors and liberation for the faithful. [There were] numerous ways in which slaves blended their African religious culture with selected aspects of Christianity to produce a sustaining, and at times defiant, religious community—"the invisible institution in the ante-bellum South."

As with so many educational enterprises, what was taught and what was learned were two different things.[12]

What whites wanted preached to blacks and what black slaves actually heard diverged not only when slave audiences attended white-sanctioned worship. In reviewing the oral histories of many ex-slaves, Thomas Webber has concluded that "Despite the fact that many slaves who lived on large plantations were forced to attend church services organized and supervised by whites, nearly all quarter communities organized their own clandestine congregation without the sanction or participation of plantation authorities." These secret religious meetings, usually held at night, formed the heart of African American Christianity in the slave communities. There slaves could testify to their own faith, build their own theological views of the world, support each other, and gain temporary emotional release. There also they could speak of the truth regarding the deep yearning for freedom. Litt Young remembered her plantation near Vicksburg, Mississippi, where there was "a nice church with glass windows and a brass cupola for the blacks." The black preacher, however, had two different messages, depending on who was listening. If the mistress was near, "She had him preach how we was to obey our master and missy if we want to go to heaven, but when she wasn't there, he come out with straight preachin' from the Bible." And the straight message was of freedom.[13]

In the congregations controlled by the slaves themselves, freedom, faith, and literacy were always linked. John Caddie, a University of Louisiana professor who interviewed many former slaves, reflected: "If there chanced to be among the slaves a man of their own race who could read and write, he generally preached and would at times and places unknown to the master, call his fellow slaves together and hold religious services with them. It was to such leaders as these that slaves owed much of their religious instruction." Many of those slaves who learned to read and write, owed their literacy to these services.[14]

EMANCIPATION, LITERACY, AND SCHOOLING

It was out of this crucible of a kind of liberation theology, the hidden institution of the black-controlled church, and a tradition of literacy that southern blacks, newly freed by the war, began to build schools. As James Anderson has reported, even before the first Reconstruction governments had been set up or the first black elected officials began to develop Southern schools, Northern visitors to the South discovered an amazing love of learning there. The abolitionist Harriet Beecher Stowe reported, "They rushed not to the grog-shop but to the schoolroom—they cried for the spelling-book as bread and pleaded for teachers as a necessity of life." And Booker T. Washington remembered in the immediate aftermath of emancipation, "Few people who were not right in the midst of the scenes can form any exact idea of the intense desire which the people of my race showed for education. It was a whole race trying to go to school. Few were too young, and none too old, to make the attempt to learn."[15]

The second thing that amazed Northern observers, whether officials of the army and the Freedman's Bureau or missionaries from Northern white churches, was that the newly freed slaves began their schools even before the first teachers had arrived. The clandestine institutions had produced enough literate people that they could now begin to teach others more openly. Indeed, the formerly hidden black-controlled congregations could now emerge into the light of day with their full range of religious and educational activities. So, as one example, Zion School in Charleston, South Carolina, began operation in December 1865 with an entirely black administration and teaching staff. A year later it had 13 teachers, an enrollment of 850 students, and an average daily attendance of 720 students.[16]

Many of the missionaries were surprised when they first entered the more remote areas of the South, prepared to begin the process of opening schools and educating illiterates. Instead, they found schools were well under way without any white help. John W. Alvord, national superintendent of schools for the Freedman's Bureau and a perceptive observer, reported in the early years of his administration that he found "native schools . . . throughout the entire South," in places that had not yet been visited by any government official or missionary. Alvord and the more open-minded of the missionaries discovered that while Northern white help was needed and welcomed, control was not. This is not to say that literacy rates were very high; general estimates are that not more than 5 percent of ex-slaves were literate at the time of emancipation. But as William Channing Gannett of the American Missionary Association wrote, "What they desire is assistance without control." The literacy of the late-night clandestine meeting or the secret instruction of a friendly teacher was too hard won to be surrendered to the control of others.[17]

Many, if not most, of the African American leaders of the Reconstruction South, both political and religious, had learned to read and write illegally. Frederick Douglas; churchmen like Bishops Henry M. Turner, Isaac Land, and Lucius H. Holsey; Louisiana's lieutenant governor, P. B. S. Pinchback; and many other nineteenth-century Southern black leaders had at least begun their literacy training in secret before the war. Anderson says, "They viewed literacy and formal education as means to liberation and freedom." The purpose of the school reinforced a set of beliefs about the nature of freedom and the social good. For the generation of black leaders immediately after the Civil War, even for those who had been taught to read by friendly whites, and even more for those who had been taught by fellow slaves or free blacks, literacy had always come at great risk, and often at a great price. It was said of Enoch Golden, who had taught many fellow slaves to read, that "On his dyin' bed he said he been de death o' many a nigger 'cause he taught so many to read and write." Thus Anderson concludes that compared to others, "emancipation extruded an ex-slave class with a fundamentally different consciousness of literacy, a class that viewed reading and writing as a contradiction of oppression." This group strongly identified literacy and liberation with the church and illiteracy and oppression with the state.[18]

For a brief period between 1863 and 1876, the state—in the form of federal troops and later federally protected Reconstruction governments—took on a very different role in relationship to the nation's African American community. After 200 years of state support for slavery, with most schooling and nearly all talk of freedom carried on underground, suddenly the federal government was the guarantor of freedom and the state governments actually were in the hands of freed blacks and their white allies. It was a dramatic change indeed. And it was during the thirteen years between the Emancipation Proclamation and the end of Republican Reconstruction with the election of 1876 that DuBois's statement, cited at the beginning of the chapter, came true. Public schooling was established in the Southern states under the leadership of free black leaders.

While the end of slavery dramatically changed the relationship of the state to African Americans, James Anderson's pioneering work shows that it changed far less in terms of African American views of education. The arrival of Union troops and the subsequent development of Reconstruction governments in the Southern states unleashed a movement already well begun in the minds of the people: "Before northern benevolent societies entered the South in 1862, before President Abraham Lincoln issued the Emancipation Proclamation in 1863, and before Congress created the Bureau of Refugees, Freedmen and Abandoned Lands (Freedmen's Bureau) in 1863, slaves and free persons of color had already begun to make plans for the systematic instruction of their illiterates." John Alvord was one of many to observe the emergence of these schools all over the South and to note their roots in passions and hidden institutions begun in slavery. Anderson reports:

> In July 1864, for instance, the black New Orleans Union commemorated the founding of the Pioneer School of Freedom, established in New Orleans in 1860, "in the midst of danger and darkness." Some schools predated the Civil War period and simply increased their activities after the war started. A black school in Savannah, Georgia, had existed unknown to the slave regime from 1833 to 1865. Its teacher, a black woman by the name of Deveaux, quickly expanded her literacy campaign during and following the war. It was this type of "self-sustaining" behavior that produced the native schools [Superintendent] Alvord observed throughout the South in 1866.[19]

Recent historical scholarship has shown that there was far more continuity in approaches to schooling before, during, and after the Civil War than previous generations had thought possible.

Beginning with the first Union victories in 1861, a new and positive link developed between previously underground African American educational activities and the government. Anderson makes the convincing case that the Freedman's Bureau and the various Northern missionary groups, such as the white Congregational American Missionary Association, augmented what was already in place while too often claiming all of the credit. However, the enterprise of establishing schools was vast, and most recognized the need for united efforts on the part of everyone who wanted to expand literacy among the newly freed.

Whether one focuses on the role of federal government agents of the Freedman's Bureau, white Northern missionaries of the American Missionary Association, or emerging black-controlled schools, the links among religion, the black church, and education remained strong. Not surprisingly, the Northern missionaries mixed Protestant Christianity with their lessons in reading and writing just as they had been doing for thirty years or more in the schools of New England and elsewhere.

The link between religion and the new school ventures was even clearer in many black-controlled schools. When black leaders started the Georgia Educational Association, forerunner of public schooling in that state, in 1865, they described their venture primarily in secular terms. In other parts of the South, the link to churches was more obvious. In many places black church-based Sabbath schools offered the first instruction to newly freed ex-slaves. "These church-sponsored schools, operated mainly in evenings and on weekends, provided basic literacy instruction." Alvord complimented them on their success in gathering groups of students "upon the Sabbath day, sometimes of many hundreds, dressed in clean Sunday garments, with eyes sparkling, intent upon elementary and Christian instruction." Another Freedmen's Bureau operative reported on the education in Kentucky in 1867: "The places of worship owned by the colored people are almost the only available school houses in the State." As had happened among whites when schools were founded in the North, so with blacks in the post-bellum South—the separation of secular and religious authority or instruction was almost impossible to make. It was a heritage that would have powerful consequences in the difficult days after 1876.[20]

In the optimistic days immediately after the war, Southern blacks and Northern whites moved quickly to establish statewide systems of public education based on Northern models. In 1867 Congress passed the Military Reconstruction Acts calling for constitutional conventions in each of the states of the former Confederacy in which blacks and whites were to draft new state constitutions. Three years later, by 1870, every Southern state had a constitution with specific provisions for a state-wide public school system financed by state funds. The transition to laws in favor of public schools in Southern states took place with amazing speed. Even after the return to white rule in the 1870s, these provisions remained in the constitutions.[21]

One of the greatest debates of the Reconstruction era had to do with the racial make up of the Southern schools. Radical Republicans ensured that Louisiana and South Carolina included provisions in their 1868 state constitutions for integrated schooling in which all public schools would be open to all children without regard to race. Most of the rest of the Southern states, as they adopted new constitutions between 1868 and 1870, called for equality in schooling but did not specifically mention integration. The largest northern white benevolent societies, especially the Peabody Fund led by its agent, Barnas Sears—Horace Mann's successor in Massachusetts—fought for "separate but equal" schools. (Actually Sears did not quite support equality; the Peabody Fund gave one-third less money to black schools because it "cost less to maintain schools for the colored children than the white.") In describing his support for segregation, Sears remarked, "We ourselves raise no questions about mixed schools. We simply take the fact that the white children do not generally attend them, without passing any judgment on the propriety or impropriety of their course." In light of his position, Sears also successfully argued against inclusion of school integration in the Civil Rights Act of 1875. Other white moderates supported Sears. Among them was William Henry Ruffner, the first superintendent of public instruction in Virginia, who did much to create a state system of education there, but who also argued that "the social repugnance between the races has not been obliterated anywhere" and therefore insistence on integration would undo the progress being made in creating schools. Thus were the foundations laid for segregation and inequality in schooling well before the end of Reconstruction in 1876 or the Supreme Court's ruling in *Plessy v. Ferguson* in 1892.[22]

Of course, the battle about universal education was not just between proponents of integrated and segregated schools. The old planter class and its allies did not want schooling for blacks in any form. The belief that "learning will spoil the nigger for work" did not die with the end of slavery.[23] White Southern clergy argued that education was a private matter belonging to families and churches. A

Baptist minister wrote that the idea of public schools was "foreign to free institutions and fatal to liberty." Robert Lewis Dabney, a white Presbyterian minister, saw public schools as an unrighteous system "wrung by a grinding taxation from an oppressed people" and a "quixotic project . . . the cunning cheat of Yankee statecraft." Such voices spoke for a widespread white Southern fear not only of integration but of black education in any form.[24]

AFTER RECONSTRUCTION

With the return to power of the white planter class which was finalized in the compromise of 1876, when the last of the Union troops were withdrawn in exchange for Southern support for the election of Republican Rutheford B. Hayes as president, the future of the recently established schools was clearly in doubt. Black school defenders were firmly excluded from power—indeed, from any voice in the affairs of their states. The planter class did not abolish the public schools, it simply radically underfunded them, both white and black. White populists began to challenge the white elite in the 1880s and 1890s. Around the turn of the century they were joined by middle-class Southern reformers, which resulted in a moderate expansion of public support for white schools in the South early in the twentieth century. Nevertheless, for the last two decades of the nineteenth century and for most of the twentieth century, Southern states lagged far behind the rest of the nation in support for the public schools. And the separate—and very unequal—school systems for white and black continued, only slowly and partially dismantled after the Supreme Court's reversal of *Plessey v. Ferguson* in the *Brown v. Board of Education* decision of 1954. Only with the Civil Rights movement in the 1950s and 1960s and the emergence of the "New South" ideology in the last third of the twentieth century did Southern support for education come to equal that in the rest of the nation.[25]

With political power firmly in white hands, with increasingly racist attitudes reinforced in state and national legislation, and with the emergence of new terrorist extra-legal organizations such as the Ku Klux Klan, the relationship of Southern African Americans to the state returned in many ways to that of the antebellum era. On the other hand, their relationship to the church was quite different. In the black church, now able to operate at least somewhat more above-ground than during slavery, blacks had an institution under their own control. The new African American Baptist and Methodist associations, the National Baptist Convention, and the African Methodist Episcopal, African Methodist Episcopal Zion, and Colored Methodist Episcopal churches took on a crucial role in all aspects of black community life, nowhere more than in the education of children.

Church-based education took many forms. The Sabbath schools continued to be important, as they had in an earlier era. And for many who were forced to work long hours, now as sharecroppers or in emerging industries, schooling on Sunday provided the route to literacy and religious education. The African Methodist Episcopal Church (AME) reported 40,000 students in its Sabbath schools in 1868. By 1885, long after white state control was complete across the South, the AME church reported "200,000 children in Sunday Schools" that offered "intellectual and moral" instruction. Literacy and religion, the Bible and the spelling book, thus were firmly linked in these critical educational institutions.[26]

Asbury P. Jones, Jr. has recently written, "Perhaps the most significant contribution to the development of black schools in the South after the Freedmen's Bureau expired was made by black Baptists."[27] Church-based schools provided the institutional basis for continued black literacy, for the expansion of black religion, for the education of a new black leadership class, and for resistance to the new forms of post-bellum oppression. The state-supported public schools offered meager fare indeed. When high schools began to be developed in the south as a result of turn of-the-century reform movements, they were for whites only. As scholars such as James Anderson and Evelyn Brooks Higginbotham have reported, "As late as 1910 no southern black community could claim a single public school offering two years of high school. In some places, such as Augusta, black education fared worse than it had in the early 1880s. It was the existence of private institutions that made black secondary education possible at all."[28] For the most part these private institutions were church based, occasionally the result of Northern white missionaries, more often the result of the work of Southern black churches.

Jones' analysis of these schools is right: " . . . much like the church, these black 'private' schools became institutions of resistance to American white supremacy, and allowed for black ideas to flourish and prosper." The evidence for this is not hard to find. Between 1888 and 1907 the black Baptists of Virginia formed twelve secondary schools.[29] In an earlier study of these schools, Lester F. Russell recorded their beginnings :

> Spiller Academy was founded at Hampton in 1891; the Ruffin Academy, at Cauthornsville in 1894; the Northern Neck Industrial Academy, at Ivondale in 1898; the Keysville Mission Industrial Academy, at Keysville in 1898; the Halifax Industrial Institute, at Houston in 1901; the Rappahannock Industrial Academy, at Ozeana in 1902; the Pittsylvania Industrial, Normal, and Collegiate Institute, at Gretna in 1903; the Bowling Green Industrial Academy, at Bowling Green in 1903; the King William Academy, at King William Court House in 1903; the Fredericksburg Normal and Industrial Institute, at Fredericksburg in 1905; and Nansemond Collegiate Institute, at Suffolk in 1905; and the Corey Memorial Institute, at Portsmouth in 1906.

Most of these schools were small, taught in local churches by local pastors, a pattern that developed in most Southern states.[30]

Russell has indicated one of the reasons for the strong support for church-based schooling in the black community: "The impetus on the part of the Black Baptist churches toward education was based on the desire of the leaders to refute the belief generally held that blacks were incapable of the mental development known to whites. Thus, education of the black race was both a test and a challenge to black ministers."[31] But proving black intellectual equality to the white world was only a part of the story. As Anderson and others have convincingly demonstrated, literacy for its own sake was deeply important in the black community. Higginbotham sums up: "There was little doubt in their minds that education stood second only to religion in enabling their survival and salvation in America."[32] And in the hardest of times, before and after emancipation, the two were linked: black-controlled and black-taught schools were embedded within the black church.

Native American Religion, Christian Missionaries, and Government Schools, 1819–1926

OFFICIAL POLICY TOWARD THE TEACHING OF RELIGION in public schools for Native Americans, like official policies toward all aspects of Native American life, can be viewed as either the great exception to or the clearest confirmation of policies for the rest of the nation's inhabitants. From the moment of the first European encounter with the earlier residents in the Americas, Europeans have been deeply ambivalent about the terms of their interaction with Native Americans. In the parts of British North America that were to become the United States, three distinct attitudes emerged quite early and remained in conflict at least until well into the twentieth century: genocide, conversion to Christianity and all attendant European ways (sometimes accomplished through isolated boarding schools), and isolation of native cultures on "protected" reserves where the Indian ways could continue more or less safe from the contamination of European greed, culture, and—sometimes—religion.

Policies of isolation, while often popular, seldom worked for long. In the 1820s some white leaders advocated the great removal of Indians from lands east of the Mississippi so that the lands to the west of the river would form one vast reservation. By the 1840s, however, white land hunger and the settlement of California and Oregon had begun a process of breaking up the western reservation. And by the 1850s the Great Plains were being chopped up into more and more farm and ranch land, less and less reservation land. In 1869 the transcontinental railroad not only linked the East and West coasts of the United States, it cut a swath through the very heart of the great plains and mountains that had been the western reservation. When in the 1890s the historian Frederick Jackson Turner proclaimed the end of the frontier between white and native settlement, he was confirming a change that the vast majority of Native Americans had experienced over the previous several decades. Such changes left really only two options, genocide or conversion. And while any thoughtful retrospective analysis leads one to see significant efforts at genocide, the growing national consensus, certainly from the 1850s onward, pointed to efforts, however half-hearted and mean-spirited, at conversion and assimilation.

In the eyes of most of the nation's leaders, efforts at assimilating a people so fundamentally different from Europeans as the Native Americans meant that the usual niceties about respect for religious rights had to be abandoned. If Native Americans were to adopt European ways, they argued, then there had to be a concerted effort to get them to give up their religious traditions and adopt some form of European Christianity. Until quite late in the twentieth century, few seemed to believe that the First Amendment applied to Indians or to Indian schools. Indeed, the contrary was true. Indian education was expected not only to westernize but Christianize the Native Americans.

Joel Spring, a historian who has devoted considerable attention to the cultural and religious conflicts inherent in European efforts to educate Native Americans, has noted the clear church-state issue in the strong link between religion and Indian education that was part of the United States government's Indian policy for most of the nation's life. "From the perspective of the late twentieth century, government support of missionaries might be considered a violation of the First Amendment prohibition against government support of religion. [But] in the minds of most white Protestants in the early nineteenth century, it probably appeared logical and correct to use missionary educators to 'civilize' Native Americans, because 'civilizing' included conversion to Christianity."[1] Indeed, most architects of the policy believed there were no alternatives.

Of course, very few of the policymakers bothered to consult with those who would be affected. When whites talked of civilizing the

Indians, Indians understood the cost. For Overtakes the Enemy, a Pawnee, moved to the reservation in the 1860s: "To do what they called civilizing us . . . was to destroy us." He understood the kind of cultural genocide involved when he continued: "You know they thought that changing us, getting rid of our old ways and language and names would make us like white men. But why should we want to be like them, cheaters and greedy? Why should we change and abandon the ways that made us men and not the beggars we became." And at about the same time, a Sioux song responded to the white efforts:

"Dakotas
be citizens,"
he said . . .
but
it will be impossible for me
the Dakota ways
Them
I love . . .

But the Sioux and Pawnee ways did not fit with the expanding capitalist culture. As President Ulysses S. Grant said, "No matter what ought to be the relations between such settlements and the aborigines, the fact is they do not harmonize well, and one or the other has to give way in the end." Grant understood which would give way, and since he also believed that "A system which looks to the extinction of a race is too horrible for a nation to adopt." he became, like many of his predecessors and successors, a firm believer in efforts at civilizing and Christianizing the Indians . . . and using the school to accomplish the task.[2]

THE MISSIONARY OPTION:
JOHN ELIOT TO THOMAS JEFFERSON

English colonization of the New World, like the earlier English colonization of Scotland and Ireland and the later colonization of Africa and India, was always done in the name of extending Protestant Christian civilization and bringing Christianity to the native populations. While the lust for land and the desire for empire was never far from the surface, the missionary impulse gave a religious justification to the effort and represented the spirit of at least a few participants. Thus very early in the first English settlement in Virginia in 1617, King James I asked the archbishops of his realm to solicit contributions for "some churches and schools for the education of the children of those barbarians." Two thousand pounds was raised in response and plans made for a college at Henrico, Virginia, which would serve Indian graduates of the tribal schools. Clearly church and school were designed to work together in the enterprise of Christianizing the Indians and bringing them fully within the sphere of Protestant English culture. The schools and college were never built, in part because the settlers kept diverting the funds to other uses and in part because by the 1620s, the relationship between the English and Virginia's native peoples had turned from cautious contact to all-out war.[3]

Farther north, in Massachusetts, Governor John Winthrop's deep hostility to Indians was countered by the work of John Eliot, pastor of the church in Roxbury and "Apostle to the Indians." While Winthrop thanked God for "making room" for the English by a visitation of smallpox on the Indians that "hereby cleared our title to this place," Eliot took time to learn some of the local languages and began his preaching in 1646, reporting sadly that his audience "rather despised what I said." Eliot did not give up, however. He formed small communities of "praying Indians," translated the Bible into Algonquian in 1663, and played a crucial role in the creation of the London-based Society for the Propagation of the Gospel, which sent missionary funds to the colonies for the next century. For Eliot, conversion to Christianity could best be supported and sustained by also embracing all of the accoutrements of English life. In 1649 he wrote, "I find it absolutely necessary to carry on civility with religion." The result was the creation of Indian towns, of which Natick was the first, with streets, houses, farm lots, and a meeting house. Eliot was thus among the first of a long line of preachers, missionaries, and government officials who believed in saving the Indians by schooling them in European civilization and European religion.[4]

On the island of Martha's Vineyard, the Reverend Thomas Mayhew had even greater success in converting the natives to his Puritan faith, translating the scriptures into Wampanoag, and laying the foundations of a continuing community of Christian Indians that continues to meet in the Baptist Church in Gay Head to this day. It has been estimated that by 1675 there were some 2,500 Christian Indians in New England representing 20 percent of the native population.[5]

While its isolation by the sea protected a small part of the Gay Head community, the overwhelming majority died of European diseases. For most of the rest of New England's natives, the impact of disease and war would be even more devastating. King Philip's War, which began in 1675, represented the end of the communities of "praying Indians" which Eliot had established. Probably half of all of the Indians of southern New England were killed in this bloody war. The missionary impulse always seemed to take second place to the ever-expanding white need for land, security, and the defining role in what constituted civilization. In 1642 Miantonomo, a Narraganset leader, warned other Indians about the English who, "having gotten our land, they with scythes cut down the grass, and with axes fell the trees; their cows and horses eat the grass, and their hogs spoil our clam banks, and we shall all be starved." Miantonomo called for resistance, "otherwise we shall all be gone shortly." He understood, earlier than most, what the true cost of European civilization was to be.[6]

The early debates in Virginia and New England set the tone for the rest of the colonial era. While efforts at assimilation into European culture and European religion continued, in the final analysis they always took second place to pure conquest, which resulted either in the extermination or expulsion of the native peoples. And after Eliot, most of those who did argue for assimilation reversed the order, seeking to assimilate the Indians into European ways and seeing conversion to Christianity as an important means of supporting the larger venture. Still, the assimilationist approach to the country's indigenous people did continue from the first contacts to the present. And for assimilation, no institution was more effective than the school and no ideology more powerful than Christianity. Thus for the natives, religion and education would be linked more clearly and more directly than for any other group of peoples.

With the coming of independence, few issues were as pressing in the new nation as Indian affairs. George Washington and his secretary of war, Henry Knox, began the process of developing policy for what they considered the independent nations of Indians. In 1791 Washington sought Congressional support for efforts aimed at offering the "blessings of civilization" to the Indians. The resulting trade and intercourse acts provided for federal support for agents assigned to teach agriculture and domestic arts, establish factories and trading houses, and generally introduce the Indians to what the government considered civilization, which included the nuclear family and, most important of all, private property. It was clear from the beginning of the nation, then, that the government's policy would be, in one way or another, to separate the Indians from tribal allegiances and their way of life, which required vast tracts of land. If Indians could be educated for and settled in English-style villages and encouraged to till the ground as farmers, then most of their land could also be sold off to white settlers and peace would prevail. If this could not be done, the only remaining alternatives contemplated by the government were continuing war or resettlement of the Indians farther and farther west. No other options—no serious respect for the rights of the Indians to their land or their way of life, including their religion— were ever considered. This was in spite of the words of the Northwest Ordinance of 1787, which had required schools for the new white communities and also required that "The utmost good faith shall always be observed towards the Indians, their lands and property shall never be taken from them without their consent and in their property, rights and liberty, they never shall be invaded or disturbed."[7]

The nation's third president, and perhaps the most famous early advocate for education for white citizens, Thomas Jefferson, began his presidency with high hopes for the trading houses as a means of building up Indian interest in owning things, entering a cash economy, accruing debt, and thus separating from both their tribes and their land. In 1803 Jefferson spoke of a "coincidence of interests" as government efforts created willingness on the part of Indians to trade land for "civilization," while European Americans had civilization to offer in exchange for land. It was not to be so easy. Encouraging Indians to embrace the benefits of private property, nuclear families, and ultimately European Christian civilization required more than merely offering a few goods.

Realizing the difficulty, Jefferson quickly moved beyond reliance on the trading houses alone. On one hand, he purchased the

Louisiana Territory, commissioned the Lewis and Clark expedition, and generally supported manifest destiny as a way of greatly expanding both white settlement and Indian distance from the settlements. On the other hand, he expanded Washington's program and requested what were then significant federal funds for the education of the Indians. In the latter part of his program, Jefferson also entered into a close alliance with the evangelical Protestant denominations whom he otherwise distrusted. While federal government agents were engaged in efforts to bring education and civilization to the Indians, under Jefferson and his successors the majority of the federal monies went to Protestant missionaries. These missionaries raised even larger funds from their supporting congregations in order to bring to the Indians the blessings of western civilization in which capitalism, individualism, and Christianity were inseparable. As Lawrence Cremin has noted, "In effect—and paradoxically, given the Jeffersonian penchant for secularism—the government ended up in patent partnership with the several Christian denominations." It was indeed an ironic twist in the career of the author of Virginia's statute for religious freedom. But until well into the twentieth century, few if any voices were raised in favor of the religious freedom of Native Americans. The notion that the pre-European inhabitants of the American lands might have religious traditions in need of respect, indeed of First Amendment protection, was simply not considered. The Indian religion was far too tightly woven into the Indian way of life—a way of life fundamentally at odds with white settlement—to receive such respect or protection.[8]

EXPANDING MISSIONARY SCHOOLING

Jefferson's successors in the White House and in Congress continued and expanded his efforts. In 1810 two of the nation's largest Protestant groups, the Presbyterians and the Congregationalists, created the American Board of Commissioners for Foreign Missions (ABCFM) and soon thereafter sent Protestant missionaries to the Iroquois in New York and to the five civilized tribes of Tennessee, Mississippi, and Arkansas. The mandate of these missionaries— supported by both church and federal funds—was to establish both tribal and more distant boarding schools so that they could raise up a generation of Indians who would be "English in their language, civilized in their habits, and Christian in their religion." Perhaps the most famous of these ABCFM missionaries, Cyrus Kingsbury, illustrated the government-church alliance when he established the Brainerd mission to the Cherokees of Georgia using church funds for the staff and government funds for mission's land and farm equipment. The Brainerd mission served as a model farm, a boarding school, and a Presbyterian church for the Cherokees.[9]

A few years later, in 1818, the House Committee on Indian Affairs recommended to Congress: "Put into the hands of their children the primer and the hoe, and they will naturally, in time take hold of the plough; and as their minds become enlightened and expanded, the Bible will be their book, and they will grow up in habits of morality and industry, leave the chase to those whose minds are less cultivated, and become useful members of society." Thus was established the policy of both the federal government and the majority of Protestant denominations toward the proper relationship of religion and public education for the Indians. In this case, far more blatantly and far more directly than in the case of schooling for whites or African Americans, church and state would join in a mutual effort aimed not only at a generalized Christian morality but at specific conversion to Protestant Christianity as one of the key ingredients in the civilization of the natives.[10]

In 1819 Congress regularized the government's alliance with Protestant missionary efforts and the commitment to Indian education for civilization—meaning private farms, nuclear families, Christianity, and the opening up of previously held Indian land for white settlement—in the passage of the Civilization Fund Act. The Civilization Fund appropriated $10,000 per year so that the president could "employ capable persons of good moral character [i.e. Protestant missionaries for the most part] to instruct them [Indians] in the mode of agriculture suited to their situation; and for teaching their children in reading, writing, and arithmetic." The fund's major advocate, Thomas L. McKenney was a Quaker by background, committed to peaceful conversion of the Indians. McKenney had been for many years the government's superintendent of Indian Trade and in 1824 became head of the new Office of Indian Affairs. He argued for the fund because he believed that "there were now several missionary stations already in operation, though on a small scale, all of them furnishing proof that a plan commensurate to the object would reform and save, and bless this long neglected, and downtrodden people." McKenney, and many in Congress and in the major Protestant missionary groups who worked with him, shared this commitment to schooling, moral uplift, and acculturation to European values.[11]

It is important to remember, in this context, that in white America, the voices of opposition to missionary efforts at civilizing and Christianizing the Indians were not those who argued for respect of indigenous land, cultural, religious, or treaty rights. They were, rather, the voices of the even more land-hungry settlers and military leaders who believed that any effort at assimilation or peace was hopeless. Andrew Jackson, the most famous of those who spoke against the educational effort, told his superior officer in 1814, "I must destroy those deluded victims doomed to destruction by their own restless and savage conduct." Another time, after a bloody battle, Jackson assured his troops of their divine mission—not to Christianize but to exterminate: "The fiends of the Tallapossa will no longer murder our women and children, or disturb the quiet of our borders. . . . They have disappeared from the face of the Earth. . . . How lamentable it is that the path to peace should lead through blood, and over the carcasses of the slain!! But it is in the dispensation of that providence, which inflicts partial evil to produce general good." Half a century before U.S. Army General Philip Sheridan's 1867 statement regarding the Cheyennes, "The only good Indians I ever saw were dead," the potential for genocide was outlined quite clearly.[12]

The basic outlines of federal policy that began under Washington and Jefferson continued throughout much of the century, but with many twists and turns. The fundamental debates between the advocates of conversion, removal, and genocide were never resolved. By the 1830s Southern whites in Georgia and Mississippi began seeking the land of the Cherokee Nation and the Choctaws. In collusion with a supportive President Jackson, they accomplished the infamous removal of these tribes to the west of the Mississippi River. Many of those who had led the earlier missionary efforts protested vigorously as these peoples were forcibly uprooted. Tribal leaders also protested, warning colleagues not to accept any removal treaty and asking those among them who might support the removal "Will you break sticks to put into the hands of the president to break your own heads with?" In 1834 Chief John Ross protested to the secretary of war, "The right of property and even the life of the Cherokee is in jeopardy, and are at the mercy of the robber and the assassin." And later he reminded President Jackson of the "assurances of protection, good neighborhood and the solemn guarantee" of the rights of the Cherokee people. All of these protests made no difference. The federal government and federal troops cooperated closely with the states in removing the Indians.[13]

Of all the Native American groups, the Cherokee and Choctaws had responded by far the most positively to the missionary efforts, welcoming the schools and the churches, setting up their own written language and printing press, becoming farmers and in some cases very successful capitalists, and converting (at least in outward appearance) to Christianity. And it was all for naught. When the pressure for land increased, they too were pushed out without recourse. Not surprisingly, missionaries who met the Choctaws and Cherokees in their new lands in the West reported considerable hostility to Christianity and to schooling that lasted for many years.[14]

While war had always been the alternative to assimilation, the great Indian wars of the plains lasted a relatively short time. Although the land east of the Mississippi had seemed sufficient for white settlers in the 1830s, by the 1840s the pressure was on again. The major nomadic tribes of the plains, the Sioux, the Cheyenne, and the Arapaho fought hard and bravely, but they were no match for the well-trained and mechanized army, especially after the Civil War. The war was not fought only on the battlefields. The army and the settlers destroyed the prairie grass and the buffalo on which Indian culture, and food, and shelter depended. In 1851 the Treaty of Fort Laramie confined many of the Plains Indians to limited reservations. The railroad and barbed wire brought settlers and settled farms. By the early 1870s the major Indian wars were over. There would be continued guerrilla warfare and the great uprising of the 1890s, but the nation's Indian wars were at an end and the Indians had lost.[15]

MISSIONARIES AND BOARDING SCHOOLS

By 1875 almost 300 years of warfare suddenly came to an end. In spite of occasional rebellions, culminating in 1890 with the great Ghost Dance revival and the massacre at Wounded Knee, South Dakota, the military superiority of the post Civil War Union army and the destruction of the buffalo and the rest of the natural infrastructure that supported the Indian way of life meant that the wars were simply at an end. The question, of course, was what would come next?

In 1869, partly in response to the end of the Indian wars and partly in response to corruption in the Office of Indian Affairs, President Ulysses S. Grant announced a new Peace Policy that included three commitments: Reservation personnel would be appointed by church boards rather than the government, government support for education would be expanded, and a group of well-known philanthropists would be appointed by the president to serve as a Board of Indian Commissioners to review and administer Indian policy. The Grant Peace Policy was short-lived. Those who profited from Indian Bureau contracts and patronage fought successfully against interference from both church groups and the lay board.

However, the Peace Policy was the beginning of a new effort. With the end of both the Grant administration and Reconstruction in the South, new efforts began to be focused on the needs of the Indians. With the wars over, more whites were willing to heed reformers like Helen Hunt Jackson, whose 1881 book, *A Century of Dishonor,* described government duplicity. The result in the 1880s was a series of reform efforts, the creation of the philanthropic Indian Rights Association, and the Lake Mohonk philanthropic conferences, which met from 1883 to 1913. The consensus among all of these groups was that the time of war was over. The time for full assimilation had arrived. The U.S. commissioner of education, William Torey Harris, told the Lake Mohonk Conference in 1895 that the time had come finally for an Indian education which included the "Christian ideal of the family," the shift from tribal loyalty to a focus the "independent citizen," and the full amalgamation of Indians into the nation. Secretary of the Interior Lucius Q. Lamar put it more bluntly when he said the "only alternative now presented to the American Indian race is speedy entrance into the pale of American civilization, or absolute extinction." In surprising ways, the policies and the rhetoric had changed very little since Washington and Jefferson or, for that matter, since Eliot and Winthrop.[16]

While the reform efforts of the 1880s were not all that new, they did represent an expansion of federally supported schooling, especially of the boarding school, which was specifically designed to enculturate young Indians by completely cutting them off from tribal influence through a long-term residential program. First, the Dawes Act, passed by Congress in 1887, called for surveying the remaining reservations, dividing the land up into 160 acre holdings for each family, selling the rest off, and giving the family the freedom to sell after twenty-five years. The long goal of shifting from tribal to private property was accomplished simply by congressional vote. Second, the government created a reservation Indian police force in 1878 and Indian courts in 1883 to shift justice from a tribal to a quasi-European-American legal system. Finally, the reformers renewed their educational efforts. The Board of Indian Commissioners asked: "If the common school is the glory and boast of our American civilization, why not extend its blessings to the 50,000 benighted children of the red men of our country, that they may share its benefits and speedily emerge from the ignorance of centuries." Why not indeed? But the common school for Indians was to be different. The community school, placed in and controlled by the community, would not do. Instead a range of reservation schools and boarding schools, controlled by the government and by continued alliance with religious missionary organizations, would raise the Indians to Christianity and civilization. Secularism was not on the agenda.[17]

A new era in federally supported Indian schools began quite accidentally in 1875 when seventy-two Indian prisoners from the Red River War of 1874 were ordered removed from their temporary prison in Fort Sill, Indian Territory, to a federal prison in St. Augustine, Florida. Including leaders and younger warriors from the Cheyenne, Arapaho, Kiowa, Comanche, and Caddo tribes, the prisoners were placed under the direction of Lieutenant Richard Henry Pratt, a veteran of the Union army in the Civil War and several years of Plains Wars. With only vague orders as to how to conduct the prison, Pratt made the decision on his own to turn it into a model school. He recruited Sarah Mather, a graduate of Mt. Holyoke and longtime teacher, and together Pratt and Mather began to teach the Indian prisoners European dress, the English language, and Christianity. As conducted by Pratt and Mather, the prison school made no distinction between sacred and secular. The effort to convert the Indians, isolated as they were by prison walls and thousands of miles from their tribes, proceeded. In time most of them adopted western ways and some seem to have converted to Christianity. Soaring

Eagle, a Cheyenne warrior, wrote: "It is good to go to church. . . . When I go home, I hope to sit down and sing God's hymns . . . I now look up to Jesus who has been so good to me and pray to him to forgive all my past sins and make me his child." Because the inducements for making such pronouncements were considerable, those who spoke them knew that they were probably the only route to eventual freedom, and the enclosed world of the prison made resistance especially difficult, it is impossible to accurately judge how effective the efforts were in terms of the prisoners' core beliefs.

What is easy to judge, however, is the degree to which the prison school was viewed as a success by white society. The Episcopal bishop Henry Benjamin Whipple, himself known for missionary efforts among the Sioux, spoke of how deeply touched he was after a visit to the school. "Here were men who had committed murder upon helpless women and children sitting like docile children at the feet of women learning to read." Harriet Beecher Stowe wrote positively of the school after her visit: "Is not here an opening for Christian enterprise? We have tried fighting and killing the Indians, and gained little by it. . . . Might not the money now constantly spent on armies, forts, and frontiers be better invested in educating young men who shall return and teach their people to live like civilized beings?" The prison school embodied a philosophy dating back to John Eliot, to Washington and Jefferson, and to the missionaries to the Cherokees and Choctaws at the beginning of the nineteenth century. But there was something different in Pratt's experiment. In total isolation it all seemed to work. Enough distance between the Indians and their tribes seemed to be the key to schooling them in civilization and Christianity. And the government was prepared to support both the schooling and the distance.

In time most of Pratt's prisoners were freed. But he continued his efforts, first in an unsuccessful alliance with another Civil War veteran, Samuel Chapman Armstrong, at the latter's American Missionary Association school for freed slaves, Hampton Normal and Industrial Institute. But Pratt had his own vision for Indian schooling. With major federal backing and authorization to recruit 125 students from the West, especially the Sioux, Pratt, again aided by Mather, opened the Carlisle Indian School in a former army barracks in Carlisle, Pennsylvania. Pratt seemed to have solved the major problem with previous efforts at Indian schooling near reservations.

Whether in day schools or boarding schools tribal culture continued to make itself felt. "We make our greatest mistake in feeding our civilization to the Indians instead of feeding the Indians to our civilization" Pratt wrote. Feeding civilization to the Indians, bit by bit, never worked according to Pratt. He had no respect for Indian culture or religion and wanted to cut individuals off from it as securely as possible, literally "feeding the Indians," one by one, into the cultural power of white America.

While historians have had decidedly mixed opinions on Pratt and the Carlisle experience, government agents of the 1880s and 1890s thought they had finally found the solution. Other schools followed in rapid succession. David Wallace Adams has chronicled the some-times tragic history of twenty-five Indian boarding schools built on the Carlisle model between 1879 and 1902. These off-reservation schools created total communities for the full acculturalization of Indians to white ways. They appealed to church and government agents who were determined to prove that Indians were not a race apart but people who could be civilized as well as anyone else. As one reformer of the day wrote: "The years of contact with ideas and with civilized men and Christian women so transform them that their faces shine with a wholly new light, for they have indeed 'communed with God.'" And they did so in government schools designed to separate them from their own culture and induct them into a wholly different world.[18]

Much has been written about the cultural elitism, indeed, the cultural genocide, of the boarding school experience. One of Pratt's most effective way of popularizing his idea was to take before-and-after pictures of the Indians—when they first arrived and at gradua-tion. From today's perspective, these pictures are filled with tragedy, showing Indians shorn of their hair, their dress, their pride. Yet that was exactly the goal of those who sought to "kill the Indian but save the man."

From the perspective of a study of the relationship between religion and public education, the boarding schools came at a unique moment. In one sense, they were the pinnacle of a century-long partnership between church and state to convert Indians to white ways and white religion. Using federal tax dollars, these schools—without apology—taught all of the accoutrements of white American life as it was lived in the late nineteenth century, including most specifically conversion to Christianity, attendance at Christian worship, and the study of Christian scriptures in the schools. At a moment in history when the public schools were finally responding to a half century of Catholic criticism and to growing Jewish immigration by shedding some of their most overtly Protestant characteristics, the federally supported Indian boarding schools showed no such inclination, either by giving any signs of respect to Indian religion or by attempting a less Protestant, more secular approach to instruction. Schools for Indians were the last place where any notion of First Amendment freedom penetrated.

An ironic twist to the story is the fact that just as the Carlisle model was expanding, so too were Catholic schools for Indians. While boarding schools at a great distance from the reservation might be the capstone of the system, much of the federal money continued to flow to missionaries who built boarding or day schools on the reservations. And with the creation of the Catholic Bureau in 1874, Catholic missionaries showed that they intended to join in the effort. Funded in part by the largess of their patron, Katharine Drexel, but also taking advantage of the same federal contracts offered to Protestant missionaries, Catholic teaching orders quickly became a major force on the reservations. During the administration of the first post-Civil War Democrat, Grover Cleveland, from 1885 to 1889, Protestant reformers such Lyman Abbott worried about "an incidental evil of this anomalous condition of affairs" that in 1886 more government contracts were going to Catholic schools than to Protestant ones. It was an ironic event indeed. For most of the nineteenth century Catholics had campaigned, with no meaningful success, for federal and state funding for Catholic parochial schools to serve their own children, especially in the largest urban areas. An alliance of Protestant and more secular forces always succeeded in blocking any such aid. But in the field of missions to the Indians, in spite of the jealously between them, Protestants and Catholics were happy to share the federal aid and use it to convert the Indians from their ancient traditions to an Americanism that seemed to include Christianity in any form.[19]

The acculturation efforts, the missionaries and the boarding schools, and all other attempts to suppress Native American culture and religion did not take place without many forms of resistance. The most dramatic, and most tragic, was that led by the Paiute Wovoka, who called himself the Indian messiah and called on his followers to wear sacred "ghost shirts" and dance the Ghost Dance to rid the land of the white invaders. For Wovoka, the religious roots of the rebellion were clear. He promised that "Big Man [Great Spirit] come. He bring back all game of every kind . . . and all white people die." To many it was an appealing promise.

A few whites saw the Ghost Dance as an appropriate religious activity. A former Indian agent, Valentine McGillycuddy, appealed to the government: "I should let the dance continue. The coming of the troops has frightened the Indians. If the Seventh-Day Adventists prepare their ascension robes for the second coming of the Savior, the United States Army is not put in motion to prevent them. Why should not the Indians have the same privilege? If the troops remain, trouble is sure to come." But the Indians were not Seventh-Day Adventists, the military leaders were not troubled by constitutional scruples, and the Ghost Dance ended in the tragic massacre of men, women, and children who were camped out at Wounded Knee, South Dakota, in 1890. As Ronald Takaki has said, "For Indian America, Wounded Knee violently symbolized the end of the frontier."[20]

After 1890 resistance was much more personal and hidden. Like the slaves who conducted their religious services away from the prying eyes of their masters, Indians continued to practice their religion and their own forms of education out of sight of white eyes. At times this resistance was simply the encouragement given by a medicine man to a family to keep a child out of the boarding school. At times it was the much-complained about tendency of young scholars to stay quietly in touch with family and friends so that "A dance is announced a week in advance, and at once you see the young mind reveling in thought until study and all thoughts of books are driven out and nothing but Indian remains, and weeks pass before the scholars get back to their regular work."[21]

Francis La Flesche, an Omaha who attended a Presbyterian mission school in the 1860s, later published his own recollections. He reported that he and his friends enjoyed the Bible stories, but most of them did not take a "serious" interest in Christianity and remained quite free of the sense of guilt and sin that the missionaries were teaching. At the same time, in La Flesche's account, the missionaries seem to have remained oblivious to the fact that while the boys showed signs of Christian religious devotion during the day, they also continued to share the Omaha myths and traditions with each other late at night after the lights were out and the missionaries gone. Such private acts of resistance maintained traditions thought to be lost and meant—as with African traditions among former slaves—that when times became slightly more tolerant, far less had been forgotten than the white world thought and hoped.[22]

THE SCHOOLS AND THE REEMERGENCE OF TRADITIONAL RELIGION

Only in the 1920s did serious questions begin to be raised about the long standing federal policies, and still only by a minority of voices. A series of investigations of the boarding schools revealed not only the attack on Indian culture but the hard work, poor food, and generally miserable conditions prevelant in what one investigator called "penal institutions—where little children were sentenced to hard labor for a term of years to expiate the crime of being born of their mothers." While Congress gave the various missions title to the land they were using on the reservations in 1922, questions began to be raised in that decade for the first time about the religious nature of the schools, forced religious instruction, and the use of federal tax funds for religious institutions. In 1926 a team of Johns Hopkins researchers began the most systemic review of Indian affairs in decades. The Meriam Report, as Louis Meriam's *The Problem of Indian Administration* was known, called for a completely different approach to Indian affairs. The report summarized much of the last century's work by noting that missionaries and government agents alike had sought to remove the Indian student "as far as possible from his home environment" whether physically in a boarding school or psychologically in an institution that did not honor Indian culture. This approach completely contradicted where education was moving in the rest of the country toward a "modern point of view in education and social work [which] lays stress on upbringing in the natural setting of home and family life."[23]

The coming of the New Deal only a few years after the Meriam Report led to vast changes for all Native Americans. Franklin Roosevelt's commissioner of Indian Affairs, John Collier, voiced a sometimes romantic and sometimes harsh view of the needs of Indians. But he did insist that "Assimilation, not into our culture but into modern life, and preservation and intensification of heritage are not hostile choices." The result was the Indian Reorganization Act of 1934, which ended the Dawes Act privatization of Indian lands and called for federal respect for tribal entities and Indian culture. While the heart of the 1934 legislation focused on protecting Indian lands and tribal identity, Commissioner Collier also noted that it repealed the brunt of the last century's educational efforts: "Through 50 years of 'individualization,' coupled with an ever-increasing amount of arbitrary supervision over the affairs of individuals and tribes so long as these individuals and tribes had any assets left, the Indians have been robbed of initiative, their spirit has been broken, their health undermined, and their native pride ground into the dust." Such words represented a sea-change in federal policy. Mission schools did not end overnight. Most denominational missionary organizations opposed Collier's prohibitions on interference with Indian religious life or ceremonies. At the same time, Collier protested a lack of funds for his efforts. There was even less support for Indian cultural and educational efforts during the Truman and Eisenhower administrations. Serious federal attention to Indian schooling was delayed until the Great Society legislation of the 1960s, when significant funds began to flow to educational efforts that respected tribal and cultural rights. The Rough Rock Demonstration School, established on the Navajo Reservation in 1966 as a truly community-controlled educational effort represented a significant further step in this direction. Cultural imperialism did not end with the Great Society, but the concerted effort to individualize, westernize, and Christianize the Indians did slowly begin to cease.[24]

Finally, in 1978, a joint resolution of Congress made it clear that the First Amendment rights did, in fact, apply to Indians. Beginning with the recognition that "the freedom of religion for all people is an inherent right, fundamental to the democratic structure of the United States and is guaranteed by the First Amendment of the United States Constitution" and recognizing that "the religious practices of the American Indian (as well as Native Alaskan and Hawaiian) are an integral part of their culture, tradition and heritage, such practices forming the basis of Indian identity and value systems," the act clearly recognized that federal policy had too long failed to recognize this right, which "has often resulted in the abridgment of religious freedom for traditional American Indians."

As a result, Congress also resolved "That henceforth it shall be the policy of the United States to protect and preserve for American Indians their inherent right of freedom to believe, express, and exercise the traditional religions of the American Indian, Eskimo, Aleut, and Native Hawaiians, including but not limited to access to sites, use and possession of sacred objects, and the freedom to worship through ceremonials and traditional rites." It was an important recognition even if very late in coming. While still honored in the breach in many cases, the act, and the long civil rights agitation that led to it, has created a very different era in the teaching of religion in Indian schools.[25]

This chapter began with the assertion that U.S. policies toward the teaching of religion—specifically Protestant Christianity—in the federally supported public schools for the Indians could be seen as either the exception or the confirmation of similar policies for all other citizens. Indian policy was the exception, because nowhere else was there such an overt emphasis on conversion to Protestant Christianity—or, later in the century, to any kind of Christianity—as in the Indian schools. This was a use of federal tax dollars that made someone like Thomas Jefferson highly uncomfortable even as he expanded the budgets for the enterprise. The *McGuffey's Readers* and the teachers and school leaders who built schools and used the textbooks certainly aimed at inculcating very similar Protestant values in the children of Protestants, Irish Catholics, and the nonreligious who might attend the schools. The missionaries who went South after the Civil War to teach the freedmen and women, and who found, to their surprise, that indigenous schools already existed, were motivated by quite similar notions of sharing Christian culture. But in neither of these cases was there the same missionary emphasis on rejecting the former religion, faith, and ways, and quite clearly converting people to Christianity, as there was in the Indian schools.

But in a larger sense, the efforts at a common American schooling were very similar. Where an 1818 congressional committee could speak of Indian schooling designed to "Put into the hands of their children the primer and the hoe . . . the Bible will be their book, and they will grow up in habits of morality and industry," half a century later, in 1863, Boston's much-respected civic leader, Edward Everett, spoke of Americanizing the city's Irish Catholic youth "not with cannons and Minie rifles, but with the spelling-book, the grammar, and the Bible!" And Jon Reyhner and Jeanne Eder, among other scholars, have explored the clear links between Indian education and the education offered to African Americans. In the nineteenth century, the common school effort—whether focused on white Protestants, white Catholics, African Americans, Native Americans, or, late in the century, other groups—had some very common elements. It was not the institution of the more laissez-faire Democrats of Jackson and his heirs who preferred to fight Indians, defend slavery, and control their individual destinies as free whites.[26]

Schooling as it developed in nineteenth-century America was a natural part of a Whig/Republican worldview that had at its heart what historian Carl F. Kaestle has called the Protestant-Republican ideology. As Kaestle says, this ideology included: "The sacredness and fragility of the republican polity (including ideas about individualism, liberty, and virtue); the importance of individual character in fostering social mobility; the central role of personal industry in defining rectitude and merit . . . the superiority of American Protestant culture; the grandeur of America's destiny; and the necessity of a determined public effort to unify America's polyglot population, chiefly through education." It was an ideology that, for better and for worse, fueled the public school movement and built it into an enterprise in which society could safely abandon having an established church; the common school would replace such a church as the purveyor of Christian morality and civic virtue. Advocates simply did not understand the fact that the same notions of morality and virtue were not held by all citizens. What was to its advocates so clearly a program of national progress, seemed like a form of incredible oppression, bordering at times on cultural genocide, to those who did not share their specific moral and religious worldview.[27]

Mary Crow Dog, a Lakota Sioux and herself a student at the St. Francis boarding school in the 1960s, summed up the policies that led to such miserable experiences for her, her mother, her grandmother, and so many other Native Americans between the early years of the nineteenth century and at least the middle of the twentieth:

Oddly enough, we owed our unspeakable boarding schools to the do-gooders, the white Indian-lovers. The schools were intended as an alternative to the outright extermination seriously advocated by generals Sherman and Sheridan, as well as by most settlers and prospectors overrunning our land. "You don't have to kill those poor benighted heathen," the do-gooders said, "in order to solve the Indian Problem. Just give us a chance to turn them into useful farmhands, laborers, and chambermaids who will break their backs for you at low wages." In that way the boarding schools were born.[28]

And so, for several generations, they continued.

From the perspective of the end of the twentieth century, it is striking how similar the attitudes of the leaders of the dominant Protestant-European-American culture have been toward the education of Catholic immigrants, African American slaves and free people, and Native Americans. As Joel Spring has argued, "In many ways, the educational plans of European Americans for Native Americans set the stage for the common school movement of the 1830s and 1840s."[29] Christianizing, generally "Protestantizing" Catholic immigrants, Southern slaves and free blacks, and the native population of the land all had the same goal: the transformation via education of a diverse population into a nation dominated by European culture and Protestant values. The older form of formally established church was, in the new United States between 1800 and 1860, to be replaced by a unified common Protestant culture, taught by a common school. The pattern had been a long time in coming before the common school era, and it continued long after.

Protestant, Catholic, Jew: Immigration and Nativism from the Blaine Amendment to the Scopes Trial, 1875–1925

AT THE CLOSE OF THE CIVIL WAR, white Protestant Americans were a deeply divided lot. The war itself had been fought largely between white Protestants of the North and white Protestants from the South. The rapid industrialization of the North, begun in the 1830s and accelerated by the war, was creating new class divisions that were far deeper than earlier ones. Jefferson's vision of a nation in which the vast majority of white citizens were agrarian democrats gathered in small towns and sharing a rough equality was receding faster and faster.

The war also hastened other changes in the country that had been developing for some time. African Americans who had been in the land for over 200 years were suddenly newly enfranchised citizens. Native Americans were still present despite two centuries of attempts at extermination. And more and more immigrants were coming to these shores who were not Protestant (as in the case of Irish and German Catholics or later in the century Russian and other European Jews and Italian and eastern European Catholics) or neither white nor Protestant (in the case of the Chinese and later Japanese and other Asians). And in the decades leading up to the Civil War, the United States had also conquered new lands in the Southwest that included a majority of mostly Roman Catholic Hispanic citizens. The United States has always been a diverse nation. From the beginnings of the colonial era, Europeans of many different cultures mixed with Native American and Africans. Before the nineteenth century had ended, the diversity would grow much greater. Nevertheless, for an adult white male Protestant in the 1860s or 1870s, the perception of the world was likely to be shaped by a sense of rapid change and a growing cultural and religious diversity which threatened a long-accepted hegemony. It was a sense of change that led to grand visions but also to crabbed and mean-spirited fears. And it would change many people's attitude toward the relationship between religion and the public schools.

THE BLAINE AMENDMENT:
RELIGION, SCHOOLS, AND THE ELECTION OF 1876

In August 1876, in the waning days of Reconstruction and in the midst of the highly convoluted presidential campaign between Republican Rutherford B. Hayes and Democratic nominee Samuel Tilden, the U. S. Senate voted on an amendment to the Constitution. Known as the Blaine Amendment, the proposed change would have applied the rights guaranteed in the First Amendment to state and local government actions with a long series of very specific added restrictions.

> No State shall make any law respecting an establishment of religion, or prohibiting the free exercise thereof; and no religious test shall ever be required as a qualification to any office or public trust under any state. No public property and no public revenue of, nor any loan of credit by or under the authority of, the United States, or any state, territory, district, or municipal corporation, shall be appropriated to or made or used for the support of any school, educational or other institution under the control of any religious or anti-religious sect, organization, or denomination, or wherein the particular creed or tenets of any organization, or denomination shall be taught. And no such particular creed or tenets shall be read or taught in any school or institution supported in whole or in part by such revenue or loan of credit; and no such appropriation or loan of credit shall be made to any religious or anti-religious sect, organization, or denomination, or to promote its interests or tenets. This article shall not be construed to prohibit the reading of the Bible in any school or institution; and it shall not have the effect to impair the rights of property already vested.

The vote fell along strict party lines with all of the Republicans supporting the amendment and all of the Democrats opposing it. While the Republicans were in the majority, they did not have the needed two-thirds vote to move the amendment along to the House and to the states.[1]

The party-line vote on this amendment revealed a great deal about the deep fissures running through American politics at the time. The original amendment, as proposed by Republican House Speaker James G. Blaine, had simply banned public funds for any school "under the control of any religious sect." In the heat of the presidential campaign, the Republican nominee Hayes, the governor of Ohio, dictated a much more detailed amendment which would allow him to campaign on a platform that showed that he and the Republican Party were clearly committed to support for the public schools and to a significant federal role in the schools, that they were absolutely opposed to any form of support for Catholic parochial schools, and that they supported Bible reading and other religious symbols in the schools as a means of unifying a Christian, and predominantly Protestant, nation. Fresh from his reelection victory in Ohio, based on a vitriolic anti-Catholic campaign, Hayes meant to campaign for the presidency on what he understood to be a winning combination of anti-Catholicism and a pro-pan-Protestant public school ideology. Hayes' decision to focus his campaign on school issues represented, in many ways, the culmination of Carl Kaestle's description of Whig/Republican ideology that supported public schools based on a belief in "the superiority of American Protestant culture; the grandeur of America's destiny; and the necessity of a determined public effort to unify America's polyglot population, chiefly through education." Seeking to succeed the great Civil War hero but discredited politician Ulysses S. Grant, Hayes and his managers thought they had hit on a winning issue.[2]

In a brilliant new work, *Religion, Race, and Reconstruction: The Public School in the Politics of the 1870s*, Ward M. McAfee has described the politics of the Blaine Amendment. It was an era in which battles over continued support for Reconstruction and the rights of Southern blacks, and battles regarding religion and schooling—whether over the question of Bible reading in public schools or the use of tax dollars to support Catholic parochial schools—were mixed in the highly charged partisan divisions. The Hayes-Tilden election is remembered for its tragic outcome in which Tilden's electoral majority was thwarted in Congress through an agreement with some Southern electors to support Hayes in return for a guarantee that he would remove the last federal troops and thus end Reconstruction. The heart of the campaign was not fought over overt issues of race and Reconstruction, however. Rather, the battle lines were drawn by Hayes and the Republicans around the issue of religion and the public schools. They developed an overtly anti-Catholic campaign strategy that had worked for Hayes in Ohio state politics. These Republicans sought to increase the role of the federal government in standardizing education, for blacks and whites, Northerners and Southerners. They also sought to resurrect the overtly Protestant nature of the schools of an earlier era through required Bible reading (from the Protestant King James version only) and an absolute prohibition on any state aid to Catholic parochial schools. Tilden, governor of the much more diverse state of New York, built his own campaign coalition around a base of Northern Catholics, who clearly wanted government aid for their schools and resisted the use of a Protestant translation of the Bible in the public schools, and Southern whites who remained deeply hostile to Reconstruction and African American civil rights, federal involvement in the affairs of the individual states, and what they often continued to see as a Northern invention—the public school. Prejudices ran deep on both sides. In retrospect there is little appealing in the prejudices of either candidate or their followers.[3]

Historians have focused a great deal on the outcome of this most contested of American presidential elections. Yet they have paid surprisingly little attention to the bitter battles about religion and the schools at the very heart of the 1876 election campaign. For anyone interested in the long history of struggles over the evolving relationship between religion and public education in the United States, it is one of the most illuminating moments in the story. Only in the context of the rapid changes brought about by the creation and growth of schools in the South under African American leadership, white Southern fear and opposition to those schools, and the parallel growth of Roman Catholic majorities in many of the cities of the North can the election's key issues be understood.

As has already been noted in chapter four, in the years immediately after the Civil War newly freed African Americans with support from the Freedmen's Bureau and Northern missionary organizations had created the first public school systems in the states of the former Confederacy. When Louisiana and South Carolina wrote their new state constitutions, both in 1868, each specifically called for a racially integrated public school system. Other Southern states also required public schools in their new constitutions, but with less clear requirements for integration. Radical Republicans in Congress supported these efforts with various proposals for both federal aid and requirements for integration. Massachusetts Republican Senator Charles Sumner's 1874 proposal for a civil rights bill included a specific requirement for school integration—North and South.[4] A backlash followed quickly.

The elections of 1874 were fought very much along the lines of the congressional civil rights bill. While the number of black elected officials grew in parts of the Deep South still under Reconstruction, the attack on schooling and on integration was a major factor in many elections. In North Carolina, the reconstruction state superintendent was defeated by a white Redeemer (as the anti-Reconstruction white politicians were known) who was militantly opposed to integrated schools and not much of a defender of schools at all. More important for the future of Reconstruction, many Northern constituencies turned out Republicans and replaced them with Democrats who had campaigned on a specifically anti-school integration platform. In Harrisburg, Pennsylvania, a Democratic newspaper asked if people were "quite ready to sleep in the same bed with their colored brethren, . . . or even to place their children in the same rooms at school with pickaninnies." After the November election, the Cleveland *Daily Plain Dealer* editorialized, "The Republican party has attempted to legislate the people up to an ideal standard of morality. . . . It has interfered with the private rights of the citizens." The powers of fear and racism were clear and for the first time since the war the anti-integration Democrats controlled the House of Representatives.[5]

The growing alliances of fearful whites, North and South, had more consequences than the outcome of the 1874 election. As early as 1871, the growing Ku Klux Klan had led riots in eastern Mississippi that included burning schools and beating teachers. Klan terrorism against blacks and against schools and teachers was encouraged after 1874 across the South. The legislature of the state of Texas had officially dismantled the public education system in 1873, and the new Democratic majority in Congress was unwilling to overturn the action. Reconstruction's end had begun, and Republicans from President Grant on down believed the party was in danger. Their retreat from the commitment to integrated schooling, to federal aid to education, and to efforts to use the schools in building a new and more just social order occurred very quickly.[6]

But debates about race and the schools were not the only educational concerns on the national agenda. The growth of the nation's Roman Catholic population, its development in certain urban areas, and the growing militancy of both American and world-wide Catholicism provided a new target for Republican efforts. With Charles Sumner's death in 1874, few white national Republican leaders were as willing to defend integrated schooling or schooling for African Americans. But anti-Catholicism offered a different route to power. And there was much to fuel the fires.

The first Vatican Council, meeting in Rome in 1869-1870 and responding far more to European events flowing from the French Revolution than to anything in the United States, had moved the Catholic church in conservative and centralizing directions. Among the council's actions had been the declaration of Papal Infallibility concerning faith and morals. For many American Protestants, these actions confirmed deeply held fears of Catholic plans for world conquest that were to begin in the United States. Bernard McQuaid, Catholic bishop of Rochester, New York feared that the council vote would exacerbate tensions. Just prior to the vote he wrote that "we can look for hard times in all countries in which Catholics and protestants are expected to live together." American newspapers, overwhelmingly Protestant owned and dominated, played up the issue.[7]

Closer to home, two other issues of particular concern to Catholics became the heart of the school debates. Since at least the 1840s when New York's Catholic bishop John Hughes had led the fight for a portion of the city's school funds, Catholics were rankled by both the anti-Catholic nature of much of the public school curriculum and by the fact that they were required to both pay taxes to support public schools and, in conscience, maintain their own separate schools at their own expense. Both issues became important on the national stage in the 1870s.[8]

The Cincinnati Bible War began in 1869 as the city in which famous antebellum evangelical Protestants like Lyman Beecher had presided gained greater and greater numbers of Catholics. While Cincinnati still had a Protestant majority in 1869, Catholics were the largest single denomination and Archbishop John Purcell was the city's leading religious figure. The city's Catholic schools enrolled 12,000 children compared to 19,000 in the public schools. Moderates on the Cincinnati School Board sought an arrangement with Purcell along somewhat similar lines to those of New York's Poughkeepsie Plan. In the Cincinnati version, the public school system would take over the Catholic schools and pay the teachers. Bible reading and hymn singing would be banned in all schools. And on weekends, the Catholic diocese would lease back the former parochial schools and offer religious instruction. It seemed like a reasonable plan to negotiators on both sides, but it was not to be.

Anti-Catholic papers in Cincinnati got word of the plan and began an attack on what they said was a means to take the Bible out of the schools. Nationally, *Harper's Weekly* attacked what its editors called a popish plot. In response, Archbishop Purcell withdrew from the negotiations and attacked the school board for not simply dividing the school funds between the public and the Catholic schools. In the battle, all moderate voices were drowned out.

In fact, there were many moderate voices. The majority of the Cincinnati School Board, on their own, decided to end Bible reading and hymn singing, although they were overturned in court appeals. In a dissent in one of the court cases, Judge Alphonso Taft, father of the future president, agreed with the school board. To him, reading the Bible in school clearly violated Ohio's Bill of Rights. It was offensive to Jews, Mormons, Buddhists, atheists, and free thinkers of many stripes. Clearly Judge Taft had a broader sense of what it meant to be an American than most of his fellow Republicans in the 1870s. He said: "The idea that a man has less conscience because he is a rationalist, or a spiritualist, or even an atheist, than the believer in any one of the accepted forms of faith, may be current, but it is not a constitutional idea in the state of Ohio." Taft paid for his liberality by never again receiving a Republican nomination for office. Beyond Taft's fate, the Cincinnati experience dramatically fueled the fear that Catholics represented an attack on the Bible in the schools and, more basically, on Protestant cultural dominance in the nation.[9]

While Cincinnati was struggling with Bible reading, New York focused on the issue of money. The infamous Boss Tweed, leader of

Tammany Hall's corrupt political ring that achieved such political power in New York in the 1860s and 1870s, succeeded where Bishop Hughes had failed. In 1869 he convinced the New York state legislature to provide state funds for religious schools with 200 or more students—in practice, this meant largely Catholic parochial schools. For New York's and many of the nation's Protestant Republicans this law represented "a direct attack upon the essential theory of our public school system." Illinois and Iowa quickly amended their state constitutions to ban any such aid. Thomas Nast, the famous anti-Tweed cartoonist, began a series of mean-spirited cartoons showing "What Sectarian Appropriations of the School Fund Is Doing and What It May Lead To" with a Catholic bishop and a racist version of the Buddha each absconding with school monies.[10] Thus the stage was set for the battle of 1876.

From the Republican perspective, the issues were clear. The Republicans did not have the courage to campaign for the rights of Southern African Americans in the face of persistent racism. But if Southern racism could be linked to Northern fear of immigrant Catholics the issues shifted dramatically. As McAfee has said, "In the South, Ku Klux Klan terrorists were then burning public schools. Accordingly, these midnight criminals demonstrated their disloyalty to American nationalism. In the North, Roman Catholics sought to remove the Bible from the public schools. Therefore, these dissenters also revealed their contempt for the nation." The only solution was a clear campaign, similar to those of the generations before, to save the nation with "the Bible, the spelling book, and the primer." The ultimate result of that campaign, as it was waged in the nation's centennial year of 1876, was a tragedy for all parties.[11]

For African Americans in the South, the end of Reconstruction meant a quick end to nearly all rights. While most Southern states did continue to operate schools, they generally did so poorly and on a clearly separate and unequal basis. Generations of Southern blacks were denied quality schooling as well as the most basic political and economic rights. Only with the great civil rights movements of the 1950s and 1960s was even a portion of the lost ground of the 1870s recovered.

For Roman Catholics, the losses were also clear. While the Blaine Amendment disappeared from consideration after the election, state aid for parochial schools never again developed a strong constituency.

When Colorado was admitted to the nation in 1876, Congress insisted that its state constitution bar state aid to any sectarian schools, and all future states were expected to include similar bans. Most older states adopted the same restrictions during the next few years. At the same time, Catholic insistence that the overtly Protestant symbols be purged from the schools continued with greater and greater success. While schools did become more secular as a result of the need to respect Catholics and others, secular schools, whatever their value, had hardly been the primary Catholic goal. In the twentieth century, the Supreme Court began to interpret the Fourteenth Amendment as applying the First Amendment's limits on the federal government to state and local governments, and in an odd way, a more liberal court enacted much of the heart of the Blaine Amendment into U.S. constitutional history. As late as 1960, when John F. Kennedy ran for president, one of the keys to his success in becoming the nation's first Catholic president was his clear disavowal of any intention of supporting federal aid for Catholic parochial schools. The prejudices of the Blaine era ran deep indeed.[12]

THE CHANGING FACE
OF AMERICAN RELIGION, 1880–1920

If the growing diversity of the nation stirred fears in the 1870s, those nativist fears only deepened as the greatest tide of immigration ever came to these shores between 1880 and 1920. The Chinese immigration had started earlier, first to California and then to many parts of the nation, beginning with the Gold Rush of 1849. Initially the Chinese had been welcomed as candidates for assimilation. The *Daily Alta California* had editorialized in 1852 that "the China boys [sic] will yet vote at the same polls, study at the same schools and bow at the same altar as our own countrymen." In these early years, education was seen as the key. If the Chinese could attend public schools, they could be taught to vote and worship correctly. Fairly quickly, however, especially as mining declined and the transcontinental railroad was completed in 1869, the Chinese began to be seen as a threat to white labor, and the racism of two centuries toward blacks and Indians expanded to include the early Asian immigrants.[13]

Late in the century Japanese, Filipino, and Korean immigrants also began coming to the United States. Many of these newest Asian immigrants went to Hawaii, which quickly become the most cosmopolitan part of the country. Because of the segregated housing on pineapple and sugar plantations, Asian culture, including Buddhist religious practice, was able to thrive there more than in other parts of the country. While the Chinese had come mostly as single men, Japanese and Filipino immigrants often came as families and children followed. With children came new conflicts about education. The white planters in Hawaii, much like their counterparts in the South, feared too much schooling. One plantation manager asked, "Why blindly continue a ruinous system that keeps a boy and girl in school at the taxpayers' expense long after they have mastered more than sufficient learning for all ordinary purposes?" A University of Hawaii student remembered a schooling in which "the children learned about democracy or at least the theory of it." This kind of education led a sugar plantation owner to respond, "we had better change our education system here as soon as possible." Because of Hawaii's racial and cultural diversity, education there has never had the same level of religious assimilationist assumptions as in other parts of the union. And in Hawaii, as elsewhere, the battle over the school's role in preparing for democratic citizenship and for second class citizenship has been fought for a long time.[14]

From the other side of the planet, Mary Antin arrived in Boston early in the new century as a young girl, a Jewish immigrant from the Russian village of Polotzk. In her romantic but enlightening autobiography, *The Promised Land*, Antin revels in the freedom of America, a freedom symbolized for her most clearly in the public school. Her experience with the school—and she was far from alone in this—was quite different from that of earlier immigrants, for at least two reasons. The first was the horror from which she had immigrated. She was old enough to remember Russia clearly. "Often we heard that the pogrom was led by a priest carrying a cross before the mob. Our enemies always held up the cross as the excuse of their cruelty to us." At the same time, by the 1890s and later, the public schools, especially in the large urban centers where Jewish immigrants settled, had been cleared of most of the outward trappings of religion. Fifty years of struggle on the part of Catholics to remove hated Protestant symbols had resulted in schools that, though still sometimes having prayers and other symbols strange to viewers from the late twentieth century, were relatively secular compared to the schools of a half century before or—more important to these new immigrants—to the Russian Orthodox schools of their homeland. As a result the schools spelled liberation. So Antin remembered, "Father himself conducted us to school. He would not have delegated that mission to the President of the United States." Here was learning and freedom in the new country.[15]

Antin also reflected a secularism common among many of the first generation of Jewish immigrants. While many held to the orthodox ways, others were more caught up in the secular world of socialism and assimilation. Antin remembered the clash that this division caused for her when she decided that she herself was an atheist.

It was Rachel Goldstein who provoked my avowal of atheism. She asked if I wasn't going to stay out of school during Passover, and I said no. Wasn't I a Jew? she wanted to know. No, I wasn't; I was a Freethinker. What was that? I didn't believe in God. Rachel was horrified. Why, Kitty Maloney believed in God, and Kitty was only a Catholic! She appealed to Kitty. "Kitty Maloney! Come over here. Don't you believe in God—There, now, Mary Antin!—Mary Antin says she doesn't believe in God!"

Antin continues the story of how she held her ground, more and more stubbornly, as the faithful of different traditions gathered on the school playground in Chelsea, Massachusetts to challenge her. The issue was resolved after recess by the teacher who: "made me understand . . . that it was proper American conduct to avoid religious arguments on school territory. I felt honored by this private initiation into the doctrine of the separation of Church and State, and I went to my seat with a good deal of dignity, my alarm about the safety of the Constitution allayed by the teacher's calmness." This is more than a charming story. It well symbolizes both the incredible religious and cultural diversity that had come to the schools of urban America by the beginning of the twentieth century and the strange forms that peer pressure as well as institutional pressure could take in these institutions.[16]

Antin can no more be taken as the typical Russian Jewish immigrant than any one story can stand for any immigrant group. The very fact that by her early thirties she was publishing her autobiography in the *Atlantic Monthly* and then with Houghton Mifflin marks her as exceptional. But the Jewish immigrant experience was different from that of earlier immigrant groups; not easier or harder, but different. The Jewish tradition of learning was part of what held the community together in the oppression of the old world. The daily insults and pogroms of czar and Orthodox church meant that there was no romanticism about what had been left behind. And the schools into which these immigrants arrived, though far from respectful of their religion, their culture, or their potential contribution, had been reshaped dramatically from those that sought so overtly to Protestantize the Irish Catholics of the 1830s and 1840s or that so thoroughly sought to purge all aspects of Native American or Asian life from their charges.

THE ROAD TO THE SCOPES TRIAL

The fears and uncertainty of a changing America continued to play out in the forum of the public schools in many different ways. After the end of Reconstruction, it was a long time—until the New Deal—before any real talk of federal aid to schools resurfaced, and only with the Great Society in the mid-1960s did anything other than the most targeted kinds of aid get through Congress. Proposals such as those considered in Congress in the late 1860s and early 1870s for a truly unified national system of education have never again surfaced. In education, the power of states and localities reigns supreme. And in large part because of the significant local power over school matters, schools have continued to be a place where much of the nation's— and different region's—self-image and cultural identity are played out. In that process, no issue has been more powerful than the proper role of religion, religious belief, and religious teachings.

At probably no other point in the nation's 200-year history of struggle with the issue of religion and the schools has the battle been joined with as much color, as much national attention, and as little clarity regarding the outcome, as in Tennessee's famous 1925 trial of John Thomas Scopes for violating state law prohibiting the teaching of evolution in the public schools.

Between the contest over the presence of the Bible in public schools and state aid to parochial schools, which came to such a dramatic head in the election of 1876 and the end of the nineteenth century, two intellectual trends began to develop in the United States that would, in the twentieth century, almost eclipse questions of Bible reading or state aid to religious schools as the dominant point of the debates about religion and the schools. As a number of thoughtful historians of American religion have shown, fundamentalism emerged as a new theological school of thought in the last years of the nineteenth century, although it had roots in the earliest Puritan movements in England and the Americas. At the same time, the publication of Charles Darwin's *Origin of Species* in 1859 dramatically shifted the teaching of science in the schools within decades of the initial printing. These two developments had virtually no impact on each other in the nineteenth century. When they did meet, the proponents of each view consciously sought to make room for the other. The collision was postponed but clearly not averted.

Darwinian teaching slowly emerged in more and more high school textbooks. Fundamentalism grew as a religious wing of many of the Protestant denominations—initially in the urban North, only later in the rural South. The great late-nineteenth-century revivalist Dwight L. Moody dismissed any potential clash between science and religion, seeking, as he always did, to shift the focus to individual salvation and skip the arguments. Moody was far from alone in his accommodationist views. While as early as 1874 Princeton theologian Charles Hodge had declared Darwinism "virtually a denial of God" and urged against allowing it in biology classes in religious colleges, most others were much more permissive. Ironically, as the debate played out, essays in *The Fundamentals,* the ultimate textbook of fundamentalism published between 1910 and 1915, made room for evolution. James Orr, author of some of the key essays in these volumes had earlier written "Assume God—as many devote evolutionists do—to be immanent in the evolutionary process, and His intelligence and purpose to be expressed in it; then evolution, so far from conflicting with theism, may become a new and heightened form of the theistic argument." He continued this line in his essay for *The Fundamentals* by saying that evolution was "coming to be recognized as but a new name for 'creation.'" And even the great William Jennings Bryan himself, in his years of campaigning for the presidency, made it clear that while he personally rejected evolution, "I do not mean to find fault with you if you want to accept the theory."[17]

Scientists and scientific textbooks were equally accommodationist, especially in the United States. Darwin himself concluded
that natural selection was both random and often cruel and left little
room for a beneficent creator. His chief English defender, T. H.
Huxley, was "sharpening up my claws and beak in readiness" for a
battle with Christianity. In the United States, however, Asa Gray,
professor of botany at Harvard and a friend and confidant of Darwin
who arranged for the publication of *Origin of Species* in the United
States, saw no conflict between that work and his own Protestant
faith. Gray told a group of Yale seminarians that "the forms and
species, in all their variety, are not mere ends in themselves, but the
whole a series of means and ends, in the contemplation of which we
may obtain higher and more comprehensive, and perhaps worthier,
as well as more consistent views of design in Nature than hereto-
fore." God's grand design, for Gray, could be seen as effectively in
evolution as anywhere else. Gray not only spoke to seminarians; his
Elements of Botany was the major high school botany text of the late
nineteenth century. In the post-Darwin editions of his text, Gray
described plant evolution as a way of showing that the various
species are "all part of one system, realizations in nature, as we may
affirm, of the conception of One Mind." The 1884 high school
geology text written by University of California geologist Joseph
LeConte described the field as "a history of the evolution of the
earth and of its inhabitants." Nevertheless, LeConte saw no conflict between his liberal Christianity and his views of geology and
warned his students against getting caught up in worry about
reconciling the details between the differing views of creation.[18]

Few students, whatever their faith or lack of faith, were likely to
be offended by these kinds of texts. Few parents, whatever their
religious backgrounds, were likely to be worried about having their
children read this sort of material. So, for the most part, nineteenth-
century theologians and scientists seemed determined to avoid a
fight. It would not be so easy in the twentieth century as the schools
became the primary battleground in which these theological and
scientific battles were waged.[19]

Many historians have attempted to come to terms with the roots
of fundamentalism in the late nineteenth century. It is not necessary
to explore all of the issues or the debates among historians surrounding this very significant theological change that began to emerge in

the post–Civil War United States to understand the basic shape of what happened. While theologians have directly associated fundamentalism with the publication of *The Fundamentals*, the religious historian George M. Marsden is correct in describing these books as "a symbolic point of reference." "When in 1920 the term 'fundamentalists' was coined," Marsden also wrote, "it called to mind the broad united front of the kind of opposition to modernism that characterized these widely known if little studied volumes." For the purposes of understanding the hostility to the teaching of evolution that exploded in the twentieth century, attention to three strands of what came to be known as fundamentalism is essential.[20]

First, fundamentalism was specifically antimodernist. In part this meant that its adherents rejected modernism in theology, specifically the emerging higher criticism of the Bible. Where theological modernists sought to understand the Bible in the social context in which it was written and apply its teachings in the contemporary context, fundamentalists increasingly focused on the unchanged word of God and became increasingly literalistic in their insistence that the Bible was specifically and infallibly God's word. It is important to note that fundamentalist leaders, contrary to most current stereotypes, have never been anti-intellectual. Indeed, far more than some of their nineteenth-century predecessors such as Dwight L. Moody and Henry Ward Beecher, they engaged in very thorough research and linked piety with rigorous theology. They just came to intellectual conclusions that were far from the mainstream of the modern world. Although its literalistic side is perhaps best known, fundamentalism was also anti-modern in another equally important way.

Since the Puritan era, American evangelicals had been believers in progress. For many, America was the place where the Kingdom of God would finally and fully blossom. Fundamentalists, for the most part, had none of this hopefulness. Moody began to speak of the change when he preached, "I look upon this world as a wrecked vessel" and continued, "God has given me a lifeboat and said to me, 'Moody, save all you can.'" It was a significant shift from an optimistic belief in Christianity's role as the ultimate agent of social and moral reform to a much more defeatist attitude toward culture and a desire to save as many individuals as possible for a better future life. As early as the 1880s, the predecessors of fundamentalism were talking more and more about the world, and the United States, "growing worse and worse." With the Red Scare at the end of World War I, this pessimism hardened into a deep distrust of all aspects of the modern world. And while fundamentalism originally began among Northern city preachers and teachers, it did take on deep roots in the rural South. After the 1920s, at least one significant aspect of fundamentalism was that it "was a focal point for the real hostility of rural America toward much of modern culture and intellect."[21]

Finally, fundamentalism was a fighting faith. In this sense, it had roots deep in Christianity's aggressive rejection of sin. The militant side of fundamentalism grew rapidly in the twentieth century. Whereas Moody, who died in 1899, could say of his opponents "Let us hold truth, but by all means let us hold it in love, and not with a theological club," his best-known successor, Reuben A. Torrey, took a clearly different approach: "Christ and His immediate disciples immediately attacked, exposed and denounced error. We are constantly told in our day that we ought not to attack error but simply teach the truth. This is the method of the coward and trimmer; it was not the method of Christ." And after 1920, few errors attracted fundamentalists more than the teaching of evolution in public schools supported by their tax funds and the primary source of their children's education.[22]

The earlier, more sociological students of fundamentalism may have missed some of its theological roots, but they did notice a powerful link being forged among many white Protestant Americans who saw their cultural dominance receding rapidly in an increasingly diverse nation. These Protestants found in fundamentalism a faith reassuring in its specific antimodernist stance, hostile attitude toward change, and militant approach to sin. By 1920 more thoughtful observers should have seen the explosion coming.

While fundamentalism was growing increasingly militant and distrustful of the nation's intellectual establishment, the next generation of American scientists and textbook authors were moving beyond the genial approach of Gray, LeConte, and their colleagues. Recommending basic curricular changes that led to the consolidation of high school botany and zoology courses in a unified biology curriculum, the journal *School Review* carried a recommendation in 1900 that "The fundamental theory of the evolution of organized life and an explanation of the powers of 'natural selection' should surely be unfolded when data enough have been mastered to make it intelligible." *Elementary Biology*, published in 1912 by James E. Peabody and Arthur E. Hunt, made its perspective clear. After describing "the struggle for existence," the text continued with a picture of Darwin and a description of "his great book on the 'Origin of Species,' published in 1859—a book which has doubtlessly influenced human thought more than any other book of modern times." In 1914, in a nationally circulated article for high school science and mathematics teachers, a teacher named Oran L. Raber stated that it was their duty to their students "to correct for them some of the ideas which previous training in the Sunday school or home has led them." This may have been good science, but it was a historic break with the confidence that at least the Protestant churches had placed in the public schools. And the textbook that John Scopes used in the biology classes that led to his trial, George William Hunter's *A Civic Biology*, was also quite clear. In Hunter's version, "Species have been modified, during a long course of descent, chiefly through the natural selection of numerous successive, slight, favorable variations." Hunter was clear in his attribution of these views to Darwin, and he left little room for intelligent design by a higher power. The issue of the randomness of the natural selection process, far more than the numbers of days, years, or millennia involved, was at the heart of the battle between the scientific and the religious worlds. While the nineteenth-century textbooks sidestepped that issue, the new texts emerging after 1900 did not.[23]

As important as the story of the changing tone and content of high school science textbooks is for understanding the explosion of the 1920s, it is equally important to recognize the changing role of the high school itself. Emerging out of the earlier college preparatory academies in the nineteenth century, the American high school remained an institution serving a very small and elite portion of the nation's young people up to the century's end. After 1900, however, the high school became the natural culmination of the common school rather than an elite educational experience. In 1890 the federal government recorded 200,000 students enrolled in all of the nation's high schools. By 1920 the number was almost 2 million. Thus by this time it was much more likely that many people's children, particularly the children of rural fundamentalists, actually would enroll in high school and study the new science texts. The site of the

Scopes trial, Dayton, Tennessee, for example, opened its first high school in 1906. In 1925, the year of the trial, Tennessee governor Austin Peay, who signed the anti-evolution law, said, "High schools have sprung up throughout the state which are the pride of their communities." And for many parents and community leaders, these new institutions, which they were so proud to have in their communities and to have their children attend, suddenly seemed to be teaching a set of theories about the creation of the world, the beneficence of God, and the origins of the human race directly the opposite to the faith in which they believed. Thus there developed a crisis in the relationship between the schools and the faith of the people that was bound to come to a head.[24]

In 1921 William Jennings Bryan added two new speeches to his repertoire, "The Menace of Darwinism," and "The Bible and Its Enemies." Darwin, Bryan charged, "does not use facts; he uses conclusions drawn from similarities." This was clearly not sufficient science for Bryan. In "The Bible and Its Enemies," Bryan went on to say that belief in evolution "leads people away from God." He also saw Darwin as linked to a survival-of-the-fittest worldview that justified war and, indeed, had laid "the foundations for the bloodiest war in history"—World War I. Finally, Bryan, the old progressive, saw in Darwin an attack on the rights of labor and all of the social legislation he had sponsored over thirty years. Much earlier he had seen in Darwin "the merciless law by which the strong crowd out and kill off the weak." For someone who had opposed capitalist robber barons for his whole career, a new justification for their greed was clearly something to fear. And Bryan's position against social Darwinism certainly had as much resonance with his increasingly Southern and rural audiences, who felt oppressed by the same national corporations, as any of his arguments about correct biology.[25]

In response to the growth of evolutionary textbooks, Bryan proposed that "in schools supported by taxation we should have a real neutrality wherever neutrality in religion is desired." Far from being the buffoon he has often been characterized as, Bryan, in fact, had a fairly nuanced approach to the issue. Unlike later "creationists," as opponents of teaching evolution came to be called, he sought only to ban the teaching of human evolution, not plant or animal evolution. He believed that a respect for religious diversity meant that the Genesis account could not be taught in the schools. But he did insist that "If the Bible cannot be defended in the schools it should not be attacked, either directly or under the guise of philosophy or science." His goal, unlike that of some of his supporters or those calling for the teaching of creationism in the latter half of the century, was simply silence on the issue.[26]

Bryan was far from alone in campaigning against the teaching of evolution in the schools. As a three-time presidential candidate, he was certainly the best-known voice, but a wide range of voices, both preachers and lay people, began the new decade by explaining to church and political audiences why the teaching of evolution must be stopped. Initially Bryan advocated moral pressure. However, when the Kentucky Baptist State Board of Missions called for outlawing the teaching of evolution in the state's schools and when a bill to do just that was introduced in the legislature in January 1922, Bryan endorsed the action. These bills linked Bryan's long-standing support for public education with his majoritarian and anti-evolutionist views. As he said, "Those who pay taxes have a right to determine what is taught; the hand that writes the pay check rules the school." And Bryan was confident what these hands would want. Similar anti-evolution bills were introduced in New York and Minnesota in 1922. While some states moved more slowly, Oklahoma became the first one to act in 1923, when a textbook bill was amended to prohibit any mention of evolution in state's texts. Before the end of the 1920s, forty-five similar bills were filed in twenty states. Needless to say, Tennessee was one of the states to enact this legislation.[27]

In fact, Tennessee came somewhat late to the issue. The anti-evolution bill was introduced in the legislature in the spring of 1925 along with other measures to increase school funding. It passed both houses and was signed by a somewhat reluctant Governor Austin Peay, who said: "Right or wrong, there is a deep and widespread belief that something is shaking the fundamentals of the country, both in religion and morals. It is the opinion of many that an abandonment of the old-fashioned faith and belief in the Bible is our trouble in a large degree. It is my own belief." Peay correctly saw the legislation as a response to a much wider cultural dis-ease and as a symbolic response. It was a way for local people to assert control over their schools and in a sense over their destinies, which seemed more and more to be shaped by forces from far away. He never expected the law to be enforced. He was in for a major surprise.[28]

The story of the trial of high school biology teacher John Thomas Scopes for teaching evolution in Dayton, Tennessee, in spite of the new state ordinance specifically prohibiting such teaching has been told often and well. Edward J. Larson's new *Summer of the Gods* certainly represents the best and most thorough account. The basic outline of the trial is clear. For the leaders of the American Civil Liberties Union (ACLU), based in New York, the passage of laws banning the teaching of evolution were more than an attack on academic freedom, they were part of a larger assault on personal liberty in the United States in the wake of the Red Scare that arose at the end of World War I. As such challenging the laws was essential and the ACLU set out to find a test case. In May 1925 it placed an advertisement in the Chattanogga *Times*. "We are looking for a Tennessee teacher who is willing to accept our services in testing this law in the courts. . . . Distinguished counsel have volunteered their services. All we need now is a willing client." They soon found a somewhat reluctant, but ultimately willing client in John Scopes.[29]

According to most accounts, a group of Dayton boosters, led by George Rappleyea, manager of the local mines, two young attorneys, Herbert E. Hicks and Sue K. Hicks, and a few friends decided that Dayton could use the national publicity of a show trial. They called the Dayton High School's twenty-four-year-old science instructor John T. Scopes, who remembered Rappleyea saying "John, we've been arguing, and I said that nobody could teach biology without teaching evolution.' 'That's right,' I said, not sure what he was leading up to." The young teacher found out soon enough. He was asked directly, "Would you be willing to stand for a test case?' Scopes was young, not particularly committed to Dayton, and had little to lose. He agreed.[30]

Two of the greatest showmen of the decade quickly took over the trial. The leading anti-evolution spokesperson, William Jennings Bryan, appeared as a counsel for the prosecution, with Clarance Darrow, probably the greatest attorney of the era, appearing for the defense. Dayton got quite a show indeed. In fact, the trial had to be moved out of the courthouse and on to the lawn to accommodate the crowds. Perhaps no trial in the first half of the twentieth century received as much publicity. For all of the hoopla, however, the legal results were quite limited. Scopes was found guilty—he had clearly broken the letter of the law—and was fined $100. Higher courts in

Tennessee overturned the case on a technicality which ensured that the ACLU could not have its dream of an appeal to the U.S. Supreme Court. The trial's impact was not in legal but in cultural, religious, and educational circles.

Darrow's withering questioning of Bryan, who appeared as an expert for the prosecution, allowed Darrow to make a fool of Bryan and, by implication, of religious fundamentalism—if not in the eyes of the Dayton audience, at least on the national stage. Bryan started explaining scripture but fell back on a seemingly lame "I believe in creation as there told, and if I am not able to explain it I will accept it." He held his ground, insisting "The only purpose Mr. Darrow has is to slur the Bible, but I will answer his questions." Darrow responded, "I am examining your fool ideas that no intelligent Christian on earth believes." H. L. Mencken, one of the best-known journalists of the era, summarized the evolution trial: "Neanderthal man is organizing in these forlorn backwaters of the land, led by a fanatic, rid of sense and devoid of conscience. . . . There are other States that had better look to their arsenals before the Hun is at their gates." Fundamentalism, indeed all of the rural South and the conservative religion associated with it, became stereotyped in much of the country as anti-intellectual and fearful of any forms of scientific thought. Mary Bryan had warned her husband that the anti-evolution crusade could easily shift from an effort to focus on the curriculum of the schools to a conservative assault on individual freedom that the Great Commoner could never support. Bryan was more confident than his wife that he could control the trial's outcome. But the result of the trial was a tarnishing of fundamentalism for decades to come. Indeed, religious fundamentalism retreated from the national stage for almost half a century after the trial, growing in churches and spreading through evangelists but avoiding legislation or the national spotlight. For many commentators, at least through the 1970s, the Scopes trial was the high-water mark of a religious fundamentalism that seemed doomed to the margins of society.[31]

Anyone looking at the impact of the Scopes trial on school curriculum, however, must conclude that the fundamentalists won more than the liberals. John Scopes committed his crime simply by citing the approved Tennessee biology text, *A Civil Biology*, which, in conflict with the law, clearly described the evolutionary process. As early as 1923, publishers Ginn and Company had changed the description of evolution in their texts from scientific truth to "a theory." After the trial *A Civil Biology* was changed dramatically. The 1927 edition dropped the identification of Darwin as "the grand old man of biology" and simply listed him as a leading biologist. All references to human evolution were omitted. Where the earlier edition had described Darwin's "wonderful discovery of the doctrine of evolution," the new edition simply referred to "His interpretation of the way in which all life changes." Most other science texts followed suit.

Herbert Kliebard and other students of textbooks have regularly noted how quickly publishers retreat from any controversy. After the Scopes trial the nation's science publishers certainly retreated very quickly from any seeming endorsement of Darwin or the teaching of evolution. Only with the revival of science teaching in response to fears of the Soviet Union in the late 1950s and the expansion of federal funding for science texts in the 1960s did evolution return to the place it had occupied in the curriculum prior to 1925. Thus for over a quarter century Bryan had the silence on the issue he had sought.[32]

This lack of attention to the topic of evolution, which reigned for much of the middle of the twentieth century, remains an unnoticed chapter in the history of the uneasy relationship between religion and the public schools. As Kliebard and others have noted, textbook publishers and many teachers often prefer silence to controversy. In the case of evolution, this was certainly true for many years, and it is still the case in some circumstances. Silence can be a kind of respectful neutrality, but it does not prepare students to be thoughtful citizens, able to engage different opinions and different world views and, ultimately, to think for themselves. Only in the last years of the century have new approaches to the relationship between science education and religion emerged. They are explored in later chapters of this volume. And the nation is still a very long way from a satisfactory resolution of the issue.

Prayer, Bible Reading, and Federal Money: The Expanding Role of Congress and the Supreme Court, 1925–1968

IN RETROSPECT, the fifty years following the Scopes trial can be seen as a time when the major battles around the relationship between religion and the schools moved from the state to the national level. No one planned it that way. No group seeking a larger or a smaller role for religion in the schools decided after 1925 to move the center of gravity to the federal government, even though the ACLU lawyers would have dearly loved a Supreme Court review of Scopes' conviction. Many people in Washington opposed the growing federal role. On the other hand, there have always been federal issues with which to contend, whether the 1791 decision to amend the federal Constitution to prohibit a religious establishment, the nineteenth-century alliances of the Bureau of Indian Affairs and the Freedman's Bureau with Protestant missionary organizations, or the efforts to amend the U.S. Constitution to specifically prohibit any level of governmental aid to Catholic parochial schools after the Civil War. But things did change in the middle of the twentieth century. With the coming of the New Deal and World War II, more and more aspects of American life were finally adjudicated in Washington, D.C. In the case of religion and the schools, two things speeded this reality.

First, the U.S. Supreme Court began to take on a larger and larger role as the appeal of last resort in determining just how the separation of church and state should be applied in school cases. Beginning in the 1920s but expanding rapidly in the 1940s and 1950s,

Prayer, Bible Reading, and Federal Money: The Expanding Role of Congress and the Supreme Court, 1925–1968

IN RETROSPECT, the fifty years following the Scopes trial can be seen as a time when the major battles around the relationship between religion and the schools moved from the state to the national level. No one planned it that way. No group seeking a larger or a smaller role for religion in the schools decided after 1925 to move the center of gravity to the federal government, even though the ACLU lawyers would have dearly loved a Supreme Court review of Scopes' conviction. Many people in Washington opposed the growing federal role. On the other hand, there have always been federal issues with which to contend, whether the 1791 decision to amend the federal Constitution to prohibit a religious establishment, the nineteenth-century alliances of the Bureau of Indian Affairs and the Freedman's Bureau with Protestant missionary organizations, or the efforts to amend the U.S. Constitution to specifically prohibit any level of governmental aid to Catholic parochial schools after the Civil War. But things did change in the middle of the twentieth century. With the coming of the New Deal and World War II, more and more aspects of American life were finally adjudicated in Washington, D.C. In the case of religion and the schools, two things speeded this reality.

First, the U.S. Supreme Court began to take on a larger and larger role as the appeal of last resort in determining just how the separation of church and state should be applied in school cases. Beginning in the 1920s but expanding rapidly in the 1940s and 1950s, the court took on a number of cases that culminated in its 1947 definitive ruling in *Everson v. Board of Education* that, at least in cases of religious freedom, the Fourteenth Amendment did in fact apply the freedoms of the First Amendment to local as well as federal decisions. The court's role expanded further in the highly debated decisions in 1962 and 1963 ending devotional prayer and Bible readings in the schools.

Second, the long national debate over whether the federal government could provide financial aid to the public schools—a goal long blocked over "state's rights" issues in regard to race and over Protestant/Catholic disagreements regarding aid to parochial schools—was finally resolved with the passage of the Elementary and Secondary Education Act as part of Lyndon Johnson's Great Society in 1965. In customary Johnson fashion, LBJ and his advisors simply sidestepped the parochial school question by having federal resources follow the child rather than go to the school. With the power of the Court's decisions and with the significant increases in congressional funding, the federal government seemed destined to play the leading role in many aspects of public education, especially the church-state struggles, for some time to come.

THE DECLINE OF PROTESTANT AMERICA

While the political crusading of fundamentalism went underground for a generation after the Scopes trial, a more generalized Protestant intolerance did not. For many Protestants, conservative and not so conservative, the belief that the United States was a fundamentally Protestant nation died hard. On numerous occasions throughout the 1920s the schools became the battle-ground for efforts to maintain the Protestant ascendancy. In 1922 a coalition of groups in Oregon, including Protestant churches and the Ku Klux Klan, initiated a successful referendum which mandated that, beginning in 1926, every child between eight and sixteen must attend public school. A number of those affected by the law, including the leaders of the state's Roman Catholic parochial schools, appealed to the Supreme Court. In its 1925 ruling in *Pierce v. Society of Sisters*, the U.S. Supreme Court struck down the law on relatively narrow grounds. Choosing not to engage in a discussion of whether the Fourteenth Amendment demanded state as well as federal respect for religious freedom, the justices, in a unanimous opinion, found that the Oregon law would have deprived Catholic and other school organizations of their property rights without due process of law.

While the Pierce case was decided as a property rights case, the conservative Justice James C. McReynolds used it and an earlier case on foreign-language schools, *Meyers v. Nebraska*, to expand the notion of property rights to include the right "to the orderly pursuit of happiness." McReynolds thus insisted:

> [W]e think it entirely plain that the Act of 1922 unreasonably interferes with the liberty of parents and guardians to direct the upbringing and education of children under their control. . . . The fundamental theory of liberty upon which all governments in this Union repose excludes any general power of the State to standardize its children by forcing them to accept instruction from public teachers only. The child is not the mere creature of the State; those who nurture him and direct his destiny have the right, coupled with the high duty, to recognize and prepare him for additional obligations.

Thus in unmistakable language, the Court made it clear that compulsory schooling did not mean compulsory *public* schooling. The rights of Catholics or other groups, whether religious or not, to maintain their own schools at their own expense was clearly affirmed. And the next quarter century represented the fastest growth of Catholic parochial schools of any time in the nation's history.[1]

The rights of Roman Catholics and others to maintain their own schools was settled in 1925, but that certainly did not signal the end of anti-Catholic or many other forms of bigotry in the nation's life. Church historian Robert Handy has described the 1920s and early 1930s as the end of the Protestant era in America. While he is also careful to note that this "does not at all mean that Protestant faith and institutions have not carried on," he also makes a convincing case that after 1935 it was no longer possible to speak of a Protestant America, as it had been in the previous century and a half. Obviously there are many who have yet to come to terms with these changes. But for many Protestants who entered the 1920s with such high hopes—the war had saved the world for democracy and prohibition had saved the nation from drink—the intervening fifteen years were difficult indeed. And the difficulties were played out on numerous fronts, many impacting the relationship between the church and the schools.[2]

For many Protestants, letting go of their dominant place in the culture was not easy. Leighton Parks, an Episcopal rector in New York City, offered the Episcopal tradition as the great bulwark against a Roman Catholic takeover of the nation. White Protestants, he urged, should protect their heritage and so "cement the spiritual union of the great race of which we form so important a part." Others were more blunt. The Imperial Wizard of the Ku Klux Klan spoke of three "great racial instincts" which were essential to the nation's future: "These are the instincts of loyalty to the white race, to the traditions of America, and to the spirit of Protestantism. . . . They are condensed into Klan slogan: 'Native, white, Protestant supremacy'." And of course, the Scopes trial itself has been interpreted, in part correctly, as one of the last gasps of this same commitment to Protestant, Christian, white, and nativist hegemony. After all, the team of lawyers who defended Scopes included Jews and represented both the nation's intellectual elite and the hated citadel of New York.[3]

Finally, the presidential election of 1928 brought all of these fears and hatreds to a new height. The fears of Catholicism, of New York, and of losing prohibition all came together when New York's governor Al Smith won the Democratic Party nomination. While historians have argued that the prosperity of the era should have guaranteed Herbert Hoover's victory over any Democratic nominee, the election brought the fears of many to the surface. One Anti-Saloon League broadside summarized the cultural divide of the campaign: "If you believe in Anglo-Saxon Protestant domination; if you believe in those principles which have made the country what it is; if you believe in prohibition, its observance and enforcement, and if you believe in a further restricted immigration rather than letting down the bars still lower, then whether you are a Republican or a Democrat, you will vote for Hoover rather than Smith." This obscure piece of campaign literature summarized the issues all too well. To be for Smith was to be for increased immigration, which meant more Catholics from southern Europe and more Jews from Eastern Europe; to be for Smith meant to be for ending the great experiment of enforced Protestant morality known as prohibition; and to be for Smith was, most of all, to be for an end to "Anglo-Saxon Protestant domination."[4]

As another historian of American religion has also noted, it was not merely the loss of racial and religious superiority that threatened Protestants, it was the growing secularization of the nation and of the very institutions in which so many Protestants had placed their greatest trust. Edwin S. Gaustad has described the change of the 1920s and 1930s: "The school, not the church, would now Americanize ethnic minorities and culturally deprived groups. The school, not the church, would now give instruction in prudence and morality—the basic niceties that became known as 'citizenship.' The school, not the church, would now plan and plot how to refashion and reform the society of America, holding national meetings and instituting ambitious programs to this end." Gaustad has seriously underestimated the degree to which the school had been taking over all of these responsibilities for at least a century—certainly since Horace Mann claimed them in the 1830s. However, he is quite correct in understanding the degree to which by the 1920s and 1930s the school ceased to take direction—at the most fundamental cultural level—from a Protestant hegemony in politics and society. A century of secularization had moved very far along. For those seeking a simpler America—less diverse, less differentiated—the past now seemed far gone.[5]

The secularization of the public schools had been a long and slow process between the 1830s and the 1930s. Even in the 1930s, schools still bore a few limited formal trappings of religion. But the situation Timothy Smith had described in the 1830s and 1840s in which Protestants could send their children to the public school, "confident that education would be 'religious' still,"[6] was long past. Where in many states the founders of the public schools—people such as Samuel Lewis, Calvin Stowe, Catharine Beecher, John Pierce, Caleb Millis and others—were either Protestant ministers or very active church people, the twentieth century school leaders were a thoroughly secular lot, although their professed secularism often masked personal roots in an evangelical tradition every bit as strong as their predecessors.

David Tyack and Elisabeth Hansot have provided a brilliant description of the changes in the philosophies of school leaders as the nineteenth century gave way to the twentieth. Giving the new turn-of-the-twentieth-century leaders the appropriate name of "administrative progressives," Tyack and Hansot note:

> The members of the "educational trust" (as the administrative progressives were sometimes called) embraced the new managerial models developed in business. Rarely self-conscious about their cultural assumptions, they incorporated many of the values of their small-town pietist upbringing into what they regarded as an objective "science of education." They sought legitimacy through expertise rather than through deference to character or through broad public participation in policy making.

These new twentieth-century leaders, with their confidence that "they possessed the instruments of scientific progress that would enable them to shape society towards 'ever nobler ends,'" continued to operate as evangelicals in terms of their missionary zeal, but the philosophy they imparted had a secular and scientific ring that suited the intellectual tenor of the new century but left many more pious parents distinctly uncomfortable and feeling slightly diminished.[7]

No less a progressive educator than John Dewey himself sought to describe what might be a "common faith" for the twentieth century when he published a book by that title in 1934. For Dewey, a new approach to the debates between religious and nonreligious people might be possible if the religious impulse could be separated from its reliance on the supernatural—however conceived—so that "what is genuinely religious will undergo an emancipation . . . then, for the first time, the religious aspect of experience will be free to develop on its own account."

For Dewey, something of this sort was essential if there was to be any religious element left in education. After all, "Nothing less than a revolution in the 'seat of intellectual authority' has taken place. . . . There is but one sure road of access to the truth—the road of patient, cooperative inquiry operating by means of observation, experiment, record and controlled reflection." And this was not a road leading thoughtful people one bit closer to any traditionally accepted view of religion, although it could be a road leading the human community to fulfill its responsibility in "conserving, transmitting, rectifying and expanding the heritage of values we have received that those who come after us may receive it more solid and secure." Dewey was confident that in this process of cultural transmission of the highest and best of human relationships resided "all the elements for a religious faith that shall not be confined to sect, class, or race." *A Common Faith* was not Dewey's most influential book, but in its gently but clearly stated rejection of all traditional forms of religious faith and relationship with a transcendent being in favor of a commitment to an ethical and scientific human community, he spoke for many of the educational leaders of his day.[8]

In their review of American educational history, Wayne Urban and Jennings Wagoner, Jr., have noted Dewey's blind spot when it came to other people's strongly held conservative religious views. Like many secular progressives, Dewey could not help seeing a more theistic worldview not as a democratic political right in need of respect, but as simply the stubborn reaction of fundamentalists in need of the ministrations of good progressive educators. During World War I, Dewey and a group of his students wrote quite critically of Polish Catholics who supported the American war effort but also the Polish monarchy and the church. He was much more comfortable with the more liberal Polish Jews who also supported the war but who, quite understandably, supported neither monarchy nor Catholic church. The toleration of beliefs that one considers deeply misguided is one of the most difficult challenges for any true believer in both democracy and religious freedom. Yet without such toleration, a pluralistic, multicultural school, indeed a free society, is impossible. Unfortunately, this tolerance does not come easily.[9]

Franklin Roosevelt's four terms as president were relatively quiet on matters of church and state, religion and the schools. One observer, Gilman Ostrander, saw the New Deal as "a secular movement such as the nation had not witnessed since the days of Jeffersonian republicanism."[10] It was an administration that had deeper links to Dewey's notions of faith than to any of the historic religious communities. President Roosevelt's own inclinations to focus on auxiliary educational agencies such as the Civilian Conservation Corps and the National Youth Administration, and his distrust of the inherent conservatism of the "educational establishment" meant that he was not likely to push federal funding for schools and therefore not likely to get caught in the historic swamp of battles over aid to parochial schools. He simply did not mean to aid any schools.

One arena where the New Deal did get into battles over issues of schooling has already been noted. Roosevelt's commissioner of Indian Affairs, John Collier, was deeply committed to supporting the "great spiritual stirring [that] had become noticeable throughout the Indian country. That awakening of the racial spirit must be sustained, if the rehabilitation of the Indian people is to be successfully carried through." Collier's—and Roosevelt's—commitment to support Indian spirituality and the clear recognition of Indians' rights to religious freedom put them at odds with many of the missionary societies that had worked among the Indians in the previous century. But the climate of the times meant that the New Deal opponents had little support for their objections. In this one realm of Indian affairs, the Democratic administration was prepared to support the growth of indigenous spirituality.[11]

THE SUPREME COURT ENTERS THE PICTURE

While the president and Congress were occupied elsewhere, the Supreme Court became increasingly involved in issues related to religion and schooling during the New Deal era. In 1935 William and Lillian Gobitas were expelled from the public schools of Minersville, Pennsylvania, for refusing to pledge allegiance to the flag. The brother and sister were Jehovah's Witnesses. They and their parents believed that the flag was a graven image and that saluting it constituted a breach of the Ten Commandments. In an extraordinarily thoughtful response, William Gobitas wrote to the authorities:

> Dear Sirs, I do not salute the flag because I have promised to do the will of God. That means that I must not worship anything out of harmony with God's law. In the twentieth chapter of Exodus it is stated, "Thou shalt not make unto thee any graven image nor bow down to them nor serve them . . . ." I do not salute the flag [not] because I do not love my country but [because] I love my country and I love God more and I must abide by His commandments.
>
> —Your pupil, Billy Gobitas

The ten-year old-student had cut to the heart of the meaning of religious freedom. The Courts, however, were slower to catch up.[12]

In previous cases involving Jehovah's Witnesses, judges had tended to rule that "The pledge of allegiance is not, by any stretch of the imagination, a religious rite." The result, for many of that faith, had been the development of their own separate schools. In this case, the Gobitases seemed to have a good base for challenging these rulings. The federal district judge who first heard the case, Albert Maris, wrote in a pretrial hearing, "Individuals have the right not only to entertain any religious belief but also to do or refrain from doing any act on conscientious grounds, which does not prejudice the safety, morals, property, or personal rights of the people." The Pennsylvania state school superintendent saw forcing a student to salute the flag as something that might take place in the growing dictatorships in Germany and Italy, but not the United States. But the Minersville superintendent, Charles Roudabush, feared that allowing one student not to salute the flag would spread dangerously. "In our mixed population where we have foreigners of every variety, it would be no time until they would form a dislike, a disregard for our flag and country." Probably without knowing it, Roudabush was joining a long line of school leaders who saw the role of the school as transmitting the common culture by Americanizing—which usually included "Protestantizing"—the immigrants so that they would join the community on its own terms rather than making their own contribution. To such a worldview, the Gobitas children did, in fact, constitute a serious threat.

The Gobitas family won the case in federal district court, but the school district appealed all the way to the Supreme Court. Unfortunately for the family, the case came before the highest court in 1940, a time when war fever was raising patriotic concerns. Ultimately the court ruled against the children. Justice Felix Frankfurter defended the state's need to emphasize patriotism. He also urged people to keep cases of this sort out of the courts. A democratic faith did not rely on courts, he argued, "for the impossible task of assuring a vigorous, mature, self-protecting and tolerant democracy by bringing responsibility . . . directly home where it belongs—to the people and their representatives themselves." The one dissenting justice, Harlan Fiske Stone, saw constitutional liberty quite differently:

> The very essence of the liberty which they guarantee is the freedom of the individual from compulsion as to what he shall think and what he shall say, at least where the compulsion is to bear false

witness to his religion. If these guarantees are to have any meaning they must, I think . . . withhold from the state any authority to compel belief or the expression of it where the expression violates religious convictions, whatever may be the legislative view of the desirability of such compulsion.

Stone was closer than his colleagues in anticipating the Court's future direction, but he was not able to protect the Gobitas children.[13]

In the weeks after the 1940 decision, mobs attacked individual Jehovah's Witnesses and vandalized their homes and meeting places. At the same time, many others began to see such intolerance as especially wrong in a nation preparing for war with Nazi tyranny. In a highly unusual step, three justices of the Supreme Court itself used another case, *Jones v. City of Opelika* (1942) to signal their change of heart when they wrote, "Since we joined in the opinion in the Gobitis case, we think this an appropriate occasion to state that we now believe that it was also wrongly decided." It was a signal to bring another case.

When *West Virginia State Board of Education v. Barnette* was heard in 1943, Harlan Stone had become Chief Justice and the Court's makeup and judgments had changed. Justice Frankfurter still argued that religious cases should be left to local preference stating "The constitutional protection of religious freedom terminated disabilities, it did not create new privileges. It gave religious equality, not civil immunity." But the court's new majority had a different opinion. Justice Robert Jackson wrote: "Those who begin coercive elimination of dissent soon find themselves exterminating dissenters. Compulsory unification of opinion achieves only the unanimity of the graveyard. . . . If there is any fixed star in our constitutional constellation, it is that no official, high or petty, can prescribe what shall be orthodox in politics, nationalism, religion, or other matters of opinion or force citizens to confess by word or act of faith therein." This ruling went far to protect individual religious conscience and liberty for much of the rest of the century.[14]

The arguments in the Barnette case went to the very heart of the purpose of public schools and especially the relationship of that purpose to religious opinion and religious rights. If schools are ultimately to create a national culture, as defined by certain leaders of the society, then the schools must, by definition, demand conformity. So Jackson argued:

Struggles to coerce uniformity of sentiment in support of some end thought essential to their time and country have been waged by many good as well as evil men. . . . As governmental pressure toward unity becomes greater, so strife becomes more bitter as to whose unity it shall be. Probably no deeper division of our people could proceed from any provocation than from finding it necessary to choose what doctrine and whose program public educational officials shall compel youth to unite in embracing. Ultimate futility of such attempts to compel coherence is the lesson of every such effort from the Roman drive to stamp out Christianity as a disturber of its pagan unity, the Inquisition, as a means to religious and dynastic unity, the Siberian exiles as a means to Russian unity, down to the fast failing efforts of our present totalitarian enemies.

For Jackson, the issue was clear. "Free public education, if faithful to the ideal of secular instruction and political neutrality, will not be partisan or enemy of any class, creed, party, or faction. If it is to impose any ideological discipline, however, each party or denomination must seek to control, or failing that, to weaken the influence of the educational system." How many battles of the century before or the half century since might have been avoided if more people had understood this concept?[15]

Ultimately a democratic system of education must embrace all citizens, with their wide range of opinions and creeds, and make all welcome and ultimately learn from them. To do anything less is always to incite battles to "control, or failing that, to weaken" the public schools of a society in which all citizens play a role, however limited, in creating the society's larger policies.

A second set of Supreme Court cases had far more limited constitutional implications but perhaps wider impact in terms of the number of children and youth involved and the actual day-to-day practice of schools in relation to the teaching of religion. Much earlier in the century, in 1914, William Wirt, the highly respected progressive superintendent in Gary, Indiana, began a program of Week Day Religious Education. WDRE, as it quickly became known, fit very well with Wirt's highly regimented approach to school organization. Wirt's goal in this gritty new steel town was to make the schools a social and intellectual center for the community. He extended school hours and set up programs to link the schools to playgrounds, parks, gymnasia, and libraries. Wirt's plan also received support because it moved students in cohort groups through these different locations and therefore allowed considerable savings in the construction of school classrooms since each desk and each classroom could serve multiple shifts of students as their colleagues were off in other settings.

As part of student rotations through different kinds of learning, Wirt also wanted to be sure that they studied religion. Aware of how contentious such study could be in a place as diverse as Gary, Wirt turned to the clergy and asked them to develop church-based programs of religious instruction in which students of different creeds could study, in the tradition which they and their parents selected, during school hours. In the years during and after World War I much of the Gary plan was attacked on the basis of charges that it attempted to include so much that it watered down the core of instruction, and Wirt's star as a progressive leader seemed to have dimmed by 1920. But the innovation of release time for students, during school hours, to study the religious tradition of their choice was too good a solution to the nation's growing diversity to be allowed to disappear with the rest of the Gary plan.[16]

As a result, school districts across the country that would never have experimented with the Gary plan developed their own Week Day Religious Education programs. In spite—or perhaps because— of the growing secularism in the larger society, the notion of an hour of school time devoted to religious instruction offered by the religious authorities of the child's own faith tradition, and at no cost to the taxpayers, rapidly grew in popularity. Not surprisingly, the arrangements were also challenged.

In 1940 Champaign, Illinois, home to the University of Illinois, became one of the school systems to embrace Week Day Religious Education. Jewish, Roman Catholic, and Protestant groups made up the Champaign Council on Religious Education which oversaw the program. Initially the separate religion classes were taught by Protestant lay people, a priest, and a rabbi. Students were asked to select Protestant, Roman Catholic, or Jewish instruction for the assigned thirty to forty-five minutes per week. Any student who did not want to attend one of the three programs could be excused. In the Champaign system, local church groups provided the instruction in assigned classrooms within the school buildings.

In the fall of 1945, Vashti McCollum selected Protestant instruction for her ten-year-old son, James. As the year went on, she became uncomfortable with the kind of Protestantism being taught, so for the 1946-1947 year she decided against having her son receive instruction. In the world of ten year olds, nonconformity is not embraced. James felt excluded and harassed. His mother protested and challenged the program in court. She and her attorneys argued "that religious teachers, employed by private religious groups, were permitted to come weekly into the school buildings during the regular hours set apart for secular teaching, and then and there for a period of thirty minutes substitute their religious teachings for the secular education provided under the compulsory education law." [17]

The United States was not a tolerant place in the late 1940s. The McCarthy era was just beginning. While young James was teased by classmates, his mother was called "a wicked, godless woman, an emissary of Satan, a Communist, and a fiend in human form." The Supreme Court took a more supportive view. Justice Hugo Black wrote the majority opinion in which he argued:

> To hold that a state cannot consistently with the First and Fourteenth Amendments utilize its public school system to aid any or all religious faiths or sects in the dissemination of their doctrines and ideals does not, as counsel urge, manifest a governmental hostility to religion or religious teachings. , For the First Amendment rests upon the premise that both religion and government can best work to achieve their lofty aims if each is left free from the other within its respective sphere . . . the First Amendment has erected a wall between Church and state which must be kept high and impregnable. Here not only are the State's tax-supported public school buildings used for the dissemination of religious doctrines. The State also affords sectarian groups an invaluable aid in that it helps to provide pupils for their religious classes through use of the State's compulsory public school machinery. This is not separation of Church and State.

Even Justice Frankfurter, usually so cautious in these kinds of cases, argued logically that "non-conformity is not an outstanding characteristic of children. The result is an obvious pressure upon children to attend." The issue of some form of religious instruction in school buildings during school hours, supported for so long by various groups and by individuals diverse as Catholic archbishop John Ireland and progressive superintendent William Wirt, seemed to be a closed case.[18]

Interestingly, as in the case of the Jehovah's Witnesses, the Court retreated rather quickly on the Week Day Religious Education issue. Authorities in New York, where such education was popular, proposed a plan whereby students would be excused from the school building altogether for religious classes. Religious groups needed to provide not only teachers but locations off public property for religious instruction. Students whose parents did not want them to attend remained in a study hall at school. Using a line of reasoning the Court would continue in future cases, the majority now held that moving the classes off public property made all the difference. Justice Douglas, who was attacked so often in later years for seeming to be antireligious, wrote the majority opinion in which he almost seemed to back off from the McCollum decision:

> We are a religious people whose institutions presuppose a Supreme Being. We guarantee the freedom to worship as one chooses. We make room for as wide a variety of beliefs and creeds as the spiritual needs of man deem necessary. . . . When the state encourages religious instruction or cooperates with religious authorities by adjusting the schedule of public events to sectarian needs, it follows the best of our traditions. . . . To hold that it may not would be to find in the Constitution a requirement that the government show a callous indifference to religious groups.

This time Justice Black found himself in a dissenting minority. For him the sole question in the case "is whether New York can use its compulsory education laws to help religious sects get attendants presumably too unenthusiastic to go unless moved to do so by the pressure of this state machinery." He would have none of it. Nevertheless, the majority voted differently and release-time programs became a popular aspect of the cultural milieu of some parts of the United States in the 1950s.[19]

FEDERAL AID,
STATE AID, AND RELIGIOUS SCHOOLS

While the issues of minority rights for Jehovah's Witnesses and others and the various compromises allowing sectarian religious instruction during school hours took up significant time in the cultural wars of the 1940s and 1950s, some of the most heated debates came back to the issue of money. In his end-of-the-war budget message and again in his January 1946 State of the Union message, President Harry S Truman proposed federal aid to "assist the States in assuring more nearly equal opportunities for a good education." Truman's proposals received widespread support. Representative Luther Patrick, Democrat of Alabama, told the House of Representatives that "If democracy means equality of opportunity—and we have long so insisted— I can think of no place more proper to apply it than in the education of the country's children." A young Estes Kefauver of Tennessee added his support for federal aid, which "is essential to an equitable distribution of the blessings of education among children of this country." But in spite of the noble rhetoric, the various proposals for federal aid submitted to Congress in the immediate postwar years went nowhere. The objection raised most often was that federal aid meant federal control and "if Federal control of education should become a reality, it would be a very long step toward totalitarianism, both in the form of control and in ideology."[20]

The fear of federal control, of course, meant many things. For some it was part of a general opposition to centralism in government in any form. Certainly this had been part of Republican opposition to the New Deal for the past decades. For others "federal control" meant federal demands for school integration. Ever since the Reconstruction Congresses had considered federal aid and mandated school desegregation, many, both North and South, opposed the former as leading to the latter. Finally, support for the Truman proposals fell apart over the issue of federal aid to parochial schools. In the spring of 1946, the National Catholic Educational Association came out strongly for federal aid plans for public and nonpublic schools. "The compelling purpose for Federal aid to education will be defeated" an April resolution of the association stated, "unless the Federal funds are distributed first, only to those areas where States and local resources are inadequate and, second, without distinction because of race, color, creed or attendance at a public or non-public school." The message was clear. Catholic educators wanted equity in the use of federal funds, and for them equity meant getting their fair share. Northern urban Democrats, from cities with large numbers of parochial schools, would not support a bill that did not provide some form of aid to parochial as well as public schools. Representatives from Protestant-majority areas would not support any aid of any sort to parochial schools. Given the number of reasons for opposing the bills, no version of a federal aid to education bill could muster a majority needed to pass Congress. And once again, as was true in the 1870s when the Blaine Amendment was under consideration, so in the 1940s an odd mixture of the nation's deep divisions over race and religion affected school policy. This was not the last time that such divisions would affect school policy.[21]

While federal aid to education remained stuck, many governors and legislatures in states with large numbers of Catholic voters sought ways to provide state aid to parochial schools. In some cases this involved providing textbooks to all students, whether they were in public or parochial schools. In others it involved providing transportation. And, not surprisingly, these forms of state support were challenged in the courts. In a case that might have been decisive, if it had not been a 5 to 4 decision, the Supreme Court in 1947 ruled in *Everson v. Board of Education* that a New Jersey statute authorizing local school districts to pay for the transportation of children to and from school, whether they attended public or parochial schools, was constitutional. In the particular test case, one New Jersey township authorized reimbursement to parents for the money they paid for bus transportation for their children to attend Catholic schools. Interpreting the First Amendment to require absolute neutrality on the part of the state in its relationships with believers and nonbelieveres, Justice Black wrote for a slim majority that "The First Amendment has erected a wall between church and state. That wall must be kept high and impregnable. We could not approve the slightest breach. New Jersey has not breached it here."[22]

Justice Jackson sarcastically remarked that Black's majority opinion reminded him of "Julia who, according to Byron's reports, whispering 'I will ne'er consent,' consented." While Jackson was sympathetic to the Catholic complaint of a double tax for public and then parochial schools, and to the argument that carfare could hardly be "a serious burden to taxpayers," he also found that providing transportation clearly constituted support for religion. So he argued, "Catholic education is the rock on which the whole structure rests, and to render tax aid to its Church school is indistinguishable to me from rendering the same aid to the Church itself."[23]

Everson was an important case. It was the first in which the Supreme Court clearly ruled that the Fourteenth Amendment meant that First Amendment protection also applied to state and local law. It was a ruling on a clear case of indirect but nevertheless real support for parochial schools. But with a close vote and a series of complex opinions, the Court's signal to the nation was less than clear. Unfortunately, in similar cases for the next half century the Court has maintained the tradition of mixed and unclear signals regarding which forms of state support to parochial schools are constitutional and which are not.[24]

The 1960 presidential election brought many of these issues into the national spotlight once again. For the second time, the Democratic Party nominated a Roman Catholic as its candidate for president, Senator John F. Kennedy of Massachusetts. And as happened in 1928, so in 1960, old Protestant-Catholic debates were brought to the surface. Kennedy decided to address the issues directly throughout his campaign. Indeed, he understood quite well that the price of his being elected was a clearer commitment than any Protestant might be asked for in terms of the separation of church and state.

Early in the campaign, before he had secured the nomination, Kennedy complained to the American Society of Newspaper Editors that the press was allowing the issue of his religion to divert the discussion from what he saw as far more important issues of foreign and domestic policy. "There is only one legitimate question" of religion, he argued: "Would you, as President of the United States, be responsive in any way to ecclesiastical pressure?" and to that he gave a resounding no. Of course, Kennedy recognized that there were other legitimate questions of public policy, though he wished they were asked of all candidates. As one example, he returned to the old fears regarding the use of federal funds: "Federal assistance to parochial schools, for example, is a very legitimate issue actually before the Congress. I am opposed to it. I believe it is clearly unconstitutional. I voted against it on the Senate floor this year, when offered by Senator [Wayne] Morse.

But interestingly enough, I was the *only* announced candidate in the Senate who did so. (Nevertheless I have not yet charged my opponents with taking orders from Rome.)" And so, with humor and candor, Kennedy continued to disarm opponents and build his base. He also uncharacteristically limited his options on this policy question long before his inauguration.[25]

BIBLE READING AND PRAYER IN THE SCHOOLS

Kennedy kept his word, and as a result, federal aid for education remained a low priority during his administration. Other forces were at work in the country, however, that would create a crisis regarding prayer and Bible reading in the schools during Kennedy's years in office. From the time of Horace Mann on, reading the Bible, "without note or comment," had been a part of the school day for many students. In deference to Catholics or to the more general religious diversity of the land, many states had ended the practice. But in others, particularly in the South and Northeast, prayer and Bible reading was still standard procedure. Thirteen states required that school be opened with Bible reading and/or prayer, and thirty-seven allowed some form of religious activities. For some people, in some areas, these activities were simply a normal part of living in a relatively homogeneous society in which church, family, and school shared a wide range of commonly held values. For many others, the same activities were a relatively perfunctory part of the day, harmless and meaningless. Yet for many others, they were an overt form of oppression, a constant reminder that they were second-class citizens in a country whose culture was defined elsewhere.

As has been seen in earlier chapters, for most of the nineteenth and early twentieth century, Catholics were the most oppressed by mandated school-based religion. But as the country became more diverse, many other groups felt similar pressures. Howard Squadron, whose parents had been part of the massive Jewish immigration from Eastern Europe, told a House of Representatives hearing in July 1995 what it was like for him to grow up in the United States in the 1950s.

> Let me recall to you what the public schools I attended were like. They had an overtly Protestant cast. Prayers and bible passages were recited daily. Prayer is not a generic form of expression and

bible passages (and translations) were not, are not, and should not be, theologically neutral. The public school religion I encountered had in every case specific theological roots and forms. The prayers said in the public school I attended were distinctly Protestant in content. The students in the schools I attended were largely Jewish; the prayers exclusively Christian.

Squadron also understood that there was a cultural agenda to these activities. They were not merely leftovers from an earlier era; rather they represented a continuity with the agendas of Horace Mann, Lyman Beecher, and others to use the schools to "Protestant-ize" the culture and to create good Americans out of a unified mold. Indeed, in many parts of the country, there was extra pressure on non-Protestant, non-European minorities to conform to the mold. Squadron continued:

> This disparity was no coincidence, nor was it simply ignorance, or even a lingering cultural tradition from a prior generation of students, teachers, and school administrators. The use of Protestant religion was a part of a deliberate effort by the public schools to suggest to the American children of Jewish immigrants that these Protestant rituals represented true Americanism, that the rituals and rhythms of our parents' houses were alien and foreign, worse, to children who desperately wished to be accepted, even "un-American." This use of religion as a means of acculturating aliens caused many painful gaps between parent and child.

Whether Squadron's classmates or indeed his teachers and school administrators understood the full impact of what was happening may be doubtful. But he has captured more clearly than most the ways in which many schools operated in the United States, whether in the 1830s, the 1950s, or the 1990s.[26]

In 1962 and 1963 the long-standing issues of prayer and Bible reading in the schools burst onto the national consciousness with two very controversial Supreme Court decisions. In many ways the roots of the dominant conservative religious organizations of the 1970s and 1980s, the Moral Majority and the Christian Coalition, lie in the public responses to these two unprecedented decisions. While the Court had become more and more involved in school issues since its

1947 ruling applying the Fourteenth Amendment to the freedom of religion and, of course, the 1954 decision on school desegregation, few cases cut more deeply to the core of the debate about the religious culture of the nation than *Engel v. Vitale* (1962) and *Abington v. Schempp* (1963). In fact, both decisions were more symbolic than specific. Many of those who objected vociferously to the rulings lived in states that had long banned both prayer and devotional reading of the Bible. It was one thing to have silence on the issue. It was quite another for the highest court in the land to so clearly announce the end of the Protestant ascendancy.

The narrower but more emotional debate came over the 1962 decision on school prayer. In the aftermath of World War II, and some would argue the McCarthy era, the New York State Board of Regents had recommended that the school day be opened with prayer. Many districts already followed such a policy. In 1958 the Regents went further, writing a specific prayer for use in the classrooms of New York state:

> Almighty God, we acknowledge our dependence upon Thee, and we beg Thy blessings upon us, our parents, our teachers and our Country.

Who could object to so generic a prayer? Only an atheist or someone who found its language so broad as to be meaningless would mind. But the prayer had multiple purposes. For some it was a continuing acknowledgment that the United States and the state of New York were still religious in a fast-changing world. The 1950s, after all, were also the time in which the phrase "under God" was added to the Pledge of Allegiance to the Flag and "In God We Trust" was added to the dollar bill. In a new atomic era, in a world where there seemed to be so much uncertainty, a little certainty about God seemed desirable. For others, requiring prayer was a way to reinforce Horace Mann's old commitment that the schools would, of course, be religious places, ensuring that New York's increasingly diverse population was reminded daily of what the nation's dominant culture believed. And for yet others, the prayer, like the pledge, was simply a way of quieting the class down before they got on to the real work of the day.[27]

Others, however, were profoundly uncomfortable with the Regents prayer. For many children, this or similar prescribed prayers created a daily dilemma. Did they stand out by refusing to comply with the prayer, or did they compromise some of their most deeply held convictions by going along to get along?

For two brothers, Joseph and Daniel Roth, the prayer caused a lot of very real pain. Looking back on the place in history they ultimately occupied, they remembered the little things. They remembered their father asking them to leave the classroom during the prayer and then, later, walking home from school in suburban Long Island in the late 1950s and being taunted "Hey, you Jew bastard!" They remembered fights with classmates and also anger at their parents for holding an un-American religion. They also remembered the teacher who "kept a statue of Christ in her third grade room. If you were bad, she would say, you would be punished by Christ." And they remembered hostility and snide comments from other teachers, especially as they began to challenge the school's policy. The Roths were hardly alone. Many Americans who did not fit with the dominant religious tenor of America in the 1950s, or in other decades, remember similar deeply painful experiences.[28]

The Roths were different, however, in the role they played in changing national policy. Their father, Lawrence Roth, was a non-practicing Jew, but he did not mean to allow the harassment of his sons to continue. He contracted the American Civil Liberties Union for help. He placed an ad in the local paper announcing "A taxpayers suit will soon be started to challenge the legality of prayers in public schools" and asking for others who would like to join in. Five parents—Lawrence Roth, David Lichtenstein, Monroe Lerner, Lenore Lyons, and Steven Engel—were ultimately selected. William Vitale, president of the local school board, decided to defend the prayer. Thus *Engel v. Vitale* was launched.

After making its way slowly through state and federal appeals, the case was heard by the U.S. Supreme Court in 1962. The plaintiffs had a simple case: "My clients say that prayer is good. But what we say here is, it's the beginning of the end of religious freedom when religious activity such as this is incorporated into the public school system of the United States." Those defending the prayer tried to cast the case in a larger cultural light. "Why are my clients here at all? They are here in the name of the free exercise of religion, if you want to put it that way. They are here because they feel very strongly that it is a deprivation of their children's right to share in our national heritage . . . to eliminate all reference to God from the whole fabric of our public life and of our public educational system." Thus the lines were drawn.

The Court responded quickly. Justice Black wrote for the majority: "We think that the constitutional prohibition against laws respecting an establishment of religion must at least mean that in this country it is no part of the business of government to compose official prayers."[29]

A year later the Court heard a second case with much more far-reaching implications. In 1959 Edward and Sidney Schempp, the Unitarian parents of two high school students, sued the Abington, Pennsylvania, Township School Board. At Abington High School, each day was opened with a student reading from the Bible and then leading the Lord's Prayer and the Pledge of Allegiance to the Flag over the public address system. The school provided the King James version but students were allowed to bring their own Bibles, Protestant, Catholic, or Jewish. Initially Schempp won in state court and overturned a 1949 Pennsylvania law requiring the reading of the Bible at the start of each school day. The state legislature then amended the law to allow students to absent themselves from the proceedings. Schempp was not satisfied and sued again, and this time the case went to the Supreme Court.

At about the same time, Madalyn Murray sued to end a similar requirement for prayer and Bible reading in Maryland. Murray, destined to become the nation's best-known and often most vilified atheist, began simply trying to protect the rights of her son William from forced participation in prayers and Bible reading. The Maryland law, similar to many adopted in the 1940s and 1950s, but continuing the Horace Mann tradition, specified opening exercises so that "each school, either collectively or in class, shall be opened by the reading, without comment, of a chapter in the Holy Bible and/or the use of the Lord's Prayer." Maryland compromised by making participation voluntary, but this was not enough for Murray. She argued that the law threatened her and her son's "religious liberty by placing a premium on belief as against non-belief and subjects their freedom of conscience to the rule of the majority . . . and thereby renders sinister, alien and suspect the beliefs and ideals" of people like the Murrays.[30]

The Supreme Court consolidated the two cases and in 1963 issued its far-reaching decision banning all required prayer (not just state written) and all devotional reading of the Bible in the schools. Justice Tom Clark spoke for a clear majority when he wrote, "In both cases the laws require religious exercises and such exercises are being conducted in direct violation of the rights of the appellees and petitioners. Nor are these required exercises mitigated by the fact that the individual students may absent themselves upon parental request, for that fact furnishes no defense to a claim of unconstitutionality under the Establishment Clause."[31]

The Court went out of its way to support the study of religion, as opposed to its practice. Clark continued: "In addition, it might well be said that one's education is not complete without a study of comparative religion or the history of religion and its relationship to the advancement of civilization." And he went on: "It certainly may be said that the Bible is worthy of study for its literary and historic qualities. Nothing we have said here indicates that such study of the Bible or of religion, when presented objectively as part of a secular program of education, may not be effected consistently with the First Amendment." The study of religion was clearly upheld. The practice of religion was clearly denied.[32]

The 1962 and 1963 rulings evoked a storm of protest. While the Abington ruling was much broader, the protests really began with Engel and stayed there. The anger was both personal and political. Lawrence Roth remembered: "We got calls, 'Don't start your car; it'll blow up.' . . . Once, kids with gas-soaked rags laid out a cross on our lawn, lit it, and left. . . . Right after the decision came out, people marched with signs, 'Roth—Godless Atheist.'" As an adult Joseph Roth remembered harassment from fellow students, local leaders, and surveillance by the Federal Bureau of Investigation. It was not an easy time for the family.[33]

The issue burst forth on the national stage. The cartoonist Herblock may have caught it best with his picture of the angry father sitting with family at the breakfast table and shouting "What Do They Expect Us to Do—Listen To The Kids Pray At Home?" President Kennedy sought to deflect the issue with a call on people to "support the Supreme Court decisions even when we may not agree with them. In addition, we have in this case a very easy remedy and that is to pray ourselves." But private prayer was not sufficient to address the cultural divide the Engel and Schempp cases had opened.[34]

Congressman Frank J. Becker of New York proposed a constitutional amendment that would have added the words "Nothing in this Constitution shall be deemed to prohibit the offering, reading from or listening to prayers or biblical scriptures, if participation therein is on a voluntary basis, in any governmental or public school, institution, or place." Becker was an effective advocate and was able to force Judiciary Committee hearings in 1964, but his amendment died in committee.[35]

Outside of Washington, polls showed significant majorities opposed to the Supreme Court decisions. Major cultural voices of the era challenged the Court. The nation's best known evangelist, Billy Graham, said "The trend of taking God and moral teaching from the schools is a diabolical scheme." Alabama's governor George Wallace responded, "I don't care what they say in Washington, we are going to keep right on praying and reading the Bible in the public schools of Alabama." And massive resistance to the Court on the issues of prayer joined with resistance on school desegregation in the rapidly cohering new right-wing agenda.

Of course, not everyone opposed the Court. Most Jews and liberal Protestants supported its decisions. Edwin H. Tuller of the National Council of Churches opposed the Becker Amendment for reasons that many people of strong belief shared. "I live in fear of identifying this with prayer," Tuller told the committee. "Because if the children are taught this prayer, then my teaching that [the act of] prayer is a vital relationship between the individual and his Creator through Jesus Christ is contrary to that teaching." Deeply held religious convictions and bland public prayers did seem like poor soul-mates.[36]

But many Americans, especially white Protestants in the Midwest and South, found the Court's decisions one more powerful reminder that they were no longer in charge of the culture. The Court had made that clear on matters of race with the Brown decision in 1954. Now it was making it equally clear on matters of religion. More and more people, with more and more differences, were being included in the schools, and on their own terms, not just as second-class citizens. The very notion of what defined the dominant culture of the United States was clearly contested terrain.

THE ELEMENTARY AND SECONDARY EDUCATION ACT: FEDERAL AID AT LAST

It is especially ironic that only two years after the Abington case, Lyndon Johnson was able to break a hundred-year deadlock and achieve the passage of federal aid to education. Such aid had been a central goal of the Reconstruction Congresses in the 1860s and 1870s, and it had been reintroduced from time to time, most vigorously by President Truman in the 1940s. And in each case, federal aid to the schools was blocked on the two issues that have been so tangled for so long—race and religion. State's rights Southerners—but not only Southerners—feared the federal mandates for school desegregation that were included, at least potentially, in all federal aid bills. Catholics opposed any aid bills that did not include aid for parochial schools, while Protestants generally opposed any possibility of tax dollars flowing to parochial schools. The result was a stand-off in which nothing could get through Congress. As on so many other issues, Johnson built a new coalition and broke the deadlock.

On January 12, 1965, Johnson submitted a special message to Congress in which he called for $3 billion in new spending for elementary and secondary education. Telling Congress that "Nothing matters more to the future of our country," Johnson also wisely made sure that everyone got a piece of the action. The initial Elementary and Secondary Education Act proposal included funds for the preschool Head Start program, direct support to public schools serving low-income families, books for school libraries "to be made available to children in public and private non-profit elementary and secondary schools," new supplementary education centers that would offer "special assistance after regular school hours" for students in both public and private schools, and strengthening of the Regional Educational Laboratories with a new focus on the development of and dissemination of new curricula for both public and private schools. Who, indeed, could object to this rich list of services? The bulk of the funds were in Title I (later Chapter I) of the bill which also provided wide leeway to states and local districts regarding how to use the funds to upgrade the education of poor students. In time Title I funds, like other parts of the act, also became available to parochial schools as well. The Elementary and Secondary Education Act of 1965 passed both houses of the Congress in record time.

This was the height of the Great Society; Johnson had wide national support and strong majorities in both houses. He signed the bill in April 1965, three months after first submitting it. At the time he said, "As President of the United States, I believe deeply no law I have signed or will ever sign means more to the future of America." It was indeed an impressive accomplishment.[37]

Twenty years later a group of veterans of the Great Society era gathered to look back on what they had accomplished. Augustus F. Hawkins, who had long served on the House Committee on Education and Labor, gave Johnson credit for resolving the two great barriers to federal aid. First Johnson resolved the fear of federal funds leading to federal involvement in desegregation not by backing off of the issue but by ensuring with the passage of the Civil Rights Act of 1964 that the federal government was going to be involved in issues of race, racism, and school desegregation, whether any federal funds flowed to the schools or not. Then, according to Hawkins, Johnson turned his attention to the next issue, "the separation of church and state." Hawkins noted that Catholics had opposed previous aid bills because they did not benefit parochial schools. But developing a new formula, Johnson changed the terms. "It was crafted on the basis that the aid was not to the school but to the individual student. This, I think, removed a lot of the opposition."[38]

The compromise at the heart of the Elementary and Secondary Education Act (ESEA) and of a number of state laws that quickly adopted similar arrangements were also quickly challenged in the courts. Did the new formulation in which "the money followed the child" pass constitutional muster? While still contested in the details, the overall structure of what aid was permissible was resolved by the U.S. Supreme Court in *Board of Education v. Allen* (1968). Even while some initial challenges to the ESEA formula were being developed, a case challenged a New York law requiring local school boards to "loan" state-approved textbooks to nonprofit private schools. The Court responded with what came to be known as "the pupil benefit theory." If the primary purpose and structure of tax-funded aid was the benefit of the individual pupil, no matter what school that pupil might attend, then support for transportation and textbooks, and perhaps other supports, was allowed.

In 1970 and 1971 the Burger Court expanded this pupil-benefit notion into what came to be known as the Lemon test, after their decision in the 1971 *Lemon v. Kurtzman* case. This three-part test would be used in all subsequent cases. "First, the statute must have a secular legislative purpose; second, its principal or primary effect must be one that neither advances nor inhibits religion; finally the statute must not foster an excessive government entanglement with religion." While still allowing considerable room for debate over the meaning of the terms in specific settings, the Lemon test has continued as the basic means by which the Court has sought, over the years since 1971, to resolve similar cases.[39]

By the end of the Great Society era, the United States was a deeply divided nation. The Civil Rights Act of 1964 and the succeeding legislation had certainly not resolved the nation's deep divisions over race and racism. The war in Vietnam had divided American society more than even the Great Depression had. The unity that had supported the passage of bills such as the Elementary and Secondary Education Act of 1965 seemed far gone. But few of those looking at the nation at the end of the 1960s could have predicted that some of the issues from early in the decade—prayer and Bible reading, the legal level of support for parochial schools, even the teaching of evolution—would become central to national debates in the next three decades. The culture wars that started over civil rights and Vietnam took more forms than most early observers or participants could ever have imagined.

Culture Wars, Creationism, and the Reagan Revolution, 1968–1990

THE YEAR 1968 WAS PIVOTAL in the history of the United States. Depending on one's perspective, the nation was either falling apart or uniting around a powerful new vision of social change and justice for all. Long the nation's best-known prophetic voice calling for an end to the savage divides of racism, Martin Luther King, Jr., in the last year of his life, linked the issues of racism, poverty, and war. In April 1967, in a speech at Riverside Church in New York City, King called on his followers to expand the civil rights agenda and "find new ways to speak for peace in Vietnam and justice throughout the developing world." In December he called for a Poor People's March on Washington in 1968 to demand "jobs, income, the demolition of the slums, and the rebuilding by the people who live there of new communities in their place; in fact, a new economic deal for the poor." In these two moves King, as the great symbolic voice of the Movement, had dramatically expanded the meaning of civil rights to include the world—especially Vietnam—and all poor people in the country. And then, in April 1968, King was struck down by an assassin's bullet. Although there were exceptions, many Americans seemed to be lined up on one side of the great divide or the other. People were for civil rights, for expanding the War on Poverty, and against the war in Vietnam, or they were on the other side on all three issues.[1]

While King was a major symbolic leader, thousands of Americans were involved in civil rights activities, the antiwar movement, and the continued efforts to organize the poor of the nation, efforts that had been so much a part of the national agenda since the early 1960s. And for people in all of these arenas, 1968 was both a heady and a frightening year. It is hard to remember how deeply shaken the nation was by the divides of civil rights, the war, and poverty. The nightly news carried scenes from the war as no previous war had been shown. And King's assassination in April was followed in June by that of Robert Kennedy, campaigning for the presidency on a King-like platform. In August the Democratic National Convention in Chicago became a literal riot, as opponents of the war and the political establishment clashed with Chicago police. And in November 1968 Richard M. Nixon was elected to the presidency he had so long sought on a platform as deeply opposed to the King-Kennedy agenda as imaginable. In fact, however, Nixon, unlike Ronald Reagan, did not roll back much of the Great Society legislation. And, in fact, Robert Kennedy had been much more deeply conservative than King or than his own campaign led people to believe. But in the symbolism of the era, the lines were being drawn with exceeding clarity. From this milieu emerged a new set of culture wars that have dominated the national discourse for the three decades since.[2]

Increased educational opportunity and school desegregation had been among the major tenets of the civil rights era. Some of Lyndon Johnson's greatest successes in the Great Society had to do with his ability to provide federal aid and federal support for education. The issues that had so divided the country during the early years of the decade of the sixties—whether a Catholic president would use the office to aid parochial schools, questions of prayer and Bible reading in the schools, quarrels about the rights of students to be excused from class time for religious instruction or excused from a flag salute in which they could not participate—all of these seemed like relics of a much simpler and long-forgotten era. In a nation so deeply divided as the United States was in 1968, few forecasters would have predicted how deeply the issue of religion and the schools would continue to perplex and divide the American people in the remaining decades of the twentieth century.

THE CULTURE WARS OF THE NIXON ERA

Nixon's 1968 presidential campaign, famous for its "southern strategy," which broke the Democratic Party's hold on the white vote of the South, and for the candidate's courting of some of the most reactionary elements of the American electorate, was also—compared to those which would follow—a very secular affair. In campaigning against Nelson Rockefeller and a late-entering Ronald Reagan for the Republican nomination, and then in the fall campaign against Democrat Hubert Humphrey and Independent George Wallace, Nixon conceded the most hardcore racists and understood that Wallace would carry the deep South. However, he sought to outflank Wallace in the border South and Humphrey in the rest of the country with a strong appeal to "law and order." For many middle-class and working-class white voters, shaken by the racial uprisings and the increasing anger in the antiwar movement, "law and order" became a code word for everything from a return to the 1950s, to an end to the reemerging issue of school desegregation, to the out and out suppression of the civil rights and antiwar movements. As Michael P. Balzano, who had served as an assistant to President Nixon, remembered the appeal to the "silent majority," it was based on a belief that the Democratic Party leadership had abandoned the core of the Roosevelt coalition, "southern Democrats, ethnics, Catholics, and labor unions." In the eyes of these strategists, the post-Johnson Democratic party had become the party of permissiveness and interest groups and was therefore easy to campaign against.

As Balzano, who was also White House liaison to many of these groups, remembered the tenor of the times: "Middle America perceived itself as the target of social policies emanating from government bureaucrats, the target of political reform of the presidential nominating process, and the target of the antiwar protest movement." Thus the culture wars began as a war of middle American values of order, stability, and meritocracy against protest, change, and social justice—especially school desegregation and affirmative action.

Looking back, a chastened Charles Colson, who served time in prison for his role in the Watergate cover-up, did see in the later stages of the Nixon era the beginning of the Reagan revolution of 1980. The Nixon team expanded its specific outreach to Catholic leaders and voters: "We brought in the U.S. Catholic Conference leaders, and we invited Cardinal Krol to sail down the Potomac on the *Sequoia*, the President's yacht. . . . We entered the aid to parochial schools case, which was one of great concern to the Catholic hierarchy and to the ethnic communities in the Northeast. We were working assiduously to win and cultivate their political support." According to Colson, the 1972 reelection campaign also differed significantly from Nixon's initial 1968 victory. "It was the first time that the principal issues in a campaign turned on social issues, the first time in modern American political history that social issues became dominant. You remember the three A's Nixon campaigned against: amnesty, abortion, and acid. He campaigned actively against busing because it was exceedingly unpopular in some of the white ethnic communities that we were appealing to." Nixon thus became the first Republican president ever to have such close ties to Catholic leaders and Catholic voters, especially those many "white ethnic" voters living in large and increasingly diverse cities. What is most interesting, however, is the degree to which the Nixon campaign—and the Nixon administration, for that matter—did not connect with conservative religious movements, especially among Protestants, and did not raise what would become among the most divisive school issues of the later 1970s, 1980s, and 1990s—school prayer, evolution, or other overt matters of religion.[3]

EVOLUTION, CREATIONISM, AND "SCOPES II"

In the midst of the tense struggles of 1968, the U.S. Supreme Court decided a case that brought only limited notice at the time. In *Epperson V. Arkansas* the Court ruled that the Arkansas law disallowing the teaching of evolution was unconstitutional. Finally, forty years after the Scopes trial, the U.S. Supreme Court had its chance to rule on the issue, and by 1968 the outcome of the Court's review seemed like a foregone conclusion. In fact, however, far from providing the final coda of a long-forgotten debate, as the Court's members and almost all of the public assumed, the ruling opened up a whole new era in battles over the teaching of evolution in the schools.[4]

The Epperson case emerged as a not-too-surprising result of the major changes of the decade before it. As was noted in chapter six, the Scopes trial had a much more powerful impact on the teaching of high school biology than has generally been noted. While many high school texts in use between 1900 and 1925 included detailed attention to the issue of evolution, publishers and textbook buyers backed off from the issue after 1925, and the work of Charles Darwin and the theory of evolution were relegated to the margins of the texts for more than a quarter of a century after the famous trial. However, in the late 1950s all of that began to change.

The Soviet launch of the Sputnik satellite in 1957, before the United States could enter space, was as powerful a cultural issue as the Scopes trial had been. The National Defense Education Act of 1958 provided federal money to upgrade science education since "The defense of this Nation depends upon the mastery of modern techniques developed from complex scientific principles." As a result, the National Science Foundation, which had been created in 1950, began to put significant federal funds into the production of first-rate high school science and mathematics texts, texts that paid full attention to scientific thought on the evolution of life. Scientists and educators in the Biological Sciences Curriculum Study developed a radically new approach to the teaching of high school biology, and state and district officials adopted the results quickly. As Herbert Kliebard has noted, "Although the major revision projects of the National Science Foundation and related programs did not have the legal power to mandate the changes they were recommending, they did transform the process of curriculum change to one in which the curriculum would be developed first by experts at a center set up for that purpose with the local school systems perceived as consumers of external initiatives." Generally unnoticed, the teaching of science, especially biology, changed significantly in the nation's high schools as the decade of the 1960s wore on as a result of these developments.[5]

One person who did notice was Susan Epperson. A native of Arkansas and holder of a master's degree in zoology from the University of Illinois, she began teaching at Little Rock's infamous Central High School in the fall off 1964. A year later she was given a new biology textbook, which restored evolution as a central part of the biology curriculum. Epperson recognized a legal bind, or at least agreed to be the plaintiff for the state teachers' organization, and so she was given an opportunity to make a stand for her own scientific principles. She was required by her job to use a textbook of which she also approved. But she was prohibited by the Arkansas law of 1928 from teaching the content of the same text. She brought her case initially in the Chancery Court of Arkansas seeking a declaration that the 1928 law was void. It was an odd case. There had been no prosecution. An unenthusiastic Justice Hugo Black, long a champion of the separation of church and state, wondered why the Supreme Court was addressing a 1928 law that the state of Arkansas seemed uninterested in enforcing. Black wondered that "Now, nearly 40 years after the law has slumbered on the books as though dead, a teacher alleging fear that the State might arouse from its lethargy and try to punish her has asked for a declaratory judgment holding the law unconstitutional."[6]

Of course there were reasons for Epperson to wonder. The new textbooks, and the national moves to change the science curriculum, meant that she would be violating the law in a way that her predecessors had not. But more was at stake in the Court's hearing the case. The new science curricula was having an impact, and the Tennessee legislature became embroiled in a debate over whether they should repeal the original laws that had led to the Scopes Trial. After a forty-year silence, Scopes himself published his own version of the original trial, *The Center of the Storm*, in 1967.[7] The issue was out in the open again, at least in a limited way. And within the Court, Justice Abraham Fortas, who had grown up as young Jewish boy in Memphis, Tennessee, in the 1920s in the midst of the Scopes controversy, seemed eager to finally have the last word. Not all of his colleagues agreed, but they gave him his chance. And Black's anger was not really focused at Epperson but at his colleague Justice Fortas who had been most anxious to review a case on which Black and others did not want to spend time. Given all of the historical baggage, it was probably inevitable that what might have been a simple case did not end up that way.

Black, although he concurred reluctantly in the Epperson decision, also wrote that he saw no reason to make the case a matter of religious freedom. After all, he said, "there is no reason I can imagine why a State is without power to withdraw from its curriculum any subject deemed too emotional and controversial for its public schools." Ironically, that had been just what William Jennings Bryan had argued forty years earlier. Fortas, however, writing the majority opinion, went further. Rejecting the pleas of other justices to overturn the law on its vagueness, Fortas insisted that "The overriding fact is that Arkansas' law selects from the body of knowledge a particular segment which it proscribes for the sole reason that it is deemed to conflict with a particular religious doctrine; that is, with a particular interpretation of the Book of Genesis by a particular religious group."

For Fortas, perhaps because of his own background, perhaps because of his adult legal philosophy, it was important to use the Epperson case to close the Scopes debate once and for all. He continued at some length: "While the study of religions and of the Bible from a literary and historic viewpoint, presented objectively as part of a secular program of education, need not collide with the First Amendment's prohibition, the State may not adopt programs or practices in its public schools or colleges which "aid or oppose" any religion. . . . This prohibition is absolute. It forbids alike the preference of a religious doctrine or the prohibition of theory which is deemed antagonistic to a particular dogma." The Arkansas statue and by implication similar laws in Tennessee and Mississippi were reversed.[8]

As Edward Larson has pointed out, however, the Fortas opinion backfired dramatically. While thinking he had closed the case, in fact Fortas had opened a new loophole and had done so with the authority of a Supreme Court ruling. Wendell R. Bird, wrote in the *Harvard Journal of Law and Public Policy:* "In Epperson v. Arkansas the Supreme Court overturned a law prohibiting instruction in evolution because its primary effect was unneutral." For Bird and many others, the problem with the Arkansas and Tennessee laws was a lack of balance. The Court had said that it was not acceptable for the state to create "an unneutral prohibition on only evolution without a similar proscription on Genesis." If that was really what the Court meant, there was also another solution—include both Darwin and Genesis in the curriculum. What could be more neutral? Now fundamentalists had a new strategy. It was clear that they could not keep the teaching of evolution out of the schools. But the Fortas opinion seemed to provide a new opening for demanding equal time. And under the banner of equal time, following Fortas' words that the old antievolution law was "an attempt to blot out a particular theory from public education," the movement was begun for demanding equal time for other theories, specifically for creation science, or the teaching of some version of the creation story as an alternative scientific theory.[9]

In the thirty years following the Epperson case, battles over the teaching of evolution—and creationism—have been much more heated than in the thirty years before the case. It did not take long before creationism began to appear in textbooks and in law. Tennessee reintroduced the issue in a 1974 law requiring "an equal amount of emphasis" on alternative theories, including the Genesis story, with that of evolution. In 1981 Arkansas and Louisiana passed laws calling for "balanced treatment" for creation science. Not surprisingly, the American Civil Liberties Union challenged the laws. The first round was settled by the Supreme Court in 1987, when the majority ruled that the Louisiana law clearly reflected "the legislature's preeminent religious purpose" since the goal had been "to restructure the science curriculum to conform with a particular religious viewpoint." For Justice William Brennan, writing for the majority, the law clearly violated the First and Fourteenth amendments. Nevertheless, Justice Antonin Scalia issued a strong dissent in which he insisted that "The people of Louisiana, including those who are Christian fundamentalists, are quite entitled, as a secular matter, to have whatever scientific evidence there may be against evolution presented in their schools, just as Mr. Scopes was entitled to present whatever scientific evidence there was for it."[10]

The creationists seem to have the fairness issue squarely on their side. When an Orange County, California, high school biology teacher, John Peloza, began teaching creationism along with the theory of evolution in 1991, he was reprimanded by the school district. In return he brought a lawsuit against the district. A thoughtful professor at nearby California State University at Fullerton remarked, "Scopes was forbidden to teach evolution and he threw down the gauntlet and taught it. Now we have somebody who is forbidden to teach what Scopes was supposed to teach, and he is throwing his own gauntlet."[11]

A number of people, from a wide range of perspectives, agree with the basic fairness premise—if it was appropriate to defend Scopes' right to teach the theory of evolution in which he believed, is it not equally important to defend the right of Orange County biology teacher John Peloaz or any other teacher to teach a belief in divine intervention in the creation process? Writing for the Rutherford Institute, a conservative think tank that "defends religious persons whose constitutional rights have been threatened or violated," John W. Whitehead has posed the dilemma created over "the teaching of human origins, a major area in which public schools have been criticized for not providing 'equal time' for a 'creationist' perspective along with teachings about evolution." He notes: "Some commentators see in modern public schools' dual goals of inculcating some 'common core' of values and equally protecting all students' viewpoints the following sort of dilemma—the public school either grants equal time to a religious perspective on a 'secular' subject, 'in which case a discrimination between religions is inevitably effected'; or it limits itself to a secular frame of reference, 'thereby belittling religion.'" From Whitehead's perspective, it seems clear that equal time represents a better solution.[12]

In what is perhaps the most exhaustive recent study of the contemporary scene, Warren Nord, a philosopher at the University of North Carolina, has also castigated the majority opinion in the *Edwards v. Aguilard* case and called for equal time for creationism in the schools. For Nord, the issue is not "the truth or falsity of any particular account" but rather the philosophical question, "What should students be taught about evolution and creation when our culture is deeply divided about the truth?" For Nord the answer is clear:

> I reject the idea that biology teachers and texts should be free to ignore religion for three reasons. First, it is one thing to teach neo-Darwinian evolution as (unchallenged) truth and another to teach it as one among several ways of thinking about origins. Scientific claims must be put into perspective if students are not to be indoctrinated. . . . Second, to divide reality into scientific and religious domains and then assume that scientists and theologians can go their separate ways without talking to one another is to convey uncritically a contested view of the relationship of science and religion and permit an intolerable level of specialization. . . . Finally, if students are to be initiated into the conversation that constitutes a liberal education, teachers and textbook authors cannot be free to ignore other voices in the conversation; they must help students make the conversation coherent (which means *they* must understand the conversation).

Nord's prescription is clearly a tall order and would require a significantly more sophisticated preparation for biology teachers than is currently offered in many places, but it seems to represent the soul of fairness.[13]

Not surprisingly, much of the scientific community does not agree with Nord or Whitehead or the more conservative parents and churches that continue to challenge what is taught in biology classrooms across the country. As Donald Kennedy, former president of Stanford University and a professor of environmental science, has noted recently, "The noted geneticist Theodosius Dobzhansky once said that 'nothing in biology makes sense except in light of evolution.' Evolution is as basic to the rest of biology as atomic structure is to physics." Given this reality, Kennedy and many others worry about what is happening in practice in the schools. Too often when teachers begin to teach good scientific biology and are challenged, they simply become quiet and move on to another topic. Kennedy worries:

> Thus it is disheartening that in many parts of the United States, high-school science classes do not teach about evolution at all, or discuss it only briefly. In other countries, students in secondary and even elementary schools study evolution. But in the United States, religious opposition to teaching evolution is deeply rooted and growing stronger. . . . Evolution is not an easy topic to teach well, and new information about it is accumulating rapidly. However, we all felt the need to deal with an increasingly intolerable situation, in which access to the most important concept in biology was being compromised by a small but determined group of fundamentalists.

The divisions seemed to be very clear.[14]

In fact, some of the more thoughtful voices are stepping back from an either/or stance. In a sophisticated review of the controversy, Stephen L. Carter has argued that the evolution-creationism debate is, like most fundamental school issues, a matter of power. Quoting one of the leading scientists who has argued that fundamentalists "have no right to control the teaching of science in the public school," Carter continues, "Very well, suppose he is right that parents who believe that God created the universe and the earth in a relatively short period of time have 'no right' to decide what gets taught as science in the public schools. Query, then: Who does have 'the right'?" That is, indeed, a fundamental question. And few progressive educators would be prepared to argue that in all cases it should be resolved in favor of scientific experts without any further discussion in a more messy and democratic dialogue. As Michael Apple has regularly reminded us, there is a clear link between the definition of "official knowledge" and who holds power in society. If experts alone rule, then the very fabric of democracy itself can be in jeopardy.[15]

Polls show the nation's citizens to be roughly evenly divided on the question of their own belief in evolution. The National Academy of Sciences reports that "Fewer than one-half of American adults believe that humans evolved from earlier species. More than one-half of Americans say that they would like to have creationism taught in public school classrooms." While few would want to have majority votes or worse, Gallup Polls determine the content of the school curriculum, especially in the sciences, these are also opinions that do need to be taken seriously.[16]

In any case, the issue of evolution, creation science and the biology curriculum of American schools is not likely to be resolved any time soon. In 1984 the National Academy of Science issued "Science and Creationism." In 1998 the National Academy provided another very thoughtful document, "Teaching About Evolution and the Nature of Science." For the authors of the most recent report, it is obviously essential that schools teach evolution: "[B]iological evolution accounts for three of the most fundamental features of the world around us: the similarities among living things, the diversity of life, and many features of the physical world we inhabit. . . . Thus, evolution is the central organizing principle that biologists use to understand the world. To teach biology without explaining evolution deprives students of a powerful concept that brings great order and coherence to our understanding of life." Thus the compromise of silence on the controversial issue, although proposed by William Jennings Bryan, implied by Justice Black, lobbied for by many parents and churches, and conceded to by more than a few teachers and schools, is unacceptable to the nation's leading scientists if Americans are to be educated citizens.

The National Academy report also rejects the possibility of equal-time proposals. The authors point out that scientists simply cannot do it:

> Those who oppose the teaching of evolution in public school sometimes ask that teachers present "the evidence against evolution." However, there is no debate within the scientific community over whether evolution occurred, and there is no evidence that evolution has not occurred. Some of the details of how evolution occurs are still being investigated. But scientists continue to debate only the particular mechanisms that result in evolution, not the overall accuracy of evolution as the explanation of life's history.

Few scientists would disagree with such a statement. Of course, some creationists will point out that this is at least partly true because no one advocating another perspective would have the slightest chance of election to the National Academy, which could be as much a political as a scientific issue. But the issue remains; calls for the teaching of "alternatives to evolution" generally are calls on scientists to provide information they simply do not have.[17]

What then is to be done? Certainly some of the wiser words on the subject appeared recently in the *Chronicle of Higher Education* when Donald Kennedy, the primary author of the National Academy report, wrote: "Perhaps the most useful lesson of these and other discussions is how important it is for scientists to treat religious convictions with respect." It seems so basic. We may not agree, but that is no excuse for as sophisticated a scientist as Richard Leakey to call those who ask for equal treatment for creation science "utterly stupid" or in turn for conservative Christians to demonize their opponents.[18]

The National Academy report is more balanced. While calling strongly for the teaching of evolution—and not creation science—the report clearly acknowledges that students will have differences that must be treated with respect. At one point, the report describes a teacher who responded to a conservative religious student: "She raised a fuss about evolution, and I told her that I wasn't going to grade her on her opinion of evolution but on her knowledge of the facts and concepts. She seemed satisfied with that and actually got an A in the class." This may be too easy a distinction, but it represents a step in the right direction. At a very minimum, no student should be put in the position of having a grade, or the respect of teachers or peers, depend on rejecting a matter of deeply held faith. Many of us learn the "facts and concepts" of many things with which we may disagree. But that certainly does not compromise us, as being required to pretend that we do believe them might.

The same teacher cited by the National Academy also noted a problem with calls for equal time. "What do you mean by both?" the teacher asks. "If you mean both evolution and creationism what kind of creationism do you want to teach? Will you teach evolution and the Bible? What about other religions like Buddhism or the views of Native Americans? It's hard to argue for 'both' when there are a whole lot more than two options." Although the report does not note this, the teacher has made two important points. First, it is true that teaching non-evolutionary science is both difficult and dubious. But it is also important to note that evolution conflicts with the worldview of others besides conservative Christians.[19]

Warren Nord may have gone further than necessary in the direction of equal time for creationism, but he does have a good point when he writes, "At a minimum, every biology text should begin with a chapter in which biology and scientific ways of thinking about nature and origins are put into historical and philosophical context."[20] There is a great deal of space between *equal time* and *some time* for the questions of the strengths and limitations of the scientific method and for a simple acknowledgment that many people of good will and of differing religious perspectives simply cannot accept the current theory of evolution. Conservative Christians may be the most visible of those who reject the theory, but there is also a clash between evolution and many other spiritual traditions, including those of Native Americans and many Eastern philosophies, which should not be forgotten. To fail to acknowledge that there is, for better or for worse, a debate about the issue going on in American society and that people of good will differ on the issue is to fail to offer contemporary students a sophisticated analysis of one of today's major issues. It also fails to allow a conservative religious student, who, due to deeply held convictions, does not accept the theory of evolution, a place at the table.

Nel Noddings provides a thoughtful response to the issues of creationism and evolution, writing "The constitutional issue should be easily settled—which is not to say that it will actually be easily settled." However, the issue for her is pedagogical, not constitutional. So she argues:

Teaching *about* religion has long been accepted. The central problem in the approach I have outlined is that religious or metaphysical questions may arise anywhere, and I have recommended not only that they be treated wherever they arise—in, say, math or physics classes—but that teachers should assume that students are continually asking such questions implicitly, and, therefore, that they should plan their lessons to include such material. Following such a plan means that students will not be able to escape the discussion of religious questions. They will at least hear (even if they decline to participate in) discussions about God, ethics, creation, religious politics, mystical love, atheism, feminism, and a host of other topics. . . . Teachers committed to pedagogical neutrality will not say to students whose parents have taught them that the world is only a few thousand years old, "That's wrong." Rather they will acknowledge the fact that some people believe this, and they will lay out what most scientists believe . . . teachers need not say, "This is true." or "I believe that . . ." They need only refer to beliefs clearly stated by others and let students weigh the evidence or decide consciously to reject it in favor of faith.

What Noddings proposes is respectful of both the scientific curriculum and the students. It also makes for very challenging teaching. But as she also notes, rejecting such challenges has resulted in a public school curriculum that has been "made intolerably boring to all but a handful of students passionately interested in the subject.[21]

One of the greatest tests of any truly liberal society—and liberal education—is its capacity to allow dissent about important issues. That is the challenge before scientists and science teachers today. It is not sufficient, as Americans United for Separation of Church and State and many other liberal groups argue, to hand the debate about evolution over to the humanities or social science classes while teaching evolution as fact in the science classes. That solution divides the world, and human knowledge, in unnatural ways. Acknowledgment of the debate, Noddings and others argue, belongs in the class where the issue is taught: in biology. Anything less is not really good science. The capacity of biology teachers of the twenty-first century, and those who prepare them and their curricular materials, to teach good scientific evolutionary biology and, at the same time, to treat dissenting students and their parents with respect and with a right to their opinions and their voice will be one of the most significant tests of whether the public schools of the new century will be engaging, multicultural educational institutions embracing all of the nation's citizens.[22]

THE TEXTBOOK CONTROVERSIES

Conservative Christians began to be more and more visible in educational issues in the mid-1970s, not only in issues related to the teaching of evolution. In 1974 Kanawha County, West Virginia, which includes the state's largest city, Charlestown, suddenly received national attention for the textbook wars raging in the community. In the spring of 1974, the board of education of the newly consolidated rural and urban district reviewed a set of textbook proposals from a group of teachers. One member of the board, Alice Moore, the wife of a local fundamentalist minister, asked to review the books before final approval. Her request was granted, and she was not pleased: "The more I read, the more I was shocked. They were full of negative references to Christianity and God. There was lots of profanity and anti-American and racist antiwhite stories. They presented a warped viewpoint of life, as if every black carried a knife, was locked into a slum, and was made to look inferior." Protests escalated quickly. The issue in this case was not evolution but anger over texts that included profanity and that seemed to reflect an elite and sophisticated cosmopolitan worldview out of keeping with the rugged individualism and fundamentalist religion of many of the county's parents.

What may have begun as a local protest quickly expanded. Mel and Norma Gabler, fast becoming national school textbook censors from their base in Texas, supported Moore. When some ministers appeared before the board to support the texts, a larger group appeared to oppose them. In the fall of 1974, with the opening of school, protests exploded into a boycott by 8,000 out of the district's 46,000 students, a counter-walkout by students supporting the texts, and firebombs and gunshots at schools, buses, and protesters. Coal miners struck in opposition to the texts, in an action that coal companies said cost $ 2 million while school facility damage cost hundreds of thousands of dollars. Parents' anger was exacerbated by their sense that they were unfairly portrayed as "poorly educated fundamentalist, rural, coal-mining 'creekers' [people living out of town—literally up the creek—who] were protesting schoolbooks in opposition to better educated professional and business people in Charleston." Liberals in teacher organizations, the media, and the national denominations were shocked by the violence and the rhetoric, such as that of one minister who prayed for the death of three school board members: "I am asking Christian people to pray that God will kill the giants that have mocked and made fun of dumb fundamentalists." It was an ugly divide.[23]

The West Virginia school wars could be a perfect case study for what Michael Apple has described: "Historically, in fact, grass-roots movements on the right, even in the 1920s, often shared two themes. These involved an opposition between a longing for and protection of self-governing, pious communities and decadent, hypocritical cosmopolitan elites. They also involved a distaste for consumerism and 'unearned benefits' such as welfare and the fostering of a morality of hard work, self-control, and self-reliance." Sensing that textbooks were being imposed on their children that had been developed by "hypocritical cosmopolitan elites," that did not reflect the values of their "pious communities," and that denigrated "self-control, and self-reliance," parents rebelled. The resulting divisions in the community persist to the present day. The failure of the local school authorities to include parents, especially rural and more conservative ones, in textbook selection as well as the larger cultural divides of the nation certainly laid the groundwork for the crisis. Once the firestorm began, it was fueled by other grievances and also by the national attention Kanawha County received. The county became a symbol for both liberal and conservative groups far beyond the realities of the immediate situation.[24]

In the end, the school board set up a complex review process involving parents and teachers. The board also adopted guidelines which included requirements that textbooks "recognize the sanctity of the home and not intrude upon the privacy of the family" and "that textbooks not contain profanity . . . [and] respect the rights of ethnic, religious and racial groups." While the National Education Association criticized the new process as so inclusive and so complex that it could virtually bring text selection to a standstill, the compromise seemed to hold.[25]

Kanawha County may have been the most famous, but it was hardly the only school system torn apart by a clash between different religious and moral values and the textbook selection process. The school board of Warsaw, Indiana banned books and fired teachers because of courses that raised issues of suicide, divorce, adultery, and drug use for class discussion. Other celebrated cases have appeared in the Island Trees district in suburban New York, Hawkins County schools in Ohio, and the city of Yucaipa, California, to name a few. There are important lessons to learn from all of these cases. This is still not a very tolerant nation. People choose up sides quickly, and people and ideas that are seen as foreign or dangerous are easily vilified. In a nation as divided as this, it is also easy for a small local case to take on symbolic proportions and to engage national figures with agendas far beyond the interests of the local combatants. But finally, school censorship cases come back to fundamental questions. Thus Michael Apple asks: "[W]hose knowledge is of most worth?" Stephen L. Carter questions, "Who does have the right [to decide curriculum]?" We need not concede ground to right-wing censors at a local or national level to agree that these questions need serious attention. Indeed, there are few better ways to fuel the increasing levels of fear and censorship than an imperious insistence on the right of experts to decide without attending to local sensitivities and to the concerns—religious or otherwise—of parents and other citizens. Arrogance on the part of an intellectual elite is one of the surest ways of building anti-intellectual movements.[26]

THE RISE OF THE RELIGIOUS RIGHT

The emergence of the religious or Christian right in the mid-1970s has been carefully analyzed by many scholars who, not surprisingly, disagree about the origins of a movement that came to national prominence fairly quickly.[27] It is not useful to review all of the debates over the issue here. If we begin with a focus on school issues, however, several developments were afoot in the United States in the late 1970s that make the rapid growth of a conservative religious agenda for schooling at least unsurprising. As has already been noted, debates over evolution and other curricular matters had been simmering for some time. The quarter century of quiet after the Scopes trial had been partly a turning inward by fundamentalists and partly a matter of their generally unnoticed victories on the textbook front. But some fundamentalists were beginning to look at social issues again at just the moment in the 1960s when the impact of the new National Science Foundation curriculum was being felt and Darwin and his theories were reemerging in the high school biology texts. The emergence of both fundamentalism and evolution played a role in the Epperson case coming before the Supreme Court in 1968 and the subsequent Louisiana case of *Edwards v. Aguillard* in which the Court ruled in 1987 that equal time for creationism, if legislated for religious reasons, did not pass constitutional muster. Both cases left many fundamentalists feeling that they had much more to do to oppose the spread of what they saw as atheistic evolutionary teachings.

Evolution was not the only issue that left conservative Christians dissatisfied with the federal government and especially the courts, however. Many evangelicals who believed that the United States should be a Christian nation continued to feel deeply the cultural losses that came in the 1960s with the Supreme Court's decisions ending school prayer and Bible reading. There seemed to be more and more signs that much of what they believed in—that the culture that many had defined as both Christian and American—was being marginalized. In a recent review of conservatism and school policy Catherine A. Lugg has concluded:

> What prompted fundamentalists to shed their self-imposed isola-
> tion was the seemingly rapid change in American social roles and
> mores during the 1960s and 1970s. Fundamentalists (and other
> social traditionalists) saw such issues as the abolition of organized
> prayer in public schools, the legalization of abortion, continuing
> campus unrest, the possible ratification of the Equal Rights
> Amendment, IRS investigations into the racial policies of funda-
> mentalist schools, mandatory busing, affirmative action, the chang-
> ing social/economic roles of American women, and the emergence
> of lesbian and gay rights movements as threatening the moral fiber
> of a "Christian" nation.

With such a list of seeming threats, political action—though long avoided in conservative churches—seemed to become much more neccesary.[28]

It is important to remember that in the 1970s, 1980s, and 1990s, many conservative Christians continued to avoid political involvement altogether, and others were closer to the politically liberal but evangelical Christian former president Jimmy Carter in the way they interpreted their faith. Still, a growing number of preachers and lay people believed that: "Involvement with political issues and campaigns, and the larger secular world, now became a religious imperative. Fundamentalists saw their (and more importantly, their children's) way of life and religious beliefs as threatened by an increasingly hostile and secular country." Clearly here was a set of issues ready to make a very significant impact in the larger political calculus of the nation.[29]

In 1976 the nation's only truly evangelical president was elected when Jimmy Carter defeated Gerald Ford in the aftermath of Nixon's

Watergate scandal and pardon. Initially Carter's election confused the politics of conservative Christians. Speaking out of his own deeply held Christian faith and Baptist tradition, having come into a close working relationship with the Southern civil rights movement, Carter reflected the language and tone of conservative and fundamentalist America as no other president had or would. Did that mean that Carter's more liberal social agenda and his clear support for public education would create a new consensus? It was not to be.

For all of Carter's genuine evangelical faith, he was too far from the nascent religious right on most policy issues for there to be much chance of an alliance. Also, once in office, Carter was true to his principles on a number of fronts, from support for the creation of a cabinet-level Department of Education—which many on the Christian right saw as a vehicle for federal control to be used against their values—to his opposition to school prayer, his support for civil rights and specifically school integration, and his support for abortion rights, gay rights, and the Equal Rights Amendment. So Richard Viguerie, one of the earliest new-right activists of the 1970s, remembered, "Not only did the Carter administration ignore the born-again Christians, it actively and aggressively sought to hurt the Christian movement in America." What did this mean? It meant several things, but fuel was certainly added to the fire when the Internal Revenue Service changed its policy in 1978 so that it took a much more critical look at racially segregated Christian schools in the South. For Ralph Reed, then only emerging as a major conservative Christian leader, the change in IRS policy, with Carter's permission, was seen by many evangelical Christians as "nothing less than a declaration of war on their schools, their churches, and their children."[30]

Not surprisingly, many have noted the degree to which this new religious right turned its back on the nation's first true evangelical in the White House, Jimmy Carter, and courted—and was courted by—the very secular movie actor Ronald Reagan. The emergence of a new phenomenon at almost the same time as the parallel expansion of the older more secular right of Barry Goldwater into the juggernaut of the Reagan campaign for the White House in 1980 brought a fundamental shift in the nation's political scene.

It is important to note, however, that the political right and the religious right, which were both so essential to Reagan's victory in 1980 and to the dramatic change in the tone of the country for the last two decades of the twentieth century, are not the same thing, although they have many important links. The United States has always had conservative political movements, and the Republican Party has certainly had more and less conservative wings for most of the twentieth century, especially as it became the anti–New Deal party after the 1930s. Nevertheless, as the discussion of the Nixon presidency noted, and as a review of Barry Goldwater's 1964 campaign for the presidency would also show, conservatism came to mean something different in the later years of the century. Well before Ronald Reagan's inauguration as president, a new mixture of issues—partly anti-communism in foreign policy, partly the domestic policy "family issues" that Kevin Phillips saw as the foundation of the new Republican majority—had emerged.

A month before the 1980 presidential election, the *Conservative Digest* summed up the changes that had taken place in conservative politics in the years leading up to Reagan's victory:

> For the past 50 years, conservatives have stressed almost exclusively economic and foreign policy. The New Right shares the same basic beliefs of other conservatives in economic and foreign policy matters, but we feel that conservatives cannot become the dominant political force in America until we stress the issues of concern to ethnic and blue-collar Americans, born again Christians, pro-life Catholics and Jews. Some of these issues are busing, abortion, pornography, education, traditional Biblical moral values and quotas.

Clearly the *Conservative Digest* saw a new consensus. They also noted that "family issues in the 1980s could be what Vietnam was in the 1960's." And they were quite clear on what they meant by family issues![31]

Thus while the religious and the secular right were and are different entities, they have plenty of overlapping concerns and constituencies. They cannot be treated as one movement, but the overlaps and alliances can—and must—be understood in order to comprehend the school politics, and the fierce battles over religion and the schools, that have dominated the politics of the United States since 1980.

One other very important political change in the 1970s that had major ramifications for religion/school politics has received insuffi-

cient notice: the broadening membership of the conservative religious coalition. Prior to the 1970s, certainly to the 1960s, nearly all
politically conservative religious movements sought the maintenance
or restoration of a Protestant America. Whether it was the Republican
advocates of the Blaine Amendment prohibiting any government aid
to parochial schools in the 1870s, the Ku Klux Klan allied with
Protestant churches seeking to close parochial schools in the 1920s,
the voices against evolution in the Scopes trial in the 1920s, the
Protestant opposition to a Catholic president in the elections of 1928
and 1960, or even most people committed to keeping prayer and
Bible reading in public schools in the early 1960s, the goal of these
activists was maintaining a Protestant hegemony in the nation and in
the education of its youth. Suddenly in the 1970s the scope was
broadened, almost without notice.

A hint of what was coming appeared in the 1960s prayer and
Bible reading debates. While Roman Catholics had long fought to
have reading from the Protestant Bible and the reciting of Protestant
prayers banned from the schools, Catholic leaders, clergy and lay, did
not generally voice enthusiasm for the Supreme Court's 1962 and
1963 decisions. By then they were more worried about how deeply
secular the schools were becoming than about keeping a Protestant
Bible out of the schools. The nation's most prominent Roman
Catholic leader in 1962, New York's archbishop Francis Cardinal
Spellman, greeted the *Engel v. Vitale* decision saying "I am shocked
and frightened that the Supreme Court has declared unconstitutional
a simple and voluntary declaration of belief in God by public school
children." His predecessor by a century, New York's archbishop John
Hughes, would not have agreed. For Hughes, the Protestant prayers
and the readings from the Protestant Bible were among the reasons
he wanted parochial schools. If Catholics had to attend public
schools, he wanted them to be as secular as possible. The Church
would do its own religious instruction on its own time. Ironically, one
of the groups opposed to the ACLU in the *Engel* case was organized
by Henry Hollenberg, an Orthodox Jew, and represented by Porter
Chandler, an attorney with experience representing the Catholic
Church. Chandler argued in favor of the Regent's Prayer in *Engel v.
Vitale* fearing the result of doing "what these petitioners are now
seeking to do, namely to eliminate all reference to God from the
whole fabric of our public life and our public educational system."

The earlier lines, which had been so stark and so simple, were clearly getting murky. But more dramatic change was to come.[32]

In 1978 Pat Robertson, certainly one of the most powerful voices of the newly emerging religious right, boasting of the power of the new force on the American stage, said that, counting both Catholics and Protestants, "we have enough votes to run the country. And when the people say, 'We've had enough,' we are going to take over."[33] *No* evangelical of any earlier generation would have said that. The *Conservative Digest's* comment from two years later that "born-again Christians, pro-life Catholics and Jews" would make up the heart of the domestic conservative agenda represented a further step in that direction. These were not the core of the Goldwater or Nixon supporters, they had not been the major activists on evolution or school prayers issues. The conservative religious agenda had become much more ecumenical, moving from hopes for a specifically Protestant restoration, to a more general Christian restoration, to an even broader religious restoration in one generation. The times they certainly were a-changing.

Many thoughtful scholars and commentators have made the important point that many different conservative evangelical groups with different agendas were emerging on the political stage in the 1970s. Many were single-issue groups. Many disagreed with each other. One of the first signs of the new activism appeared in 1974 when John Conlan, an Arizona congressman, and Bill Bright, longtime leader of Campus Crusade for Christ, created Third Century Publishers and also laid plans for activities in every congressional district in the country. However, they were quickly surpassed by others.

In the late 1970s Jerry Falwell, leader of the Moral Majority, seemed poised to be the single most powerful leader of the religious right. Falwell used his base as pastor of the Thomas Road Baptist Church in Virginia, his "Old Time Gospel Hour" broadcasts, his 1976 "I Love America" tour of state capitals, and his strategic alliances with Anita Bryant and Phyllis Schlafly to oppose gay rights and the Equal Rights Amendment, abortion rights and the *Roe v. Wade* decision, and to forge closer ties to Howard Phillips, Paul Weyrich, and other more secular right-wing leaders.

Under Falwell's leadership, the Moral Majority also supported the development of a network of Christian schools and critiqued public schools for teaching evolution as fact, for the absence of prayer, and for sex education. With affiliates in all fifty states, the Moral Majority saw itself—and was seen by others—as a major force in the 1980 election, helping to elect a number of conservatives, the most visible of whom was Ronald Reagan. Perhaps as important for future developments, in the same election that made Reagan president, two Moral Majority candidates were elected to the Lee County School Board in Florida. Here was a grass-roots, conservative religious organization to be reckoned with, in the White House, the halls of Congress, and local school boards.[34]

RONALD REAGAN, RELIGION, AND THE SCHOOLS

Ronald Reagan knew how to pay his political debts, and the debt to the Moral Majority and many other sympathetic individuals and organizations was one that the new president found easily compatible with his own beliefs. Catherine A. Lugg has carefully chronicled the educational agenda of the early years of the Reagan administration, a policy influenced by both the Moral Majority and by Reagan's longer-standing ties to the conservative movement in the United States. The administration came to power with a basic but ill-defined commitment to abolish the Department of Education and drastically reduce federal aid to education. Such steps were in keeping with Reagan's basic anti-Washington stance. "From our schools to our farms, Washington bureaucrats were trying to dictate to Americans what they could or could not do, and were portraying bureaucratic control as the price Americans must pay for federal aid." The president clearly intended to end both the bureaucracy and the aid.[35]

In addition to bureaucracy and money, however, the Reagan administration also had a social agenda. In March 1981, two months into his administration, Reagan said: "We have one agenda. Just as surely as we seek to put our financial house in order and rebuild our nation's defenses, so too we seek to protect the unborn, to end the manipulation of school children by utopian planners, and permit the acknowledgment of a Supreme Being in our classrooms just as we allow such acknowledgments in other public institutions." By 1982, some of the meaning of these statements were emerging. In January of that year at the urging of Mississippi Republican congressman Trent Lott, the administration announced that it was backing off of

Carter, Ford, and Nixon era tax policies that since 1970 had led the IRS to rule that segregated private schools were not eligible for federal tax exemptions and that, since 1978, had included segregated but church-related private schools. It should not have been a surprise. The 1980 Republican platform had said: "We will halt the unconstitutional regulatory vendetta launched by Mr. Carter's IRS Commissioner against independent schools."[36]

In April 1982 the president announced a tuition tax credit proposal to the National Catholic Education Association. Asked if such a proposal could be used to support schools for better-off citizens or segregated academies, Reagan, as he often did, made up the facts to suit his argument. He insisted that the bulk of the support would be for poor people and that "we have a proviso in the legislation we're going to send up that it cannot be used in any way to promote segregation." There was little factual basis for either assertion, but such a lack seldom bothered the genial president. More seriously, the tax credit proposal ran into trouble with David Stockman's efforts to balance the budget and increase military spending. While it never went anywhere, the tax credit played very well with some of the core members of the now powerful emerging Republican majority.

Finally, in May of the same year, the president announced the third and most powerful symbolic part of his agenda, a school prayer amendment to the Constitution. Reagan accused the Supreme Court of misunderstanding the First Amendment.

> The first amendment is to protect not government from religion, but religion from government tyranny. It says that the government will neither respect nor obstruct—or will neither institute nor obstruct religious practice. . . . I think what most people in this country—and the polls show that it is overwhelming, the percentage of people who want prayer restored—is the idea that by doing away with it, was almost as if there was an anti religious bias. It was as if saying to the children that this is no longer important.

For all his tangled grammar, the president had struck a nerve. Twenty years after the Supreme Court's actions, this conservative was going to set things right.[37]

In a May 17 message to Congress, Reagan proposed an amendment for congressional action that read:

> Nothing in this Constitution shall be construed to prohibit individual or group prayer in public schools or other public institutions. No person shall be required by the United States or by any State to participate in prayer.

The amendment never got out of committee, but submitting it did allow the president, for the rest of his career, to insist that he was the proud agent of letting "God back into the classroom and [permitting] voluntary prayer there." Not much came of any of the Reagan administration proposals. They remained locked in congressional debate, and the president gave them lip service while he and his core staff devoted their primary attention to the administration's foreign and economic policy agendas. By 1983 wily Terrell Bell, Reagan's previously unnoticed Secretary of Education, had launched his report, *A Nation at Risk*, and the focus of education policy had shifted once again.[38]

The most significant result of Ronald Reagan's proposed school-prayer amendment seems to have been somewhat accidental. While the Senate was reviewing the amendment, Mark Hatfield, a liberal Republican from Oregon, raised the question of making allowance for students who wanted to pray before or after school. As a result, both houses of Congress held hearings on the question of equal access to school property for religious activities in 1983 and 1984. One witness summarized the opinion of many when he told the Senate committee: "Our problem is this: the Supreme Court's decisions have only invalidated teacher-led, school-initiated, government-sponsored prayer. Now this committee has heard accurate statements from around the country that there are school principals who say, 'We cannot allow the Fellowship of Christian Athletes to have a meeting at our school, even though we permit the key club and the rodeo club to meet.'" The witness went on to blame Reagan and others for the misunderstanding. "Do you know why they think that? They think that, in part, because the President of the United States and many distinguished Members of Congress have for many years been misleading the American people by constantly stating that the U.S. Supreme Court has forbidden all prayer in the public schools. That is just not true." If enough people claimed that "God had been kicked out of the schools," it should not have been surprising that some people, including school administrators, would come to believe that such was the case. But if it was a misunderstanding, congressional action could easily correct it.[39]

As a result, in 1984 Congress passed the Equal Access Act, which allowed student political and religious groups the same rights as any other groups, as those rights were defined by the local school district. In other words, a district could bar all meetings or allow all meetings, but it could not allow secular meetings and bar religious or political ones. The so-called limited open forum gave districts a level of discretion, but it did require that "It shall be unlawful for any public secondary school which receives Federal financial assistance and which has a limited open forum to deny equal access or a fair opportunity to, or discriminate against, any students who wish to conduct a meeting within that limited open forum on the basis of the religious, political, philosophical, or other content of the speech at such meetings." The law further required that the district could not attempt to influence any religious activity and could not require staff to participate when such participation violated their religious scruples.[40]

The Equal Access Act was upheld by the Supreme Court in *Board of Education of the Westside Community Schools v. Mergens* in 1990. In this particular case, a high school student, Bridget Mergens, was denied official school recognition and meeting space for a Christian club that she proposed. Mergens' club was to be open to any student who wished to participate in Bible reading, discussion, and prayer. As the case made its way to the Supreme Court, a number of different groups filed friend of the court briefs on both sides. In an unclear and complex ruling, the Court's majority sided with Mergens and with the Equal Access Law. Justice Sandra Day O'Connor wrote the majority opinion which said that the school's denial of the student's request "constitutes a denial of 'equal access' to the school's limited open forum" and therefore violated the 1984 law. More important, the Court also ruled that the 1984 law was constitutional, although it issued three different and contradictory concurring opinions to arrive at that decision. In spite of the Court's inability to speak with a clear voice, the Equal Access Law did provide significant opportunities for students to meet, pray, and study the Bible—or other sacred literature of various traditions—on school property but on their own time.[41]

The Rutherford Institute, a conservative public policy and religious think tank that had supported Bridget Mergens, emerged from the case as a major resource to religious students around the country who wanted to use school facilities to meet, pray, and study. The institute's lawyers have successfully defended a student in Florida who handed out Bibles to his classmates, students in Colorado who handed out a religious newspaper, and similar groups of students in California, Pennsylvania, and elsewhere. Their *Rights of Religious Persons in Public Education* by their attorney, John W. Whitehead, is a popular publication with students and organizations claiming Equal Access protection.[42]

In spite of the success of the Equal Access movement, which seemed to many a reasonable resolution of the long-standing debates, neither liberals nor conservatives were satisfied with the way the issue had been resolved. Most evangelicals enjoyed Ronald Reagan's rhetoric but never fully trusted the speaker. Ronald Reagan, and especially the succeeding Republican standard bearers, George Bush and Robert Dole, may have enjoyed the support of and been willing to cater to religious conservatives, but when it came time to spend precious political capital, the emphasis went elsewhere. Yet it is important not to underestimate the power of symbolism. By the time Reagan departed for California in 1989, even though few of his educational initiatives—other than massive cuts in funds—had been initiated, the basic nature of the national dialogue about education had shifted quite dramatically. The bully pulpit of the White House has power beyond regulation and legislation. And few presidents in the nation's history had understood that better than Ronald Reagan. His legacy in that arena continues undiluted.[43]

For the Christian right, Ronald Reagan had always been a mixed blessing. He was clearly preferable to Jimmy Carter, although in the nominating process leading up to the 1980 convention many wished for a truer conservative Christian. Californian Richard Zone of the *Christian Voice* said of the former California governor, "Reagan was not the best Christian who ever walked the face of the earth, but we really didn't have a choice." And while Reagan was seen as much better than Carter, he was also seen as better than George Bush or Robert Dole in terms of his conservative credentials. While the religious right could dominate conventions and platforms, as it did with especially disastrous results for George Bush in 1992, it never really dominated the choice of Republican nominees, much as it tried with Pat Robertson's 1988 campaign. And as Ralph Reed viewed Reagan's departure from the White House in 1989, he reflected, "When Ronald Reagan got on that helicopter, a great deal of the pro-family political capital went with him." Unlike the president, however, the movement did not go into retirement.[44]

Changing School Boards,
Curriculum, and the Constitution, 1990–

ON JUNE 4, 1998, a majority of members of the United States House of Representatives voted in favor of an amendment to the United States Constitution that read:

> To secure the people's right to acknowledge God according to the dictates of conscience: Neither the United States nor any State shall establish any official religion, but the people's right to pray and to recognize their religious beliefs, heritage, or traditions on public property, including schools, shall not be infringed. Neither the United States nor any State shall require any person to join in prayer or other religious activity, prescribe school prayers, discriminate against religion, or deny equal access to a benefit on account of religion.

The vote on the proposed Religious Freedom Amendment, a revised version of one sponsored since November 1995 by Representative Ernest Istook of Oklahoma, with vigorous support from the Christian Coalition, was 224 to 203. Since an amendment to the Constitution requires a two-thirds vote of both Houses before it can proceed to the states for ratification, the amendment died despite the majority vote. But the fact that it reached the floor and the fact that it garnered such strong support, after previous amendments had been bottled up in committees, and in spite of some concessions on the issue by the Democratic administration, was a sign of the political muscle of religious conservatives, especially the Christian Coalition, at all levels of national life in the United States at the end of the 1990s. No one on either side of the issue thought that the last had been heard on the topic when Congress adjourned after the vote.[1]

THE CHRISTIAN COALITION TAKES THE LEAD

For a time after Ronald Reagan's retirement, it seemed as if the religious right had passed from the stage as quickly as it had been born. The Moral Majority closed up shop in 1989. Sean Wilentz, writing in the *New Republic* in the spring of 1988, saw the end of its influence: "Rarely in modern times, has a movement of such reputed potential self-destructed so suddenly. Free thinkers may want to reconsider their skepticism about divine intervention." But reports of the religious right's demise were, as they saying goes, significantly premature.[2]

There were several reasons for assuming that the religious right had reached the end of the road in 1988-1989. The end of the Moral Majority and Jerry Falwell's political leadership, the replacement of Reagan with the "kinder, gentler"—and even more secular— George Bush, and the obvious failure of Pat Robertson's campaign for the Republican nomination against Bush all seemed to signal the end of political campaigns based on conservative religion. If Robertson's crushing defeat in the primaries was a measure of the religious right's influence, it was clearly limited. However, for observers willing to take a longer view, the Robertson campaign could be seen more in terms of Barry Goldwater's 1964 campaign— the opening salvo in a long war for the heart and soul of both the Republican party and the nation.

As a recent insightful study of the Christian Coalition by Justin Watson has shown, Pat Robertson was the logical heir of both Falwell's Moral Majority and many of the themes invoked in Reagan's presidential campaigns. He was certainly not a "typical" conservative religious leader, if "typical" meant a product of the poorer, more rural, and less educated parts of the nation. Robertson's father, A. Willis Robertson, had been the Democratic U.S. Senator from Virginia for twenty years. After graduating from Washington and Lee University in 1950 and serving in the Marine Corps in Korea, Robertson earned a law degree from Yale in 1955. A year after receiving that degree, while living in New York City—hardly the normal seedbed of conservative religious movements—Robertson had a religious conversion experience and began moving toward a Pentecostal-style faith. He then earned a Bachelor of Divinity degree from New York's Biblical Seminary in 1959. In 1960 he returned to Virginia and was ordained as a Southern Baptist minister, and he began WYAH-TV in Norfolk in 1961. Throughout the 1960s, Robertson's station grew into the Christian Broadcasting Network and he became a national figure with *The 700 Club,* which mixed news, evangelism, and healing. While few secular commentators have taken the time to understand the differences, Pentecostals, with their emphasis on direct inspiration from the Holy Spirit, represent a very different strand of the conservative religious movement than fundamentalists like Falwell, who give primary evidence to the literal words of the Bible for inspiration. Robertson moved into politics cautiously, having high hopes for the evangelical Carter in 1976 but breaking with him soon after the inauguration. In 1980 he was cochair of the "Washington for Jesus" rally, which drew hundreds of thousands to the Mall the April before Reagan's election.

Through the Reagan years, Robertson began more and more to position himself as Reagan's successor. He tried to combine a persona as a successful businessman, as head of the Christian Broadcasting Network, and as a conservative religious leader. He certainly received support from many in the conservative movement who distrusted the conservative credentials of Reagan's vice president, George Bush. The heart of Robertson's nascent campaign, however, was always his appeal to the religious right to "Restore the Greatness of America Through Moral Strength." He warned of the "antichrist spirit" and worried. "[T]he people in a society begin to throw off the restraints of history, then the restraints of written law, then accepted standards of morality, then established religion, and finally, God Himself." As Watson has said, "Both his supporters and his opponents seemed to understand that he was not only calling merely for a renewal of traditional morality, but a restoration of 'Christian America.'" It was not a hard theme to catch.[3]

For many Americans who were feeling the brunt of the economic downturn of Reaganomics, who were disappointed with the president's seeming inability to legislate changes in school prayer or teaching about evolution, who continued to feel marginalized by what they saw as a distant and increasingly secular society, Robertson had a powerful appeal. As Richard Cizik of the National Association of Evangelicals said, "Those who follow Robertson tend to feel discriminated against. They have a bunker mentality. They feel modernity is against them—in matters dealing with sex, crime, pornography, education." The heirs of Bryan's followers were alive and well in American politics. And even more than in the 1920s, by the 1980s, many felt themselves to be victims of "anti-Christian bigotry."[4]

The importance of Robertson's presidential campaign therefore must be seen in the themes into which it tapped and the successful efforts to mobilize these themes in turning people out in caucuses and primary elections. After his defeat in the primaries, Robertson outlined the next part of the agenda: "We are going to place Pat Robertson people on city councils, school boards and legislatures all over this country." And the vehicle for doing that was born a little over a year later when Robertson, in a new alliance with the organizing genius Ralph Reed, announced the formation of the Christian Coalition designed to create a grass-roots campaign to "make government more responsive to the concerns of Evangelical Christians and pro-family Catholics." It was to be a powerful alliance. In the decade ahead the impact on school boards and other local entities was to be significant indeed.[5]

As it emerged in the 1990s, the Christian Coalition was clearly the most visible and powerful—but not the only—voice of conservative religious dissent in the country. Robertson and Reed were able to mobilize citizens through a series of publications, most notably the *Christian America* magazine, through Reed's Christian Coalition Live broadcasts as well as Robertson's continuing *700 Club* and through their Web site http://www.cc.org. They also created a nationwide network of "Church Liaisons" which distribute Coalition information and voter guides, and recruit voters, in congregations across the country. Most influential, the Christian Coalition has recruited and supported candidates in many local elections. They describe their approach to politics as "Think like Jesus. Lead like Moses. Fight like David. Run like Lincoln." In 1996 Reed told the National Press Club that "There are an estimated 2,000 religious conservatives who now serve on school boards, city councils, state legislatures and in Congress." Even giving room for Reed's optimism, this is a powerful cadre of Davids and Lincolns—people ready to influence local policy, especially school policy, along the lines of the Coalition's agenda.[6]

While the Christian Coalition had multiple agenda items—including tax relief for charitable giving and for empowerment zones, tough approaches to drugs, crime, abortion rights, and other things they perceived as pro-family—they also had a significant concern about for the schools. Underlying all of the specifics of their educational goals, the leaders of the Christian Coalition had a decidedly negative view of the public schools. For Pat Robertson the "public school cartel" represented a "basic denial of the value of Western tradition and a repudiation of the role of religion in the welfare of the community."

Ralph Reed, always the more cautious of the two Coalition leaders, stated that he was simply defending "the rights of parents to mold and shape the souls of their children [which] should be respected" and who should run for school boards across the country to protect those rights. Robertson, as usual, pushed the agenda further. For him, the National Education Association (NEA), the nation's major teacher union, has, as part of its agenda, a goal "to wean children away from loyalty to 'the outdated religious superstitions,' loyalty to the family, loyalty to the United States, and belief in free market economics, and then to introduce them to socialism and world citizenship." While such an agenda might be news to the leaders and members of the NEA, such fears cannot easily be dismissed. Speaking of both Falwell and Robertson, Stephen Carter has written that, "Secular liberals have rarely appreciated and have never seemed sympathetic to what Falwell instinctively understood: the powerful sense of an America spinning out of control in ways that are, for many religious people, profoundly threatening." Such views may be wrong. They may well be manipulated for many other ends by leaders like Falwell and Robertson. But they exist and they cannot be ignored.[7]

When Robertson and Reed spell out what they want done for schools to respond to their fears, they have multiple agendas. The Coalition begins with a fundamental belief that, as Robertson said on *The 700 Club,* "The public education movement has also been an anti-Christian movement. . . . We can change education in America if you put Christian principles in and Christian pedagogy in." And they know what they mean by Christian principles and pedagogy. High on the Coalition's agenda is the Religious Freedom Amendment. As originally submitted by Representative Ernest Istook in November 1995, the amendment read:

To secure the people's right to acknowledge God according to the dictates of conscience: Nothing in this Constitution shall prohibit acknowledgments of the religious heritage, beliefs, or traditions of the people, or prohibit student-sponsored prayer in public schools. Neither the United States nor any State shall compose any official prayer or compel joining in prayer, or discriminate against religious expression or belief.

The Coalition continues to see the amendment as a very important part of their agenda "to protect people of faith from discrimination in the public square," through support for prayer and faith-based affirmations in schools.[8]

The Coalition also supports tax credits and vouchers to allow religious people to send their children to religious schools that would be free of the taint of NEA and the public school cartel ideology. Prior to the June 1998 congressional vote, the Istook amendment was also expanded by a few words, prohibiting any level of government from denying "equal access to a benefit on account of religion." As critics noted, those few additional words expanded the amendment's focus beyond prayer to ensure state funding for faith-based social agencies and religious schools. It was a significant expansion. While lawyers would have debated the proper interpretation for some time to come, if the amendment has passed it would certainly have undermined one of the clearest constitutional arguments against vouchers and other forms of public funding for parochial and other private religious schools. Having a recorded vote on the amendment also allowed the Coalition to enter the fall 1998 election campaign with a clear litmus test for use in its voter guides to the candidates.

In addition to campaigns to put prayer and other religious observances into schools and efforts to secure public funding for religious school alternatives, the Christian Coalition's leaders also insisted, again and again, that they wanted to be sure that their views, and those of their supporters, are—at minimum—respected in the public schools. Ralph Reed has used the language of multicultural-ism to defend the rights of conservative religious people. He says: "African-American parents do not want their third-grader learning language that denigrates their race. Deeply religious parents do not want their children taught ideas about morality that directly contra-dict their religious beliefs. . . . [The school's] primary job is to reinforce the basic values taught at home, not experiment with alternative value systems." This interesting analogy draws sympathetic support from many.[9]

In his thoughtful survey of the Christian Coalition, Justin Watson has concluded that there is a deep fissure that seems to run through all of the Coalition's rhetoric and organizational materials. As he says: "There is an obvious and fundamental tension between the calls for the restoration of a Christian America and the demands for recognition of evangelical Christians as a persecuted group. The calls for restoration involve a rejection of the legitimacy of social and religious pluralism as an accepted norm of American society. The demands for recognition, in contrast, depend on the norms of pluralism for legitimation." Once the Coalition is viewed as Watson sees it, the "fundamental tension" appears more and more often, especially in its stance regarding public education. Ultimately Watson, who has certainly observed the Coalition more closely than most outsiders, concludes that Coalition members want both. "They want 'their place at the table' and they want everyone at the table to agree with them. They want a Christian nation and religious freedom. As contradictory as it may seem, they want to have their cake *and* to eat it too." Watson's evidence for this contradictory stance is convincing.[10]

A much clearer understanding of both the aims and the popularity of the Christian Coalition can be gained by dividing the two issues, as Watson does. People need not debate whether or to what degree conservative Christians are a "persecuted group" (it probably depends a great deal on other contextual matters) to believe that a pluralistic society demands freedom and respect for all members— even those with whom people may disagree sharply And most people would agree that the schools of a pluralistic and free society should treat all of the students, including the daughters and sons of Christian Coalition members, with respect. Reed's analogy with multiculturalism is not a bad one. Schools ought to respect the culture of all students; more than that, they ought to be places where students learn about each other, each other's cultural heritage and beliefs, and each other's rights. Embracing that part of the Coalition's agenda makes logical sense to anyone who believes in a democratic society. It is probably also good politics. Also implied in Watson's dichotomy is the assumption that if at least many of those who are attracted to the Christian Coalition begin to feel that the larger society does respect them, their values and traditions, then they will be less likely to support the part of the Coalition agenda that calls for imposing their values on others.

The demand for a "restoration" of a Christian America (whether "restoration" is the historically correct term or not), the demand that "everyone at the table agree with them"—and these demands certainly appear often enough in Christian Coalition rhetoric—are reminders that the Coalition has lurking within it a potential for cultural tyranny that could, if its adherents achieved sufficient power, make the schools and the larger society an oppressive place for many dissenting citizens. For all of its complaints about centralized governmental authority and "statism," there is an authoritarian vein within the Christian Coalition that leaves precious little room for the religious, moral, and cultural values of many, many citizens of this country.

Of course, it is also important to remember that the Christian Coalition is far from the only conservative religious group on the national scene. When Pat Buchanan declared a "religious war" for America at the Republican Convention in Houston in 1992, and when he campaigned for the presidency in 1996 on similar themes, his "peasants with pitchforks" campaign frightened Reed and Robertson. According to Reed, he told Buchanan early on that he would remain neutral in 1996, but predicted that Dole would win the nomination. Buchanan responded, "You just keep working on those school board races and leave the presidency to me." The Buchanan campaign, organized around an outsider, anti-abortion, antigovernment, protectionist agenda, with a Roman Catholic candidate, certainly represented a powerful, but different, part of the religious right in America.[11]

The Eagle Forum, founded by Phyllis Schlafly in 1972, is less overtly religious in focus but is also closely linked with other religious and political right-wing organizations. Nevertheless, Schafly militantly keeps control of her organization. Initially the Eagle Forum focused on defeating the Equal Rights Amendment. In the mid-1980s, Schafly shifted the focus to education following the publication of her book, *Child Abuse in the Classroom*. She and the Eagle Forum are strong supporters of home-schooling. Within public schools, she opposed outcome-based-education, she supports a "Pupil Rights Amendment" to restrict psychological testing in school, and she worries about what she sees as efforts in schools to "deprive children of their free-exercise-of-religion-rights, or impose on children courses in explicit sex or alternate lifestyles, profane or immoral fiction or videos, New Age practices, anti-Biblical materials, or 'Politically Correct' liberal attitudes about social and economic issues." Through it's monthly publications, "Education Reporter" and "The Phyllis Schafly Report," the Forum reaches a wide audience but does not have the organizational and political power of some of its counterparts.[12]

Many other voices also present their own interpretation of how conservative religious people should approach public schools. In *The Culture War in America: A Society in Chaos,* Bob Rosio, pastor of Cheswick Christian Fellowship and founder of Cheswick Christian Academy in Pennsylvania, takes a more extreme stance than other better-known voices. There are many, like Rosio, in premellennialist churches who see the current culture wars as a necessary enactment of the battle between God and Satan prior to the end of the world. For Rosio, educational policy is one of the prime battlegrounds in this war. John Dewey, clearly on the devil's team, "held nothing to be eternal, sacred, or absolute, his interest and energies were devoted exclusively to affecting life in the here and now. . . . Dewey, who rejected the idea of traditional authority (i.e., religion, family, tradition), opened the door to educational chaos." For Rosio, the federal Department of Education's proposals for values clarification—which are "attack[s] on godly absolutes," and advocate tolerance of different lifestyles—represent a lowering of the moral common denominator that will lead only to rule by an unethical elite who reject God and traditional values. The alternative, for Christians, is to fight without compromise for a society in which "All legitimate authority is based on God's authority. God's authority is a bulwark against the spiritual forces in the universe and the very laws of nature (beginning with the Fall of Man) which are constantly moving everything toward breakdown, dissolution, and disintegration." While many conservative Christians—and many who are not so conservative—would be horrified by the kind of theocracy Rosio seems to be proposing, the language he uses is very familiar to some in the evangelical tradition.[13]

LIBERAL RESPONSES

In spite of the conservative tenor of the times, conservative religious groups do not have the stage to themselves in the educational debates. Indeed, a wide range of opponents exists. The two best-known organizations that constantly monitor and usually oppose the institutions of the religious right are Americans United for Separation of Church and State and People for the American Way. Americans United, the older of the two groups, was created in 1947 specifically to oppose federal funding for private religious schools when President Truman first proposed federal aid to education. It recently celebrated its fiftieth anniversary as an organization that "works exclusively to protect and defend the constitutional principle of church/state separation." People for the American Way was founded after Ronald Reagan's electoral victory by a group including television producer Norman Lear, former Notre Dame University president Father Theodore Hesburgh, and former congresswoman Barbara Jordan specifically to monitor the influence of the Moral Majority and later the Christian Coalition and to counter the "political agenda of the Religious Right." People for the American Way is much more specifically focused on the Christian Coalition and describes itself as "the single most effective organization standing between the Christian Coalition and its allies on the critical issues of our time."[14]

Americans United for Separation of Church and State has 50,000 members. Its primary organ is its monthly magazine, *Church & State*, although it also publishes a wide range of brochures and other materials and cultivates links with print media, radio, and television. A significant part of its work is also conducted through its legal program, which files and supports lawsuits and amicus curiae briefs on church-state matters and offers legal assistance to others challenging the "wall of separation" between church and state. Americans United has been active in many current court cases, including challenges to Wisconsin's voucher program, which allows funding for parochial schools, opposition to the Supreme Court's 1997 *Agostini v. Felton* decision in which the Court reversed itself and allowed Title I-supported teachers once again to deliver services inside the buildings of parochial and other religious schools in New York. In addition to school funding cases, Americans United successfully challenged Alabama's "Student-Initiated Prayer Statute," which allowed many kinds of prayer and Bible distribution in schools, and it has worked closely with the American Civil Liberties Union in opposing obvious religious displays and other observances on public property.[15]

Better known, in part because of its 300,000 members and their direct high-profile challenges to the Christian Coalition, People for the American Way monitors and challenges the Christian Coalition's every move. In November 1996 People for the American Way was among the groups opposing the Christian Coalition sponsored "Colorado parental rights amendment," that included the right to censor school books, place limits on drug awareness and other programs, and on school investigations of cases of suspected child abuse, and probably would have led to fights over creationism and school vouchers. When Colorado voters rejected the amendment 57 percent to 43 percent, People for the American Way claimed much of the credit. The organization has been equally involved in school board elections in Texas and California, and it publicizes every one of these issues widely through its networks.[16]

Comparison of a topic covered in the publications of People for the American Way and its allies and in those of the Christian Coalition and its allies would lead to questions of where the truth may lie. Both organizations are adept at painting a picture in which all virtue rests entirely on one side of the argument. For example in 1992 two candidates, John Tyndall and Joyce Lee, ran on a "pro-family and anti-teacher union" platform for the school board in Vista, California, a small town near San Diego. They both won. Both conservative and liberal national organizations followed the results closely. The new board members raised considerable concern because of their positions, especially Tyndall who worked for one of the major producers of scientific creationism materials.

The conservative journal *Focus on the Family Citizen* provided a detailed report on the election and its aftermath. According to an article in its October 16, 1995, issue, Tyndall and Lee were quickly scapegoated because they were pro-family conservative Christians. The Vista Teachers Association was certainly distrustful because the two newcomers had defeated incumbents who were seen as allies of the union. Tyndall and Lee increased the apprehension of many voters when they were part of a board majority voting for an abstinence-based sexuality curriculum.

The heart of the battles came over the teaching of evolution, however. Interestingly, Tyndall denied that this was a major issue for him. He told the *Focus on the Family Citizen* reporter, "During the campaign, I was asked about putting the subject of creation into science classes. . . . I replied that it wasn't a concern of mine." Liberals had reason to wonder about the comment. Tyndall's employer, the Institute for Creation Research, was part of a network of organizations in El Cajon, California, that had been founded in the 1970s to support "scientific creationism." One of the network's founders, Henry Morris, had insisted in 1978: "[W]e must stress once again that this question of creation or evolution is not merely a peripheral scientific issue, but rather is nothing less than the age-long conflict between God and Satan. There are only two basic world-views. One is a God-centered view of life and meaning and purpose—the other is a creature-centered view. Any educational system for the training of the coming generation must and will seek to inculcate one or the other." Could Tyndall's views really be so different from those of Morris? At least there was some reason for liberal voters and liberal organizations to be concerned with his possible actions.

Not surprisingly, hidden agendas and stealth tactics create a high level of distrust. The People for the American Way report on the events in San Diego County quoted Ralph Reed as having said, "I want to be invisible, I do guerrilla warfare, I paint my face and travel at night. You don't know it's over until you're in a body bag." They also noted that Tyndall described the Institute for Creation Research as simply a research institution without noting that the focus of the research is creationism. As a spokesperson for a local anti-Christian Coalition group, the Mainstream Voters Project (MVP), said, "One of the things that concern[ed] MVP" is that these conservative candidates appear to be "approaching this from a moral standpoint, as though they are on the side of morality. And yet we see various things in their campaigns that don't appear to be moral, ethical or legal." In such battles, the stakes are very high, and vilification is not a surprising result. In the long run, however, less stealth and more honesty is likely to build a higher level of trust.

In any case, Tyndall and Lee were voted out in a recall election in November 1994. *Focus on the Family Citizen* reported the vote as one for peace at any price in a community that was tired of controversy. Michael Hudson of People for the American Way saw the vote as an important step in organizing a new majority. "The challenge of all challenges," he wrote, "will be how organizationally we can replicate what we were able to do in San Diego in hundreds, if not thousands, of communities." From People for the American Way's perspective, Vista was a small town that had been targeted for infiltration by a national conservative movement. People for the American Way gave only a bit of help to the local reform efforts. For the Christian Coalition, the opposite was true. Local conservatives with no special ties to national organizations had engaged in their democratic right to run for office. They had been targeted and vilified by national organizations and the national media because their honest opinions went against the national grain. It is ironic, however, the degree to which national organizations claim distance, rather than more credit, for their local efforts. In spite of Ralph Reed's proud boast of 2,000 conservative Christians on school boards across the country, each side sought to portray the Vista fight as primarily a local issue in which the national organizations were only marginally involved.[17]

Formal organizations are not the only opponents conservative religious groups face. The visibility of conservative religious activists at the 1992 Republican Convention in Houston, Texas, was seen by many as an important element in George Bush's defeat in the polls that fall. Certainly Bob Dole, the 1996 nominee, made sure that his nomination was not tarnished in the same way. And many educators have been challenging the ideology of the religious right in local and national forums.

In August 1996 David C. Berliner, a well-known educational psychologist and coauthor of *The Manufactured Crisis: Myths, Fraud, and the Attack on America's Public Schools* (1995), gave the E. L. Thorndike Award Address at the American Psychologist Association meeting in Toronto, Canada. In that speech, which he later published in the *Teachers College Record,* Berliner outlined what he sees as the impossibility of any accommodation with the Christian right given its inability to compromise, its fear of losing control, and its deep dislike of many of the elements of a pluralistic democracy, not the least of them being the separation of church and state. While recognizing that "members of the Christian right do not, of course, talk with unanimity on most subjects and, for that matter, neither do the members of the educational psychology community," Berliner sought to outline the basic differences between the two camps. While he may tend to overgeneralize about what he calls the Christian Right, much of what he says is very consistent with what members of the movement have said about themselves.[18]

Berliner sees several main themes in the Christian Right's goals. For some, such as Robert Thoburn, there is only one way to turn the tide against what he sees as the humanism of the schools: "abolish the public schools. We need to get the government out of the education business." For others, such as Robert Simonds, the goal is to take over the schools and restore the values of a Christian America in them. So Simonds writes: "We need strong board members who know right from wrong. The Bible, being the only true source on right and wrong, should be the guide of board members. Only godly Christians can truly qualify for this critically important position." Simonds' organization, Citizens for Excellence in Education, makes more boastful claims than Reed, seeing the Christian Right as having over 7,000 school board members. Simonds does not end there, however. Berliner reports how Simonds focuses on what he sees as the demonic nature of the schools and the persecution of Christians in both schools and the larger society. According to his newsletter: "it now appears that Christians in America are beginning to share the treatment Jews received in Nazi Germany." Bunker mentality, indeed![19]

Of course we might ask just how representative Simonds is of the Christian Right. But there is another question worth asking, as Watson did of the Christian Coalition, and that is: Aren't there fundamental discontinuities within the rhetoric? For Berliner, the campaign to take over school boards is part of a stealth campaign to eventually undermine and abolish public schools. It may be. But it may also be that the themes of undermining the schools, taking the schools over, and protecting the rights of conservative religious students represent an internally contradictory agenda by groups that are not sure if they want a place at a diverse table, a chance to withdraw from the table and be alone, or total control of the table. The differences are very important for the future of the schools and the society.

Berliner goes on to outline several points of disagreement between the Christian Right and most other educators and educational psychologists. The Christian Right representatives generally want vouchers so that individuals can withdraw from the schools. Many on the right, including Pat Robertson, are deeply hostile to the whole progressive legacy in education and specifically to outcomes-based education. Robertson has said that "the newest application of Dewey's model is outcomes-based education (OBE), which holds that it doesn't matter whether or not children know the specific facts so long as they feel good about themselves and develop 'tolerance for cultural diversity.'" For conservatives, there are many forms of diversity that should not be tolerated, and a focus on facts is essential to supporting an orderly, hierarchical worldview.[20]

Berliner also notes that some conservatives, such as James Dobson, are advocates of physical punishment and breaking the will of the child. Dobson writes, "A child learns to yield to the authority of God by first learning to submit to the leadership of his parents." Such submission, as Berliner notes, is hardly consistent with most of modern psychology, which rejects violence and supports the idea that children learn best through discovery.[21]

It may be in the arena of making sense of the world, more than in the emphasis on physical punishment, that most of modern educational psychology and conservative Christians disagree. Much of contemporary curriculum reform, such as the recommendations of the National Council of Teachers of Mathematics, calls for an approach that is based on a "belief that learning mathematics is a sense-making experience." For many conservatives such a focus on sense-making, in mathematics or elsewhere, truly undermines a faith in absolute values and a divinely ordered world. Thus their opposition to "new math," "whole language instruction," and other similar reforms is not as quirky as it might seem to an external observer, but part of an alternative worldview that rejects ambiguity in the name of moral, religious, and educational absolutes.[22]

Given these deep divisions, Berliner believes that "negotiations on many issues is impossible." Indeed, he credits religious conservatives with understanding the depth of the divide more than many liberals who want to span it. For Berliner: "All who are interested in the preservation of our public schools must be polite to the Christian Right and respectful of their concerns—some of which are shared by all of us. But we must also be extraordinary vigilant to prevent them from gaining control of the public's common schools." It is a line in the sand as clear as any drawn by Pat Robertson.[23]

Whether Berliner is right that the differences between the religious right and the current more liberal philosophies underlining public education are too great to bridge, or whether more moderate voices who hope for some level of reconciliation are correct, one thing is particularly striking about the liberal response to the religious right:

It has not developed the same level of grassroots base as the Christian Coalition and similar organizations. While People for the American Way and Americans United are membership organizations, their primary focus is on publicity and on court challenges. Liberals and the right meet regularly on talk shows and in courtrooms, while their newsletters, magazines, and web sites do regular verbal battle. But in the arena of grassroots political organizing and in nominating and electing candidates for offices from school board to Congress, the right is far ahead of its competitors.

Stephen Carter has made an important point regarding the political organizing of the religious right.

> If, as Tip O'Neill used to say, all politics is local, then the defeat of the Christian right will not come about because smart philosophers dream up clever but naked versions of the public square, that is, it will not be an *intellectual* defeat. It will not come about because thoughtful judges engage in a fruitless effort to rule religious motivations for government activity out of bounds, which is to say, it will not be a *legal* defeat. It will not come about because concerned citizens issue comprehensive lists of all the many sins that the religious right has committed, which is to say, it will not be a *public relations* defeat. No, the defeat of the Christian right—if indeed defeat is to be—will come in precisely the arena that Tip O'Neill would doubtless say that it must: local politics.

Local politics is a difficult arena in which to work. It takes time and getting to know one's neighbors. It involves mobilizing large numbers of people and providing a compelling vision of a different society that is appealing enough to engage lasting energy. And as the civil rights and anti-war movements, like many before them, have shown, it is the only way lasting change happens.[24]

SCHOOL PRAYER IN THE CLINTON ERA

Looking at the United States during the last years of the twentieth century, one sees a wide range of issues, like those outlined by David Berliner in which a conservative religious movement and a usually more secular liberal movement are contesting terrain. Lawyers for the Christian Coalition and its affiliate, the American Center for Law and Justice, or one of their allied organizations, appear in courts across the country in battles with the legal program of Americans United for the Separation of Church and State, People for the American Way, the American Civil Liberties Union, or one of their allies. At century's end, lawyers from the two sides can be found facing each other in battles over school prayer in DeKalb and Talladega Counties, Alabama; in school funding and voucher cases in Wisconsin; in equal access for religious group cases in San Diego, California; and in 1997 lawyers for both sides appeared once again before the Supreme Court debating the proper funding of programs offered under the federal Elementary and Secondary Education Act. In addition, representatives of both groups and their local affiliates and friends battle over school board races and other local campaigns in almost every state in the union. While this can be viewed as the continued healthy working out of disagreement in a democratic society or as an unfortunate diversion of time and energy from other issues, one thing is certain: The battles over the proper relationship of religion and the schools are still raging in every corner of the nation and look to continue well into the twenty-first century.

The election of Democrat Bill Clinton in the 1992 presidential elections did not end the battles over religion and the schools in Washington. Indeed, having a Democratic president in office seemed to free up many conservatives in Congress to push much further for issues of concern to them, especially after the Republican Contract with America and subsequent victory in the congressional elections of 1994.

Even before the 1994 Republican congressional sweep, a Democratic majority Congress passed the Religious Freedom Restoration Act in the spring of 1993. The act, which had unusual bipartisan support, was specifically aimed at countering a 1990 Supreme Court ruling in *Employment Division of Oregon v. Smith,* a case that, at least in the eyes of many in Congress, had overturned a long-standing precedent that "Government had to demonstrate that it had a compelling State interest in burdening the free exercise of religion and that it used the least restrictive means of furthering that interest." The act simply made the requirement of "compelling state interest" into law and required that when there was a compelling interest to limit a religious freedom, it should be done through "the least restrictive means of furthering that compelling governmental interest."

The Religious Freedom Restoration Act (RFRA) had unusually widespread support from many groups, from Americans United for the Separation of Church and State, the National Council of Churches, and the American Jewish Congress, to the National Association of Evangelicals, and the Home School Defense Fund. Attorney General Janet Reno strongly supported the act. While some school officials worried that "Students may attempt to use RFRA to get prayer in school or at school-sponsored activities," the National School Board Association's Council of School Attorneys seemed comfortable that "it is exceedingly doubtful that a RFRA claim would be upheld in any situation because of the option students have to pray silently in school or aloud in non-school locations." The 1993 act was hardly as controversial as many that had come before or would come after, but it was a symbol of the times: many felt that the Supreme Court had tipped the balance too far toward a neutrality bordering on hostility toward religion rather than mere separation of the two realms. In fact, the Court overturned the act in 1997. A majority of justices, in a 6 to 3 decision, said that "Congress does not enforce a constitutional right by changing what the right is." The results of the Court decision are unclear, although some religious groups, such as the Amish or Seventh Day Adventists, who need accommodation may find it more difficult in the future.[25]

The Supreme Court generally has not helped bring clarity in church-state-school matters; indeed the lack of clarity is the source of a great deal of contemporary anger. Writing in 1990, the religious historian Edwin Scott Gaustad reviewed the history of the Supreme Court cases on religion and public education since the 1947 Everson decision, including one 1977 case in which the justices issued seven separate dissents to one or more parts of the decision and concluded that "a rough road lay ahead." So when Gaustad looked at the 1960s, 1970s, and 1980s, he saw more and more 5 to 4 decisions, more angry rejoinders, and concluded:

> [T]he complexity of the case began to resemble a theater of the
> absurd as "Mr. Justice Brennan concurred in part and dissented in
> part" and filed an opinion in which two other justices joined. "Mr.
> Chief Justice Burger concurred in the judgment in part and
> dissented in part and filed opinion. Mr. Justice Rehnquist con-
> curred in the judgment in part and dissented in part and filed

opinion" in which another justice joined. Did anybody know which way the compass pointed, or did magnetic north just keep jumping around?

Constitutional scholars might debate the fine nuances of these cases for years to come, but for lowly school board members or teachers, seeking to find their way through the labyrinth of opinions to the right thing to do in response to a given situation in a given school, the signals were far from clear. While Earl Warren had persuaded his colleagues that compromise was essential so that the Court would speak to the nation with one unanimous voice in the historic *Brown v. Board of Education* decision in 1954, on matters of religion and the schools, the philosophy of the Burger and Rehnquist Courts seems closer to "let a thousand flowers bloom."[26]

Throughout the 1990s, heated debates about school prayer continued. When the Supreme Court had originally delivered its 1962 and 1963 decisions banning formalized prayer in the schools, Alabama governor George Wallace, who was already locked in a battle with the Court and the federal government over school desegregation, added prayer to his list. He said at the time, "I don't care what they say in Washington, we are going to keep right on praying and reading the Bible in the public schools of Alabama." Nullification of federal requirements was taking on new and interesting dimensions. In fact, many schools in many states seem to have simply ignored the Supreme Court from the 1960s to the 1980s. If someone objected and the case went to court, federal law usually prevailed. In a homogeneous community, if everyone kept quiet—out of conviction or peer pressure—little was done to challenge many forms of prayer and religious observance.

By the mid-1980s, half of the states had sought compromise in laws requiring a moment of silence in the public schools. A Massachusetts law required: "At the commencement of the first class of each day in all grades in all public schools the teacher in charge of the room in which each such class is held shall announce that a period of silence not to exceed one minute in duration shall be observed for meditation or prayer, and during any such period silence shall be maintained and no activities engaged in." This law survived a federal court challenge in 1976, when District Court judge Frank Murray ruled "In our view plaintiffs have failed to show the absence of a neutral, secular purpose for the opening moment of silence."

In 1982 Kentucky had followed Massachusetts' lead, but the U.S. District Court in that state found that the law violated the First Amendment. A year later the federal district court in New Mexico found that a similar law there was a "transparent ruse meant to divert attention from the statue's true purpose." A New Jersey law was also overturned based on the federal court's focus on the legislature's intention, which seemed clearly "to evade Engel and Abington Township." In spite of the Massachusetts precedent, the scorecard was not running in favor of moments of silence.

The Supreme Court finally became involved in the question when it ruled that an Alabama law authorizing a "1-minute period of silence in all public schools for meditation or voluntary prayer" constituted an establishment of religion and violated the First Amendment. For the majority of the Court, the issue was clear-cut. Justice John Paul Stevens wrote the majority opinion in which he said: "The record . . . reveals that the enactment of [the Alabama statute] was not motivated by any clearly secular purpose—indeed, the statute had no secular purpose. The sponsor of the bill . . . Senator Donald Holmes, inserted into the legislative record . . . a statement indicating that the legislation was an 'effort to return voluntary prayer' to the public schools." The Court's majority clearly found this unacceptable and ruled against mandated moments of silence. As with so many decisions, however, the Court was less than completely clear. A minority challenged the concept of basing a ruling on the legislature's debate about the law rather than focusing specifically on what the law said. And the majority did not close the door on any moment of silence if the legislation could show a clearly nonreligious purpose.[27]

Another school prayer case that produced both anger and confusion was the Court's decision in *Lee v. Weisman* in 1992. Daniel Weisman had objected to the prayers at his eldest daughter's Rhode Island middle-school graduation ceremony in 1989, which had been offered by a Baptist minister. The local school authorities had tried to placate Weisman, who was Jewish, by having a rabbi offer the prayers, but he still objected and sought legal relief to ensure that future students would not be required to sit through possibly uncomfortable prayers.

A divided Court ruled 5 to 4 in Weisman's favor. Justice Anthony Kennedy, writing for the majority, wrote: "The government involvement with religious activity in this case is pervasive, to the point of creating a state-sponsored and state-directed religious exercise in a public school. . . . It is beyond dispute that, at a minimum, the Constitution guarantees that government may not coerce anyone to support or participate in religion or its exercise. . . . The State's involvement in school prayers challenged today violates these central principles." Ironically, five of the nine justices ruling on the *Lee v. Weisman* case were Reagan and Bush appointees, but the divisions remained and the majority's opinion differed from those of the two presidents who had placed them on the court.

Nevertheless, the minority opinion was clear and scornful. Justices Rehnquist, Scalia, White, and Thomas issued a dissent that said in part: "Nothing, absolutely nothing, is so inclined to foster among religious believers of various faiths a toleration, no, an affection for one another than voluntarily joining in prayer together to the God whom they all worship and seek. Needless to say, no one should be compelled to do that. But it is a shame to deprive our public culture of the opportunity, indeed the encouragement for people to do it voluntarily. . . . To deprive our society of that important unifying mechanism in order to spare the non believer what seems to be the minimal inconvenience of standing or even sitting in respectful nonparticipation is senseless." While critics noted that the minority assumed, as did many conservatives, that the only reason for discomfort at the prayers was nonbelief rather than a different belief about the nature of prayer, the lines were continuing to be drawn, although not with any assuring clarity.[28]

A year after the *Lee v. Weisman* case, in June 1993, the Supreme Court declined to review a decision by the federal Fifth Circuit Court of Appeals that did allow student-led prayers at graduation after the high school seniors had conducted a vote on whether to include them. The appeals court found that student-voted and student-led prayers "place less psychological pressure on students than the prayers at issue in Lee because all students, after having participated in the decision of whether prayers will be given, are aware that any prayers represent the will of their peers, who are less able to coerce participation than an authority figure from the state or clergy." Many psychologists and other wise observers might disagree with the Court on the power of peer pressure, and others debated the student-led prayer case following predictable lines. According to a report on ABC's *World News Tonight*, Pat Robertson responded to the appeals court ruling by sending letters to 15,000 high schools urging students to initiate graduation prayers. Lawyers from the expected organizations lined up on either side of the case, but the Supreme Court continued to side-step the issue.[29]

In spite of the lack of any clarity or resolution—indeed, perhaps because of their lack—debates about school prayer remained extremely heated throughout the 1990s. In early February 1994 the Senate voted 75 to 22 in favor of an amendment to the president's Goals 2000 legislation, sponsored by Senator Helms of North Carolina and Lott of Mississippi, that said:

> No funds made available through the Department of Education under this act, or any other act, shall be available to any state or local educational agency which has a policy of denying, or which effectively prevents participation in, constitutionally protected prayer in public schools by individuals on a voluntary basis. Neither the United States nor any state nor any local educational agency shall require any person to participate in prayer or influence the form or content of any constitutionally-protected prayer in such public schools.

Given the Supreme Court's vagueness, the exact meaning of "constitutionally protected prayer" remains a bit unclear, but for Helms and Lott, this amendment was an important step toward improving the school-prayer climate. To Helms' considerable rage, however, the House-Senate Conference Committee removed the amendment before the final Goals 2000 legislation returned to the Senate later in the spring, but that simply provided one more opportunity for him to voice his frustration that the will of the people, as he saw it, was not being heard on the question of school prayer.[30]

In the fall of 1994, Helms engaged in a filibuster to block a Senate vote on the reauthorization of the Elementary and Secondary Education Act, originally passed in 1965. As with Goals 2000, Helms wanted his school-prayer amendment included before he would allow the act to get to the Senate floor. While in 1965 Lyndon Johnson had finessed the religion issues—then focusing primarily on federal money for parochial schools—the Senate leadership of 1994 clearly had no such luck with the divisive issue of school prayer, and the reauthorization battle lasted far longer, and was far more bitter, than the original passage of the Elementary and Secondary Education Act had been. It was a sign of the divided times in which Congress was meeting.[31]

In July 1995 President Bill Clinton, working with Attorney General Janet Reno and Secretary of Education Richard Riley, issued a detailed set of guidelines designed to govern various expressions of religion and prayer in the schools. The guidelines were also, no doubt, aimed at offsetting the growing pressure from the Christian Coalition and others for an amendment to the Constitution and, not incidentally, for a Republican president who might more easily support such an amendment. While the Christian Coalition's May 1995 "Contract with the American Family" said, "With each passing year, people of faith grow increasingly distressed by the hostility of public institutions toward religious expression. We have witnessed the steady erosion of the time-honored rights of religious Americans. . . . The time has now come to amend the Constitution to restore freedom of speech for America's people of faith," the president took a far more optimistic view.[32]

In the presidential guidelines issued in 1995, Clinton began by noting that "The First Amendment permits—and protects—a greater degree of religious expression in public schools than many Americans may now understand." In this the president was certainly correct. Fearful of overstepping the line, especially in light of the Supreme Court's murky guidelines, many school administrators had limited student rights in terms of private prayer, carrying or reading Bibles, wearing religious attire, or gathering for after-school prayer meetings and Bible study. And each time such a limitation was imposed, conservative groups jumped on it as one more sure sign that government—at all levels—was not neutral but actively antireligious. For the students experiencing such inappropriate limitations, government certainly seemed to be acting in just such antireligious ways. The time had come, the president and his senior cabinet officers seemed to be saying, for much more care in such matters.

Thus the 1995 federal guidelines continued with an introduction outlining the rights to religious expression that federal law protected for students:

The Establishment Clause of the First Amendment does not prohibit purely private religious speech by students. Students therefore have the same right to engage in individual or group prayer and religious discussion during the school day as they do to engage in other comparable activity. For example, students may read their bibles or other scriptures, say grace before meals, and pray before tests to the same extent they may engage in comparable nondisruptive activities. Local school authorities possess substantial discretion to impose rules of order and other pedagogical restrictions on student activities, but they may not discriminate against religious activity or speech.

Students clearly had significant rights, and the 1995 federal guidelines, revised in 1998, were designed to maintain them.[33]

The question of just what was and was not acceptable and protected religious activity for students at their public schools came into national consciousness again in a series of tense encounters in northern Alabama in the fall of 1997. Michael Candler, an assistant principal in DeKalb County, had charged that schools throughout the district were violating federal law when officials supported prayers at graduation and at the start of football games, including prayers over the school intercom, allowed the Gideons International to distribute Bibles at schools, and supported student assemblies with religious themes and student-led prayers in classes. On October 30, 1997, federal district judge Ira DeMent, who had already overturned a 1993 Alabama state law allowing student-led, nonproselytizing voluntary prayer in the schools, expanded his orders. Noting the widespread nature of the prayers, DeMent ordered the school district to provide in-service training for the staff on "the general issue of school officials' tolerance for diversity in religious opinion and duty of neutrality in matters of religion." He also appointed a court monitor to ensure compliance.

The reaction was swift and strong. Steven Green of Americans United for Separation of Church and State said, "This is a reminder that the Constitution still rules in Alabama." But Alabama's Republican governor, Fob James, challenged the judge's ruling at its most fundamental level, arguing that, contrary to forty years of court rulings, the First Amendment did not apply to state law. The governor's special counsel added: "The order is so stridently worded toward school officials that it is going to make them afraid to allow anything. . . . DeKalb County was just doing what most districts were doing in Alabama." And the governor stated that appointing the monitor amounted to the creation of a secret police, which "will comb the schools looking for 'these dangerous criminals' who might, in a public setting, pray for the Father's blessing on this nation." A local judge, Roy S. Moore of Etowah County Circuit Court, who had already gotten into major battles over his insistence on keeping a tablet of the Ten Commandments behind his bench, issued an order from his court that the federal order was "an unconstitutional abuse of power" and inoperable in Etowah Country. For all the posturing, a major constitutional standoff seemed in the making.

While the courts and political leaders argued, large numbers of students also became involved. Hundreds of students walked out of Boaz High School to pray on the tennis courts. A group of students from Alabama Avenue Middle School in Albertville left school to march to city hall and pray there. The November 8 *New York Times* front page was dominated by students at Sardis High School kneeling in prayer in front of the school. A senior at Boaz High School told the *Times*, "Everyone around here is God-believing. . . . Everyone around here believes in Christ, as far as I know. Having Jesus in our school is something that we need. It gives us strength." Another Boaz student told a demonstrating group of students, "We can't let this judge keep us from praying."

The demonstrations were not confined to Alabama. In Decatur, Georgia, school administrators responded to the stabbing death of a student by asking the pastor of the New Missionary Baptist Church to conduct a worship service at the local high school during school hours to support the grieving students. The public safety commissioner turned the service into one more protest when he announced at the service, "We are here in defiance of the Supreme Court, calling the name of Jesus Christ."[34]

Finally, tragically, in West Paducah, Kentucky, a fourteen-year-old high school freshman at Heath High School came to school on December 1 and started shooting into a circle of praying students. Three students were killed and five more wounded. The accused student, who had never been in any trouble previously, told authorities he had no idea why he had done it. While clearly the West Paducah case was an isolated case, it was also a symbol of a nation deeply and violently divided over the appropriate place of student prayer in and around the public schools.[35]

THE RELIGIOUS FREEDOM AMENDMENT

Given the widely divided opinions on the place of religion in the schools, given the depth of the debates in the courts, the Congress, and school boards across the country, it was not surprising that the ultimate resolution—an amendment to the Constitution—remained so popular with so many. When the House of Representatives convened on June 4, 1998, to vote on a proposed Religious Freedom Amendment to the United States Constitution, it was both a historic and a highly charged occasion. Randy Tate, the new executive director of the Christian Coalition, who had recently replaced Ralph Reed who had gone on to found his own political consulting organization, had written to all members of the House the week before the vote reminding them that this was the first time in twenty seven years that the full House had considered an amendment to the Constitution on school prayer and "the fundamental right of an American citizen to publicly acknowledge his or her religious faith." And, just in case anyone missed the point, his letter also reminded the representatives that "in a recent poll in which voters were asked about moral issues confronting the nation, almost 70% agreed that America needed a religious Freedom Amendment that would allow voluntary school prayer." The Christian Coalition had spent $550,000 in the week before the vote lobbying members in their home districts. If anyone thought that school prayer and related issues of religious observations on public property had been resolved in the 1960s, they were sadly mistaken.[36]

For Representative Istook and the other sponsors of the amendment, the issues were clear. Because of the trail of Supreme Court decisions and administrative rulings, they argued, an amendment to the Constitution specifically securing "the people's right to acknowledge God . . . [and] the people's right to pray and recognize their religious beliefs, heritage, or traditions on public property, including schools," was required in order to set the record straight. The amendment also included clauses insisting that no person be required "to join in prayer or other religious activity" and also mandating that the government could not "deny equal access to a benefit on account of religion." As several speakers noted, the heart of the battle was the opening clause on school prayer and the last clause, which would have meant that the government could not refuse funding for social service programs to agencies with distinctly religious or sectarian programs, presumably including religious schools. Like so many battles over the previous two centuries, the debate came down to prayer and money.[37]

For Representative Canaday of Florida, who led the floor fight in favor of the amendment, it was needed to correct what he saw as the Supreme Court's misreading of the First Amendment. It was "a measure which responds to the public's valid concern that certain court rulings have been hostile to religion, have erected barriers to religious expression and exercise, and have attempted to remove religious influences from the public arena." Not only conservative organizations like the Christian Coalition or conservative politicians like Ronald Reagan, but a number of thoughtful scholars like Thomas C. Hunt and James C. Carper, Stephen Carter and Warren Nord, had raised similar issues in the course of the 1990s.

For Canady, the issues focused on what he saw as an erosion of religious freedom through a series of Court decisions that had begun with *Everson v. Board of Education* in 1947. Thus he argued:

> In an effort to satisfy this extra-constitutional and extreme theory of separation of church and State, courts have confused governmental neutrality towards religion with the concept of required public secularism, thus moving toward a public arena with no mention or sign of religion at all. The result of this distorted view of the first amendment is that, wherever government goes, religion must retreat, and in our time there are few places government does not go. Thus, religion is slowly being eliminated from more and more of our public life. . . . All too often, religious Americans of all faiths find that their speech is curtailed specifically because of its religious character. Under the prevailing understanding of the first amendment in many quarters, there are scrupulous concerns to ensure that no person be exposed to any unwanted religious influence but woefully inadequate concern for the religious person whose expression of faith is not publicly tolerated.

Here Canady had seemed to state the heart of the matter, as many were arguing it. Whether it was the advocates for equal time for creationism and evolution, or the requirement in the Equal Access Act of 1984 that religious groups have as much access to public facilities, especially schools, as nonreligious groups, or those arguing that those who wanted to pray should have equal rights with those who did not want to pray, redressing the balance between religious and secular concerns seemed imperative to many.

Beyond Canady and his colleagues' arguments on the basis of fairness or "equal time for religion," sponsors of the amendment also argued for it on the basis of many examples they produced of people, especially school students, who "had been subjected to discrimination simply because of their religious faith." They cited a long list.

Representative Istook told the story of Zacharia Hood, a first grader in Medford, New Jersey, who "was told, because they had a reading contest in school, you get to read the story you want, to class." Hood wanted to read the story of Jacob and Esau from his *Beginners Bible*. According to Istook, the young student was told by school authorities, the school board, and eventually a federal court that the separation of church and state prohibited use of the story he wanted to read.

Istook also returned to *Engel v. Vitale* (1962), to a 1980 case that prohibited displaying the Ten Commandments in school, and to the Supreme Court's 1985 overturning of Alabama's "moment of silence" and its 1992 decision that clergy may not offer prayers at graduation ceremonies.

Representative Armey from Texas, the Republican majority leader, had his own stories: "a Florida student was suspended for handing out religious literature before and after school hours. Two students in Texas were told by their principal they could not wear their rosaries, because he thought it meant they were part of a gang; and maybe they were, part of God's gang. But rosaries? An elementary student received a zero because she wrote a thesis on her hero, and her hero happened to be Jesus, and that offended somebody."

For these members of Congress the lists of government officials, high and low, who seemed bent on ensuring that no mention of God or religion appeared in any public place, especially schools, seemed endless.

Those opposed to the amendment had their own arguments and their own examples. First, they argued that the First Amendment and the "wall of separation" had made the United States one of the world's most religious and religiously peaceful societies and that an attack on the work of Jefferson and Madison would seriously undermine the Bill of Rights under which "we have enjoyed centuries of peace, free from the religious divisions that continue to mar the lives of millions of people across the globe."

Representative Scott, leader of the opposition to the amendment, thus argued against it on multiple grounds:

> The language of the proposed amendment ends the church-State separation by allowing religious groups to be directly funded by the government. So what happens when the Catholics must compete with the Baptists for limited school funding? How much safer will society be if only people willing to practice certain religions are able to get treatment for drug addiction? Which religious groups would and would not be funded? How safer will our schools be when children begin fighting over which prayers will be said or which religious expressions should or should not take place before each class day? How much better off will churches be once they become dependent on government funding?

Scott was clearly concerned about the basic attack on church-state separation contained in the amendment and also with the specific changes, both those fostering prayer and those fostering governmental aid to religious organizations.

Other voices picked up each of these themes. Representative Capps of California, who had replaced her late husband only a few months before, spoke, "As a school nurse for over 20 years, my concern is what this bill would do in our schools. For example, it would permit students to use the school intercom to lead captive classroom audience in prayer, creating a host of troubling questions, such as whose prayer will be prayed?" Opponents of the amendment reminded their audience—which was really a national audience, not primarily other members of the House, who generally had their minds made up—of the dangerous sorts of oppression that could come from majority mandated prayers. Representative Wexler of Florida shared Capps' concern about whose prayer will be prayed and what would happen to children who were outvoted when the prayers were selected.

> They will be humiliated. They will be scorned. In the worst-case scenario, they will be beaten up and involved in fights. Why? Because they had the courageousness of their convictions to say that one of the most beautiful things about being an American is that no matter how powerful or influential a person or a group is, you cannot tell me how to pray, and you also cannot tell me to sit down or shut up, and do it respectfully, while somebody else tells me how they are going to pray at their school, at their commencement.

The tendency of religion to be divisive was clearly on the minds of many.

Finally, opponents argued very strongly that the fact that some school authorities were perhaps overzealous in keeping religion out of the schools could be corrected by better information rather than by amending the fundamental law of the land. Capps insisted, "I firmly support the current constitutionally protected role of religion in our schools. Students can now pray and read the Bible privately, say grace at lunch, distribute religious materials to their friends, and join voluntary religious clubs." Scott reminded his colleagues:

> [W]e should not be misled by inaccurate anecdotes. The proponents of H.J.Res. 78 often mention incidents where children are told they cannot bring Bibles to school or say grace before eating lunches. These are clearly permissible under current law. In fact, it is this kind of anecdotal evidence, of a need for a constitutional amendment, that is misleading in large part because most, if not all, of the examples used by the proponents of this amendment result from misstatements of fact or misinterpretations of current law.

To the degree that proponents of the amendment offered examples of excessive limitations on students' private prayers, Bible reading, or on-campus, after-school gatherings for religious activities, the amendment's opponents were clear that the mistakes could be corrected and, in fact, that the new U.S. Department of Education guidelines were specifically designed to do just that.

Representative Barney Frank of Massachusetts was blunt: "There is no constitutional prohibition against children praying in school. Yes, teachers have told children not to read the Bible on the school bus or say grace before meals. Those teachers were wrong. Teachers are not infallible. Children have the right to do that. At all of those many moments during the school day when, without disrupting the regular procedure, children are free to talk, to read, to decide what to do, they may themselves pray, if they have been taught to do so." Of course, Frank reminded his audience, that did mean that parents needed to teach their children some prayers to say, an option he clearly preferred to what he saw as the real goal of the amendment: "They want to use the coercive school mechanism, so that children who would not otherwise pray will be pressured into doing so, or pressured into doing so in a certain way. Religion does not need now, as it has not in the past, the help of these self-appointed volunteers." For Frank, the issue of protecting religious rights for the religious was clearly a stalking horse for imposing a certain majority-determined religion on all students, including the nonreligious and also those whose religions, however fervent, differed from the majority view.

Running through the debate was also a deep division regarding what it meant for an individual or a nation to be religious. Representative Jones of North Carolina argued that "America was founded on Judeo-Christian principles." And Henry Hyde argued that the amendment "restores free speech to the original dimensions that we find in the Declaration of Independence, where God is mentioned four times." On the other hand, opponents found the generic references to "Judeo-Christian principles" or God in the Declaration of Independence to be too generic. Representative Leach of Iowa told of one school visit in which the students were divided on the question of prayer, but most wanted private prayer. "'Group prayer,' one 9th grader told me, 'would embarrass too many of my friends . . . it would be unfair.'" Leach argued that there were good reasons for this kind of embarrassment, for there were many different kinds of prayer.

For some, a "non-denominational" prayer that makes no mention of Jesus Christ would lack depth. For Protestants and Roman Catholics, the difference regarding the status of Mary and the saints and the role of the church hierarchy is profound. For Jews and

Christians, piety takes very different expressions. For Muslims, prayer involves turning toward Mecca and prostrating one's self. For Islam prayer is adoration of Allah, involving no requests and asking no blessings, as most Christians do. For the son or daughter of Vietnamese-American Buddhists a "voluntary" prayer satisfactory to Southern Baptists or the Eastern Orthodox is likely to be unintelligible.

One-size-fits-all religion clearly did not fit any in Leach's view.

While Congress has strict rules of decorum, it was not a pleasant debate. The role of the Christian Coalition's $550,000 lobbying effort came in for special note. Representative Jackson-Lee of Texas, where the Christian Coalition had brought extra pressure on the members of Congress, responded, "I resent being accused of being nonreligious and nonspiritual. It is a private issue. It is an issue that we have died for." Representative Doggett, also of Texas, saw the amendment opening up the kinds of religious divides found elsewhere in the world. Doggett said: "But indeed, we have our own religious Ayatollahs right here in this country. Some of them unjustly attacked our colleague the gentleman from Texas (Mr. Edwards), and others like Jerry Falwell have declared, 'I hope to live to see the day when there will be no public schools. What a happy day that will be.' This is what this amendment is all about, the movement to destroy public education and to substitute religious arrogance for religious freedom."

Representative Hefner of North Carolina, originally a supporter of the amendment, turned against it, reminding the Congress:

> The Christian Coalition is sending out a letter that says this is going to be on the report card; if Members vote against the Istook amendment, we are going to get them in the next election. Some of this posturing reminds me of the Pharisees when they stood in the temple and said, "Lord, look at me. I have given all this money, and I have done all of this." The people that have labored in the vineyard, that have helped the hungry and the needy, went about their business of praying in private. Give me that crowd rather than the ones that posture and try to make political mileage out of something that is so precious to all of us.

The Christian Coalition had made some new enemies as well as new friends in this campaign.

With the historic but inconclusive vote at day's end, when a majority of members, but not the two-thirds majority needed to launch a constitutional change, voted for the amendment, the resolution was defeated for the time. Nevertheless, a majority vote in the U. S. House of Representatives clearly indicates some strong winds blowing across the nation. The debate provided a first-rate snapshot of the widely disparate views of many Americans on the question of school prayer and the related issue of government support for religious activities and institutions, including religious schools. There is little reason to assume that the debates will die down anytime soon in the new century. As the members of the House knew very well, the Christian Coalition report card would follow them, not only in the fall elections but well into the future. The future of school prayer and of governmental financial support for religious organizations, including especially religious schools, was clearly going to be a major issue in Congress, school committees, churches, and meeting halls across the nation for some time to come.[38]

Divisions that the authors of the First Amendment to the Constitution, reformers of the common-school era like Horace Mann, leaders of the Reconstruction Congress of the 1870s, and a long string of twentieth-century Supreme Court justices all thought they had finally resolved were as deep and wide as ever as the United States entered the twenty-first century. There were no simple solutions, and the more complex ones were clearly caught in a wide range of other issues. The meaning of respect for religious opinions and rights—indeed the fundamental nature of the civic culture of the United States—remains far from clear.

What's Next?
Prayers, Vouchers, and Creationism:
The Battle for the Schools of the
Twenty-First Century

Historians make very poor prophets, yet few of us can resist the temptation to try. A careful look at the struggles over religion and public education in the United States for the last many decades, and an examination of the climate of the country on the eve of the new millennium, leads this historian to conclude that many issues about the proper relationship between religion and the schools are likely to be lively ones for a long time to come. This chapter explores some of the issues that are very much on the horizon at this time and likely to continue for decades—prayer, vouchers, evolution and creationism, and finally—and most importantly—the question of how we live together in an increasingly diverse nation.

SCHOOL PRAYER

Alabama's minirebellion against the federal district court and in favor of school prayer in the fall of 1997, and the June 1998 vote by a majority of the members of the U.S. House of Representatives to amend the Constitution to guarantee a right to pray in school both show that the issue of school prayer is going to be a heated one for many years to come. Henry Hyde, chair of the House Judiciary Committee, had gotten to the heart of the Religious Freedom

Amendment while it was being debated by the House when he said, "Essentially stripped of all the verbiage, this amendment seeks a couple of things: basically to permit and to guarantee a right to pray in schools and, secondly, to afford equality of treatment between faith-based social service providers and treat them the same as secular ones." An amendment to the Constitution specifically allowing prayer in the schools would have resolved the rebellion in Alabama. It would have legalized the unofficial practices that take place in many classrooms across the country. It would also leave many Americans profoundly uncomfortable. It is clearly both a specific and symbolic issue.[1]

In many ways the Equal Access Law and the federal Department of Education guidelines ought to have resolved the issue. It is ironic that there is such heat on the issue of school prayer when today's federal guidelines support students who wish to pray more clearly than has been the case since the early 1960s. The revised standards for Religious Expression in Public Schools issued in May 1998 by U. S. Secretary of Education Richard W. Riley are clear:

> Generally, students may pray in a nondisruptive manner when not engaged in school activities or instruction, and subject to the rules that normally pertain in the applicable setting. Specifically, students in informal settings, such as cafeterias and hallways, may pray and discuss their religious views with each other, subject to the same rules of order as apply to other student activities and speech. Students may also speak to, and attempt to persuade, their peers about religious topics just as they do with regard to political topics. School officials, however, should intercede to stop student speech that constitutes harassment aimed at a student or a group of students. Students may also participate in before or after school events with religious content such as "see you at the flag pole" gatherings. . . .

According to these regulations, the kinds of limitations on private prayer of which many conservatives sometimes complain are improper.[2]

In his Saturday radio speech supporting the new regulations and opposing a constitutional amendment, President Clinton noted the same thing:

> [N]othing in the Constitution requires schools to be religion-free zones, where children must leave their faiths at the schoolhouse door. . . .[S]tudents have the right to say grace at lunchtime. They have the right to meet in religious groups on school grounds and to use school facilities, just like any other club. They have the right to read the Bible or any religious text during study hall or free class time. They also have the right to be free from coercion to participate in any kind of religious activity.

Ironically, the freedom to pray, or not pray, free from coercion, is what most people on all sides of the issue say they want.[3]

As Congressman Barney Frank argued during the debate on the constitutional amendment, many of the current complaints about school restrictions on prayer and other religious activity are based on misunderstanding or overzealous cautiousness, or the antireligious bias of teachers. So Frank reminded the House that while some teachers may have limited the rights of students to read the Bible or pray, "[t]hose teachers were wrong." But for others, simply clarifying the issue and maintaining currently existing rights is not enough. So in the same debate Representative Cook of Utah argued:

> In the last 20 years, our right to free, personal religious expression has been virtually destroyed by misguided court rulings and wrong-headed public policy. We now live in a world where birth control devices can be dispensed at public schools but a voluntary moment of silent worship is often forbidden. We have become so afraid of personal religious expression in schools and public places that in my State, ironically a State founded by those fleeing religious persecution, and on a national level, teacher unions are decrying a return to conservative values and, in particular, personal religious expression.

And the way to counter the trend, for Cook and a majority of his colleagues, seems to be to amend the Constitution to overturn *Engel v. Vitale* and put prayer back as a regular part of the formal exercises of the school day.[4]

Any proposals to formalize prayer in school classrooms, whether done through constitutional amendment or local custom carried on in defiance of the courts, is also going to create resistance. One of the greatest mistakes that advocates of formalized school prayer make is assuming that their opponents are primarily nonbelievers. While there certainly have been atheists and agnostics among those challenging school prayer, well before *Engel v. Vitale*, and also ever since, they have never been the majority of objectors. In fact it might be easier for a nonbeliever, who viewed the whole exercise as meaningless superstition, to sit through a formal prayer than for a believer whose form of belief was insulted by the prayer.

For most of the nineteenth century, Roman Catholics were insulted by the very Protestant prayers offered in the public schools. Jews have regularly been assaulted by Christian prayers, as were traditional Native Americans forced into Christian missionary schools until well into the twentieth century. Today, a devout Muslim, who believes that prayers should be made facing East and giving praise to Allah, a Buddhist who seeks quiet meditation rather than spoken words to God, or a follower of a modern Wiccan tradition who believes in "relinking, with the divine within and with Her outer manifestations in all of the human and natural world" are all likely to be deeply offended by most school prayers, most especially those seeking Divine intervention for the nation or the local football team.[5]

Those who ask, "What's the harm?" of a generic prayer, or who view it as a way to quiet students down and begin the school day on a reflective note need to hear the experience of Martin Buber, the great Jewish mystic and theologian who remembered the pain he experienced as a Jewish student experiencing Christian rituals in school.

> The obligatory daily standing in the room resounding with the strange service affected me worse than an act of intolerance could have affected me. Compulsory guests, having to participate as a thing in a sacral event in which no dram of my person could or would take part, and this for eight long years morning after morning: that stamped itself upon the life-substance of the boy.

Such use of prayer as cultural imposition should give pause to most people of faith who are serious about their own prayers. In a multicultural nation, such monocultural events are deeply troubling.[6]

Nevertheless, anyone who believes that the debate is closed is seriously out of touch with the main currents of American society.

Opponents of formal and organized school prayer may argue, with Nel Noddings, that "Some of us honestly believe that prayer in public school has rightly been declared unconstitutional [and, by implication, that the Constitution should not be changed], others fear that nondenominational exercises will rapidly slide over into overtly denominational ones, and still others simply want to preserve all children from the pain experienced by Buber." On the other hand, advocates of school prayer believe, with equal fervor, that it is an essential means of returning the nation to its religious heritage, of reminding students of the spiritual roots on which life and learning rest, of restoring public morality, and that the court rulings banning formal organized prayer from schools are based on a misreading of the Constitution. It is a difference of opinion not easy to resolve.[7]

VOUCHERS, SCHOOL CHOICE, PUBLIC FUNDING OF RELIGIOUS SCHOOLS

The second half of the constitutional amendment that Congress considered so seriously in June 1998 would, if it became the law of the land, provide significant ammunition to those who want to dramatically increase the level of governmental support for private religious schools. However, far short of a constitutional amendment, the issue of potential government funding for private schools, including religious schools, seemed to be making progress at century's end. Two other developments in 1997 and 1998 gave hope to those who argued that government funding should be allocated to private religious schools.

In June 1997 the U.S. Supreme Court took the unusual step of directly reversing itself on a case it had previously decided. In a 5 to 4 decision, the justices ruled that their 1985 decision in *Aguilar v. Felton* was "no longer good law." The 1985 decision, which was based on a New York City case, barred public school teachers who were funded under Title I of the Elementary and Secondary Education Act, and other similar programs, from delivering their services inside private religious schools. For twenty years between the Johnson compromise of 1965 and the 1985 ruling, Title I of ESEA had funded teachers who delivered services, usually reading and mathematics remediation, in classrooms within religious schools. A group called the Committee for Public Education and Religious Liberty challenged the practice in New York, claiming that having public teachers supported by public funds inside parochial schools created a symbolic union of church and state. The result was the 1985 decision stopping the practice. New York and other cities continued to offer the services but in trailers or adjacent public buildings, not in the religious school premises. The New York City Board of Education led the fight to have Aguilar overturned, citing the high cost of $100,000 per mobile classroom which had added up to $100 million in the years since Aguilar. New York's mayor Rudolph Giuliani and the Clinton administration supported the school board. The result of the challenge was the 1997 *Agostini v. Felton* decision that allowed the teachers to return to the school buildings to deliver their services. Title I classes again could be offered directly in the parochial school classroom. The students did not need to walk to a mobile school or another building.

While the majority of schools affected by the Agostini decision are Catholic parochial schools, many other religious schools will also feel the effect. In New York's case, the affected Title I programs involve 21,000 students in 259 nonpublic schools. In addition to the Catholic majority, the program also serves Jewish, Lutheran, Greek Orthodox, Episcopal, Seventh-Day Adventist, and Islamic schools. Protestant church schools, such as the one conducted at the former congressman Reverend Floyd Flake's Allen African Methodist Episcopal Church in Queens, are likely to benefit from the Agostini ruling. While the public-private split was historically a Protestant-Catholic split, that is no longer the case. Many Protestants, and many other religious groups, in many parts of the nation are sponsoring their own schools. The list is growing.

Jewish day schools have been increasing for decades. Alvin Schiff's *The Jewish Day School in America* describes the rapid growth of such schools between 1940 and 1965. By 1964, 65,000 students were attending 306 of these schools. Beginning with Orthodox Jews, who sought a high degree of separation to maintain their traditions and who remain the strongest supporters of separate schooling, other Jews have followed. Rabbi Robert Abramson, director of the education department of the United Synagogue of Conservative Judaism, sees the growth of similar schools among other Jewish groups as a significant change for what has been seen as an assimilationist-oriented community. "For many of the Orthodox, they were looking for isolation from American culture. . . . That certainly is not what our schools were founded for. They were founded as a way to embrace modernity and tradition." For Jews, for Muslims, for Conservative Protestants, and for many others, such combinations of "modernity and tradition" may be more and more appealing. And given this appeal, public funding for these kinds of experiments is likely to become more and more desirable to their proponents.[8]

Many have debated the significance of the Agostini decision for all such schools. At one level it is simply a matter of administrative convenience, allowing teachers to enter the student's familiar turf and diverting money from mobile classrooms to direct instruction. For many of the teachers and the school administrators involved, "being back inside the building" created more effective surroundings for instruction and far less wasted time in moving students. Others saw significant problems with the decision, particularly with Justice Sandra Day O'Connor's statement that "We no longer presume that public employees will inculcate religion simply because they happen to be in a sectarian environment." Did that mean that the Court was going to affirm other forms of public support? One of those challenging O'Connor was Justice David Souter, who said in dissent that the ruling's impact was to "authorize direct state aid to religious institutions on an unparalleled scale." Americans United for Separation of Church and State worried about an "impermissible 'symbolic union,'" and more seriously they worried that the decision "may also embolden supporters of 'charitable choice' legislation [efforts to use churches and religious institutions to administer social service programs]." Still, Americans United took comfort in the fact that all the decision did was allow public employees to offer secular services in a religious environment. It did not allow for any funds to go to religious staff for secular or religious instruction, which vouchers or charitable choice programs would do. But the door was clearly open to more.[9]

One step much farther down the road to public funding for private religious schools was a June 1998 decision by the state of Wisconsin Supreme Court that declared constitutional a Milwaukee voucher plan which specifically provided for the use of public funds to pay tuition at private religious schools. Under the plan up to 15,000 out of the 104,000 Milwaukee public school children may be able to receive a voucher good for $5,000 in tuition at a private or parochial school in the city. Critics call it a $75 million drain of taxpayers money from the Milwaukee Public Schools. Supporters see it as "the second

Emancipation Proclamation" for Milwaukee parents. The issue has split Milwaukee's African American community. One of the main sponsors of the plan is Annette Polly Williams, an African American state representative from the city. On the other hand, the Reverend Rolen Womack, a member of the Milwaukee Minority Ministers Alliance, argues, "If we put as much resources and intellect into solving the problems in our public schools as we put into what I call 'the Pat Robertson paradigm,' then we'd take a tremendous step."[10]

Looking at this situation, the historian of education Robert Lowe has written: "Despite the grave inadequacies of public education today, however, throwing schools open to the marketplace will promote neither excellence nor equality for all. Rather, it will enhance the freedom of the privileged to pursue their advancement unfettered by obligation to community." Horace Mann could not have said it better. Lowe understands the appeal of voucher programs to people who, for whatever reason, have given up on the public schools as a vehicle for providing a quality education for their children.

> At the same time, sustained inequities in educational outcomes between white students and students of color seriously undermined faith in public schools' capacity to provide equal educational opportunity. In such an environment, a new private school choice program that emphasized opportunities for low-income students of color was linked with a new, more public relations oriented defense of the educational marketplace. This approach met considerable success in creating the illusion that choice would serve all.

Clearly it is an approach that has persuaded a number of people in Lowe's hometown of Milwaukee.[11]

Milwaukee was not the first city to allow students to use tax-funded vouchers for tuition at religious schools. Cleveland had already begun such a program. And vouchers have found a powerful advocate in New York City's Floyd Flake, whose church in Queens operates its own Allen Christian School. For Flake, whose students currently pay tuition, the call for private religious schools, and for vouchers, is "a response to the unrealized hopes and expectations of the public school system in most urban communities. . . . I don't think the average educator understands the pain that the urban community is suffering because of this lack of education."[12]

The best-known school voucher advocates are not poor, urban, or African American. John E. Chubb and Terry M. Moe helped launch the current round of interest in vouchers and related school-choice campaigns with their *Politics, Markets, and America's Schools*, published in 1989. Legal scholar Michael W. McConnell asks whether the belief that a single public school system is essential to national unity is not just a new version of the eighteenth-century belief that a single church was essential. So, he argues:

> To the extent that you agree with the claim that all education has an inescapably religious component to it, the idea that we should all go to the same public school becomes as intolerable as the notion that we should all go to the same church. . . . Previously in history, religion itself had been the glue that held most nations together; the experiment of having citizens attend whatever church they wanted was rather a scary proposition. It has worked rather well, and I am inclined to think it would work well for education, too, in that it depoliticizes the culture war.

The Christian Coalition, perhaps less interested in depoliticizing the culture wars, also has certainly embraced vouchers and other means of diversifying school choice enthusiastically. Their 1995 "Contract with the American Family" calls on Congress to promote school choice through vouchers, tax credits, and charter schools. They support demonstration programs in which vouchers would be provided to students in some of the nation's poorest school districts as a means to "spur grassroots efforts to reform education and give parents greater choice in selecting the best school for their children."[13]

The opposition to various voucher proposals is also widespread. U.S. Secretary of Education Richard W. Riley called a recent congressional proposal for vouchers called HELP Scholarships "fiddling on the margins and refusing to get serious about advancing public education." People for the American Way views vouchers as part of a right-wing stealth campaign to eliminate public education. As one press release said, "By standing in the way of meaningful school reform, the Right hopes to delay improving school performance long enough to sustain the anxiety that drives many Americans to embrace vouchers."

Lee Berg, a Baptist minister and staff member of the National Education Association, insists, "the bottom line is that a lot of the people who support vouchers are not concerned about making public education better, they're interested in the end of public education as we know it." Others would respond: "that's just the point."

Just prior to its July 1998 convention, the American Federation of Teachers (AFT) held a three-day civil rights conference that focused on the issue of school vouchers. The conference became a debate between the AFT's president, Sandra Feldman, and her long-time political ally, Floyd Flake. For Flake, the issue is clear. Deeply troubled students who were getting nowhere in the New York City public schools came to his church's school and "changed their whole attitude and their whole approach to education." Feldman countered, calling it "outrageous" that civil rights leaders are supporting vouchers and telling Flake, "You're dangerous because you're very effective and because you really don't represent the real power behind this movement . . . and I am afraid that you are providing them cover that they don't deserve." The debate between Flake and Feldman is only a new chapter in a struggle that is at least as old as New York Bishop John Hughes's fight with the Public School Society in the 1840s over who would get public funds for whose schools. But it is alive and well and likely to be a major item on the educational scene for some time to come.[14]

EQUAL TIME: EVOLUTION, CREATIONISM, AND THE CONTINUING DEBATE

When the American Civil Liberties Union submitted its brief to the U.S. Supreme Court in the *Epperson v. Arkansas* case, it began by saying "The Union, having been intimately associated with *Scopes v. Tennessee* 40 years ago, when this issue first arose in the courts, looks forward to its final resolution in this case." Seldom have less accurate predictions been made. As the discussion of the case in chapter eight has shown, the Epperson case did close one phase of the evolution battles—since then few have tried to keep the teaching of evolution out of the schools, at least through the courts—but it opened another surprising chapter. In the wake of the Epperson decision, demands for equal time for alternative views of the origins of life, primarily views based on the Genesis account of creation, have expanded rapidly. As Donald Kennedy of the National Academy of Sciences has noted, "in the United States, religious opposition to teaching evolution is deeply rooted and growing stronger" thirty years after Epperson. Few issues are further from final resolution.[15]

People who are concerned with good science struggle with the kind of openness recommended in the National Academy of Science material that Kennedy supports. Some scientists seem susceptible to a charge of an unbecoming rigidity. Carl Sagan, one of the nation's most famous and respected scientists, published a best-selling book in 1996 titled *The Demon-Haunted World: Science as a Candle in the Dark*. For Sagan, the light of science is needed to drive out what seems to be the gathering darkness of far too much religiosity in the United States today. "Is this worshipping at the altar of science?" Sagan asks. His answer, he says, is based only on evidence. "If something else worked better, I would advocate that something else." But it is pretty clear from reading Sagan's work that he does not think it likely that the "something else" is going to come along any time soon.

To illustrate his discomfort with other worldviews, Sagan creates a story of someone who believes that "a fire-breathing dragon lives in my garage." When the scientist seeks any evidence, the believer insists that the dragon is invisible, floats in air, has fire that is heatless, and is incorporeal. As a scientist, of course, Sagan asks, "what's the difference between an invisible, incorporeal, floating dragon who spits heatless fire and no dragon at all?" The answer is clear: "Claims that cannot be tested, assertions immune to disproof are veridically worthless, whatever value they may have in inspiring us or in exciting our sense of wonder." But for some people, "inspiring us or exciting our sense of wonder" is just the point. When ancient biblical writers defined faith as "the assurance of things hoped for, the conviction of things not seen," perhaps they were talking about realities far more powerful than Sagan's mythical dragon.

Donald Kennedy's approach is more embracing of difference as he reminds his readers "how important it is for scientists to treat religious conviction with respect—in particular, not to suggest, even indirectly, that science and religion are unalterably opposed." After all, many scientists are religious, just as many are not. And what, it must be asked, is wrong with a bit of wonder and inspiration? David Baltimore, also one of the nation's premier scientists, has recently written, "Scientists know that questions are not settled; rather, they are given provisional answers for which it is contingent upon the imagination of followers to find more illuminating solutions. Practitioners of science are different from artists in that they give primacy to logic and evidence, but the most fundamental progress in science is achieved through hunch, analogy, insight, and creativity." It is not a concession to "creation science" to argue that high school science, like college and the most advanced research-level sciences, must never be taught as dogmatic theology but as a never-ending process of "seeking more illuminating solutions" and doing so not only through sifting the evidence but with "hunch, analogy, insight, and creativity."[16]

In this context, Nel Noddings has argued for a similar approach that includes openness, compassion, and curiosity. She begins with a basic point on which most educators would agree. She reminds high school science teachers that, when faced with a fundamentalist student who rejects evolution, it is important to remember that "Clearly, it is not intelligent to censor or proscribe full discussion of any view passionately held by one or more participant." Indeed, such a debate can become a wonderful "teachable moment" for an informed teacher who is committed to creating a classroom that is safe and engaging for all students.

> To approach questions about our origins intelligently, we should tell the full story as nearly as we can. All cultures have creation stories, and telling them or encouraging students to find and tell them presents a wonderful opportunity for multicultural education. Here our predilection for dichotomies and other rigidly marked categories leads us to insist that, if those stories be told at all, they be included in literature or history classes—not science. . . . [But] intelligent educators must be willing to cross the lines. Science teachers should begin by acknowledging the eternal human quest for solutions to the puzzle of our existence. As science teachers, they have a special obligation to pass on to students the most widely accepted contemporary beliefs in science together with the evidence used to support them. But as educators, they have an even greater responsibility to acknowledge and present with great sensitivity the full range of solutions explored by their fellow human beings. Again, such discussions do not have to end with, "Now here's the truth." The best teachers will be prepared to

present not only the full spectrum of belief but also the variety of plausible ways in which people have tried to reconcile their religious and scientific beliefs.

To do less is to rob our students of the very process of critical inquiry that is fundamental not only to science but to an intelligent approach to all aspects of the universe of learning.[17]

THE "OBJECTIVE" TEACHING OF RELIGION

Thomas C. Hunt and James C. Carper have recently written, "In company with authors like Stephen Carter *[The Culture of Disbelief: How American Law and Politics Trivialize Religious Devotion]* and Warren Nord *[Religion & American Education: Rethinking a National Dilemma]*, we believe that the United States has become publicly a secular nation, largely devoid of theistic religious influence in its institutions, including its schools. This, despite the fact that most Americans embrace, in diverse ways, a theistic belief system."[18] Clearly schools do not need to be this secular.

For all of the confusion sown by the Supreme Court's divided and seemingly contradictory opinions, the Court has been clear and consistent in ruling that the study of religion is acceptable in the schools. Justice Tom C. Clark made a point, subsequently reaffirmed by the justices again and again, in the famous 1963 *Abington v. Schemp* decision disallowing official prayers and devotional reading of the Bible. "Nothing we have said here indicates that such study of the Bible or of religion, when presented objectively as part of a secular program of education, may not be effected consistently with the First Amendment." When Justice Abraham Fortas wrote what became his controversial opinion ending any state prohibitions on the teaching of evolution for religious reasons in *Epperson v. Arkansas*, he again went out of his way to reiterate Justice Clark's opinion: "While the study of religions and of the Bible from a literary and historic viewpoint, presented objectively as part of a secular program of education, need not collide with the First Amendment's prohibition, the State may not adopt programs or practices in its public schools or colleges which 'aid or oppose' any religion." On this point, there should be no confusion. The growing secularization of the school curriculum is thus a result of a secular bias on the part of curriculum developers, fear of controversy over disputed issues, or a clear misreading of the laws and court rulings.[19]

Warren Nord's exhaustive *Religion & American Education: Rethinking a National Dilemma* represents a powerful call for a middle way. Nord begins with the assumption that "We need not make schools Christian or eliminate all religion from public education; there are alternatives." For Nord, an essential starting point is educating educators. "The conventional wisdom among educators is that religion is irrelevant to virtually everything that is taken to be true and important." The result, from an objective view, is that schools thus really do seem to reflect a religion of secularism. "One reason our situation is so difficult is that most educators are not very well educated about religion." In response to this situation, Nord sets out to educate the educators in better and more open ways to view religion, the study of history, science, morality, and the specific field of religious studies. Taking Nord, and others including Hunt, Carper, and more and more new voices appearing on the stage, seriously means a radical rethinking of the textbooks and curriculum of the schools and of the knowledge and attitudes required for effective teachers in those schools.[20]

Where Nord and most of those who seek to expand the teaching of religion in the schools focus on increasing the discussion of religious themes in history, literature, and the sciences, Nel Noddings focuses on perennial human questions that often have religious themes and that certainly cannot be discussed without references to the transcendent. She reminds her readers that most students, whatever their religious or nonreligious background, ask such questions as part of the process of maturing as young people and adults. Just to remind adults of this reality, Noddings quotes a recent comic strip, Calvin and Hobbes, in which the ever inquisitive Calvin raises a question that may not be in the syllabus but is certainly in the minds of many very real children and adults. In this strip, Calvin's teacher, ready to move to a new activity, asks if any of the students has a question:

> Calvin: What's the point of human existence?
> Teacher: I meant any questions about the subject at hand.
> Calvin: Oh. (Staring at his book, he mumbles, "Frankly, I'd like to have the issue resolved before I expend any more energy on this.")

Anyone who has taught school or spent time with children and youth has experienced just this sort of question—often at an awkward moment, or at least at a time when orderly adult minds were preparing to move to the next item on the agenda. As Noddings says so well, failure to attend to such questions, when they arise and in the context in which they arise, is failure to be the kind of open and engaged teacher that most good instructors want to be.[21]

Schools have tended to shy away from the "What's the point of human existence?" questions, however. In part it is a fear of controversy. In part it is an understandable worry about conflict with family and community norms. In part it is worry about "covering the curriculum," especially in our test- and measurement-driven educational atmosphere. In part it is sheer intellectual cowardice. But children are asking the questions. Indeed, as Noddings says, "People of all kinds—of all times and places—have asked questions about gods, existence, and the meaning of life." To put those questions aside is to compartmentalize not only the curriculum but the life of the mind and the life of the human spirit. Noddings also says, for example:

> Children in the Catholic faith learn that the purpose of life is "to know and love God . . . ," but since they rarely hear the notion discussed in "important" areas of schooling, they learn to compartmentalize their curiosity and, worse, their longings. Spiritual longing is semi-satisfied in ritual; existential longing is sacrificed to the pursuit of material goals. One starts with good grades, "solid" courses, the right schools, and proceeds to a good job. Inside, a small voice may continue to ask (in English, of course), Quo vadis? Quo vadis?

For Noddings, for many thoughtful observers, to close schools off from the realm of ultimate questions is to impoverish both schools and children.[22]

At the same time, it is very important to note that the kind of schooling that Noddings and Nord or others talk about is not easy to create. In fact, while nearly every thoughtful observer supports "the objective teaching of religion in the schools," this is not nearly as easy in practice as it is in theory. For one thing, religious faith, by definition, is not objective. Many of us have had the experience of hearing someone else describe our own faith and saying "That's not quite right." After all, Protestants believe many different things and disagree passionately with each other. So do Catholics, Jews, Muslims, Hindus, and atheists. A person so inclined could argue that part of the evidence for considering secular humanism a religion is that its adherents do not agree with each other on many things either. Teaching usually involves generalizing, and generalizing about religion often involves getting it wrong. In addition, as with many fields, it is hard to teach about the topic of religion without providing students with experience with the topic. Science classes without labs are second-rate science classes. But the primary hands-on experience of religion is the worship of believers. School visits to church, synagogue, mosque, or ashram move very close to the fine line of separation between church and state. And many believers are properly wary of simply being observed, as if they are some sort of lab specimen. So—important as the study of religion is, as right as its advocates are in arguing that we cannot understand our culture in any fundamental way without attending to matters of faith— we have not set ourselves an easy task when we seek to move forward on that front.

There are those who argue that we are best served by keeping religion a private matter while the common areas—the public square—is secular. Secular need not be hostile to religion. It can, indeed, be respectful to religion—many *different* religions. But there are things, and personal faith may be one of them, that do not thrive best when receiving the constant exposure of the public arena. Certainly the argument can be made that some matters are best attended to at home, in specifically faith-based communities, in subsets of the society where people who share common assumptions and passions can share them freely, without worry about imposition on others and without needing to explain themselves to others.

In 1965 a young Baptist theologian, Harvey Cox, published *The Secular City*. Cox's celebration of the intellectual and spiritual freedom of modern urban life, and of the ways in which God could, in fact, be found in the energetic and ever-changing cross-currents of city life, became an immediate best-seller. Twenty-five years later, looking back at the theses he had argued, Cox confessed a bit of sheepishness at some of his conclusions but also held fast to the main theme.

If anything, I believe these developments make the central thesis of *The Secular City* even more credible. I argued then that secularization—if it is not permitted to calcify into an ideology (which I called "secular*ism*")—is not everywhere and always an evil. It frees religious groups from their own theocratic pretensions and allows people to choose among a wider range of ethical and spiritual options. Today, in parallel fashion, it seems obvious that the resurgence of religion in the world is not everywhere and always a *good* thing. . . . Wouldn't a modest sprinkling of secularization, a dereligionizing of the issues come as a welcome relief in Ulster, and help resolve the murderous tensions in Kashmir and the Gaza Strip?

One cannot help wondering if some of those who participated in the congressional debate on the Religious Freedom Amendment or who tried to wend their way through the school prayer crisis in DeKalb County, Alabama, not to mention the grieving citizens of West Paducha, Kentucky, wouldn't ask some similar questions.[23]

In fact, in the midst of the congressional debate on the Religious Freedom Amendment in June, 1998, Representative Wise of West Virginia told his colleagues:

Madam Speaker, my faith, I want to get personal for a minute, comes from my heart. I seek, and I know many do, God in many ways, and we each find him in our own way through our parents, through our churches, through our community groups, through our pain, through our joy, through our many errors. That is how we find God. I take comfort in Matthew, Chapter 6 and Verse 6, 'and when thou prayest, pray to thy father in private and he shall hear you.' I think those are important words because that is the prayer that the Lord hears. Madam Speaker, I have great respect for everyone in this Chamber, men and women devoted to their government and to doing right. But with all due respect, I want this Chamber writing laws, I want us writing budgets, I want us writing resolutions. I do not want politicians writing my children's prayers. Let my children find God as we all must find God, through ourselves and our churches and our communities and our parents and our upbringings and our many experiences.[24]

There are, Congressman Wise seems to be saying, some very important arenas of life best left alone by Congress and the schools . . . and religion may well be one of them.

FINDING NEW WAYS
TO RESPECT A DIVERSE STUDENT BODY

In 1966, somewhat facetiously, Supreme Court Justice William O. Douglas reminded Americans that Islam is one of the fastest-growing religions in the world, including in the United States. "In time Moslems will control some of our school boards. In time devout Moslems may want their prayer in our schools; and if Protestant sects can get their prayers past the barriers of the First Amendment, the same passage would be guaranteed for Moslems." Is that really what the advocates of prayer in school wanted? Douglas asked.[25]

A third of a century later, schools in some major urban areas may well have a Muslim majority. There are districts with Buddhist majorities, just as there are districts with Mormon, with Catholic, with Jewish, and with Baptist majorities. The United States is rapidly becoming more and more diverse, far more so than many citizens realize. For some the answer is simple: Let the majority decide. For others who have been in the minority position too long, or fear what it may entail, the issues are much more complex.

Far more than most people have realized, the United States is a very different country at the dawn of a new century from what it was thirty years ago. The last years of the twentieth century have seen immigration on almost the same scale as the beginning years. And the immigration has been from the farthest reaches of the world: Asia, Latin America, eastern Europe, the Middle East. In addition, many people already in the country are moving frequently. As a result, many assumptions about the ethnic and religious character of the nation's people no longer hold. This is especially true in the nation's major cities.

As Shirley Brice Heath and Milbrey W. McLaughlin have shown in *Identity and Inner-City Youth: Beyond Ethnicity and Gender*, notions of race and ethnicity that motivate many contemporary public policy discussions are far removed from the changing mix of African American, Latino, Asian, and European American youth who are in the housing projects and neighborhoods, the schools, the religious organizations, and human service agencies of many of today's cities. Because of the radical changes in immigration—both from other countries and within the urban areas themselves—housing projects and other institutions are much more racially mixed than they were twenty-five years ago. As a result, "Ethnicity seemed, from the youth perspective, to be more often a label assigned to them by outsiders than an indication of their real sense of self."[26]

Urban turf conflicts in the 1960s and 1970s were often seen as black-white divisions, with most of the blacks coming from a Protestant background and most of the whites coming from Catholic, or in some cases Eastern Orthodox, backgrounds. Today's mix includes youth whose background may be any of the above but may be equally Buddhist, Muslim, Latin American evangelical, Hindu, or others. And for many youth, religion and religious institutions have little bearing on their daily reality.

A striking difference between the effective and the not-so-effective youth organizations described in *Identity and Inner-City Youth* has to do with their conceptions of youth. The majority of youth-serving programs view youth as a problem and try to fix, remedy, control, or prevent some sort of behavior. "The youth organizations that attracted and sustained young people's involvement gave visible and ongoing voice to a conception of youth as a resource to be developed and as persons of value to themselves and to society." As schools and social agencies, teachers and policymakers, take this admonition to heart, there will be significant steps in the direction of a more open future for urban youth and for the society as a whole.[27]

Looking at a different group that sees itself as marginal to the dominant society, Justin Watson, in *The Christian Coalition*, makes clear that many members of the Coalition and many other conservative religious people are torn between feeling like members of an oppressed minority who simply want the same rights as any other citizens and believing that they are the rightful arbiters of society—the appropriate definers of the dominant culture of what should be a Christian nation—temporarily pushed aside in a secular age. The reality is that a democratic society cannot have one group of citizens who define the culture for others. All citizens must together shape the culture. At the same time, a democratic culture must always respect minority rights—for all minorities.[28]

In this context of minority rights, too many contemporary voices create an unhelpful either/or dichotomy. The usually thoughtful Stephen Carter seriously missed the point when he wrote:

> Consider two examples. Imagine that you are the parent of a child in a public school, and you discover that the school, instead of offering the child a fair and balanced picture of the world—including your lifestyle choice—is teaching things that seem to the child to prove your lifestyle an inferior and perhaps irrational one. If the school's teachings are offensive to you because you are gay or black or disabled the chances are that the school will at least give you a hearing and, if it does not, that many liberals will flock to your side and you will find a sympathetic ear in the media. But if you do not like the way the school talks about religion, or if you believe that the school is inciting your children to abandon their religion, you will probably find that the media will mock you, the liberal establishment will announce that you are engaged in censorship, and the courts will toss you out on your ear.

Now, Carter must visit different schools from the ones I do. In America at the end of the twentieth century, there are still many schools where the rights of gay students, students of color, and disabled students are far from receiving respect and where those who challenge such practices are also tossed out on their ears.[29]

In supposedly liberal Boston, where I live and work, many school buildings are in violation of the legal requirements for access for disabled students, I have heard gay and lesbian students—and teachers—mocked, and I have heard terrible racist slurs. However, Carter is half right. I also have seen teachers and intellectual leaders who have a seemingly irrational fear of any mention of religion and especially of any religious passion in any form. The question is: Why should Carter, or anyone else, treat one form of discrimination differently from another? Why should Carter assume that some forms of discrimination are solved (when they are not) and then assume that other forms now merit all of our attention? There certainly are schools in America that are sensitive to the rights of students of different sexual orientations or races but not to students of different religions. There are also schools—I suspect many more if we look at the nation as a whole—that are highly sensitive to student's religious orientation but not to diversity in race, gender, or sexual orientation.

The bottom line is simple. Discrimination, in any form, is wrong. An engaged and democratic and yes, multicultural, society must make a place for all of its citizens, not merely as tolerated guests but as citizens—with all the rights, responsibilities, and contributions expected from citizens. Any hierarchy of oppression misses the point. Oppression, in any form, should not be tolerated in the schools of a democracy. To allow it is to cheapen the discussion of democracy and ultimately to impoverish the richness of the dialogue that a democratic classroom ought to sustain.

WHERE DO WE GO FROM HERE, CHAOS OR COMMUNITY?

In 1967 Martin Luther King, Jr., issued one of his great challenges to the nation, and to many in the civil rights movement, with a small book, *Where Do We Go from Here, Chaos or Community?* In that book, he told a story that was really a parable for most of his life's work.

> Some years ago a famous novelist died. Among his papers was found a list of suggested plots for future stories, the most prominently underscored being this one: "A widely separated family inherits a house in which they have to live together." This is the great new problem of mankind. We have inherited a large house, a great "world house" in which we have to live together—black and white, Eastern and Western, Gentile and Jew, Catholic and Protestant, Moslem and Hindu—a family unduly separated in ideas, culture and interest, who because we can never again live apart, must learn somehow to live with each other in peace.

Race and religion have long been two great fault lines in American society. In the next century the same challenge King raised is likely to continue to apply in both realms. As King never tired of reminding his generation, we must choose between "chaos and community," in many areas. And religion is far from the least of them.[30]

Justin Watson's brilliant analysis of the Christian Coalition applies to a far wider number of people than the Coalition's members. There is a deep ambivalence within the Coalition, Watson argues, between those demanding a rightful recognition, a respect for their rights as citizens who are also conservative Christians—which every citizen of every persuasion ought to demand—and those wanting something much more far reaching and ominous: a dream of a Protestant restoration, a longing for a past in which Protestant religion and Protestant values dominated all aspects of the nation's life, especially the curriculum and moral tone of the public schools. It is not odd that these two hopes could remain in the same organization, indeed in the same person. Most of those who embraced religious disestablishment at the time of the First Amendment had similar ambivalence. We would prefer an establishment of our particular beliefs, many seemed to say, but if we cannot have that, at least give us tolerance and do not establish someone else's beliefs. How little has changed in 220 years?

Speaking of the religious views of many who are currently most alienated from the schools, Stephen Arons, another scholar who has examined the issue, says: "As expected, the values expressed and fought for by these dissidents are, more often than not, unattractive, wrong-headed, and contrary to the accepted wisdom of the majority. Dissent, by definition, is unpopular. Yet they have acted on conscience, have shown clear commitment to their children, and have expressed fears common to many of us. It is, therefore, inappropriate for the majority to dismiss the dissidents as deranged or to congratulate itself that lack of involvement in school politics is healthy." Democracy, Arons is saying, is by definition messy. It is also a much healthier polity in which to air religious and educational differences than any other.[31]

There is, of course, the old civil liberties saying, "I may disagree with what you have to say, but I'll die for your right to say it." As an educator deeply concerned with the schooling of today's students and with the issues of this volume, I will say it a bit differently: "I may find much to disagree with in many of the claims of the religious Right; I may find creationism to be bad science and wrong-headed; I may find Robertson and Reed and many of their allies mean-spirited and dangerous in their political agenda; but I will fight with all my strength to be sure that their children, and more likely the children of their followers, are treated with as much respect as my own children or any other child in the public schools of this nation." The same, of course, must be said with equal force for the atheist or the agnostic, the Sikh, the Sufi, or the Christian Scientist. Anything less invites a retreat into private schools and ultimately undermines public education. Anything less betrays the best goals of public schools as open and engaging institutions for all of the public. Anything less is fundamentally undemocratic. Many conservative Christians will find what I am saying to be far too little, and many of my closest political and intellectual allies will find that I have engaged in dangerous accommodations with the enemy in this statement. Nevertheless, I believe that at least this degree of openness remains an essential stance for anyone who seriously believes in democracy and in a democratic and multicultural approach to American education.

In a recent essay, Michael Apple has brilliantly stated the case for a more tolerant, open, and welcoming school. Speaking of the growing power of reactionary politics, especially in relation to struggles over schools and their curricula, he writes: "When school bureaucracies do not listen respectfully to criticism, when our definitions of 'professionalism' are used to exclude power-sharing arrangements, when a curriculum seems imposed, when community members feel their voices are ignored—all of this makes rightist arguments seem sensible, even among those people who are not usually sympathetic to such ideological positions." This statement applies with considerable force to the issue of religion in the schools. To the degree religious people have been marginalized and driven into the arms of political conservatives, who are not otherwise their allies, to that degree, educational liberals, secular and not quite so secular have failed. Apple continues: "Thus, the conditions for growth of rightist anti-school and anti-public movements are often created at a local level. Making schools more open and responsive is not 'just' important because it may raise achievement scores or it may get more parents involved in supporting what 'we' want. It is also absolutely crucial for interrupting the growth of rightist social movements."[32]

If we follow Watson's analysis of the Christian Coalition and of the so-called religious right, which extends far beyond membership in the Coalition, the split between those who want to reassert cultural hegemony and those who simply want the right to hold their own beliefs and traditions is very real. And if that split does exist, the latter group need not be driven into the arms of the former. To the degree that the United States allows any return to the cultural hegemony of Protestant or Christian culture in the schools or other institutions, it will be a less humane and democratic society for all of its citizens—including those of us who are Protestant Christians. Tyranny is inhumane for all who are involved in it, even the tyrants. But as Apple notes so well, the way to avoid religious tyranny is not to impose a different, perhaps milder, tyranny of the bureaucrat, the professional, and the curriculum expert.

The way to a better future is through an inclusive and engaging education in which schools encourage all of their citizens—students, teachers, and administrators—to listen respectfully, where power is shared, where all voices are heard and given their due rights. We may not agree with all of the voices; indeed, we *will* not. That is the nature of democratic dialogue. But our education will be richer, our cultural diversity will be strengthened, and our most fundamental democratic sensibilities will be more deeply engaged if we extend a welcoming hand to religious people, to fundamentalists, to believers in creationism, and equally to Native Americans who claim their ancient spirituality, to Muslims of many varieties, to orthodox and not-so-orthodox Jews, to followers of emerging New Age spirituality, and to militant atheists and cautious agnostics. All have a right to a place at the table, all have much to learn from and contribute to the ever-changing American culture, and all are part of the rich tapestry of multicultural America that is emerging in the opening years of a new century.

NOTES

INTRODUCTION

1. Thomas Paine, cited in Mark E. Dudley, *Engel v. Vitale (1962): Religion in the Schools* (New York: 1995), p. 13.
2. John Dewey, *The School and Society* (Chicago: 1899, 2nd ed., 1915), p. 29.
3. Neil G. McCluskey, S.J., *Catholic Education in America: A Documentary History* (New York: 1964), pp. 20-21.

CHAPTER ONE

1. *The New England Primer,* edited with an introduction by Paul Leicester Ford (New York, 1962).
2. Nathaniel B. Shurtleff, ed., *Records of the Governor and Company of the Massachusetts Bay in New England* (5 vols.) (Boston, 1853-1854), II, 203.
3. Quoted in Samuel Eliot Morison, *The Intellectual Life of Colonial New England* (Ithaca, NY, 1936, 1956), p. 66.
4. Cotton Mather, *Manuductio ad Ministerium: Directions for a Candidate for the Ministry* (Boston, 1726), p. 50.
5. "Proceedings of the Virginia Assembly, 1619," in Lyon Gardiner Tyler, ed., *Narratives of Early Virginia*, 1606-1625, cited in Lawrence A. Cremin, *American Education: The Colonial Experience, 1607-1783* (New York, 1970), p. 150.
6. Colonial legislation is cited and described in Lawrence A. Cremin, *American Education: The Colonial Experience*, pp. 125-126.
7. The Constitution of the United States, The National Archives, Washington, D.C.
8. Sidney E. Mead, *The Lively Experiment: The Shaping of Christianity in America* (New York, 1963), p. 2.
9. Mead, p. 17.
10. quotations cited in Mead, p. 17.
11. For a far more detailed version of this story see chapters 1 and 2 in Mead.
12. Mead, p. 4.
13. Mead, p. 21.
14. Mead, chapters 3 and 4 explores these issues in considerably more detail.
15. Thomas Jefferson, "A Bill for Establishing Religious Freedom," in Julian P. Boyd, editor, *The Papers of Thomas Jefferson* (Princeton, NJ, 1950), 2: pp. 545-547.
16. Thomas Jefferson, to Messrs. Nehemiah Dodge, Ephraim Robbins, and Stephen S. Nelson, A Committee of the Danbury Baptist Association, the State

of Connecticut, Washington, January 1, 1802, cited in Gordon C. Lee, *Crusade Against Ignorance: Thomas Jefferson on Education* (New York, 1961), p. 69.

17. Thomas Jefferson to Rev. Samuel Miller, Washington, January 23, 1808, in Lee, p. 70.

18. Mead, p. 66.

CHAPTER TWO

1. Francis N. Thorpe, ed., *Federal and State Constitutions, Colonial Charters, and Other Organic Laws of the States* (7 vols.) (Washington, D.C., 1909).

2. Richard J. Purcell, *Connecticut in Transition, 1775-1818* (Washington, D.C., 1918), remains the best study of this little-noted story. See also my *Pedagogue for God's Kingdom: Lyman Beecher and the Second Great Awakening* (Lanham, MD, 1985).

3. All citations here are from Horace Mann, "Twelfth Report," in Lawrence A. Cremin, ed., *The Republic and the School: Horace Mann On the Education of Free Men* (New York, 1957). Mann's reports have been printed in various formats, all with different page numbering, since their original publication by the Commonwealth of Massachusetts during Mann's tenure.

4. Mann, "Twelfth Report" in Cremin, ed., *The Republic and the School.*

5. Mann, "Twelfth Report" in Cremin, ed., *The Republic and the School.*

6. Mary Peabody Mann, *Life of Horace Mann* (Boston, 1891), p. 14. See also Jonathan Messerli, *Horace Mann: A Biography* (New York, 1972), for a thorough account of Mann's life and work.

7. Carl F. Kaestle and Maris A. Vinovskis, *Education and Social Change in Nineteenth-Century Massachusetts* (Cambridge, 1980).

8. Report of the Committee on Education, Massachusetts House of Representatives, March 7, 1840, *The Common School Journal*, 2:15 (August 1, 1840): 225.

9. *The Common School Journal*, p. 227.

10. *The Common School Journal*, p. 227.

11. *The Common School Journal*, p. 228. For a thoughtful and detailed analysis of Mann's battles with the legislature and other religious groups in Massachusetts, see Kaestle and Vinovskis, *Education and Social Change in Nineteenth-Century Massachusetts*, and Charles Leslie Glenn, Jr., *The Myth of the Common School* (Amherst, MA, 1988).

12. Much of the material on Lyman Beecher is from my earlier study, *Pedagogue for God's Kingdom: Lyman Beecher and The Second Great Awakening* (Lanham, MD, 1985). For more detail, see that study.

13. Assumptions that the word "evangelical" means the same thing in the early nineteenth and late twentieth centuries has led to a great deal of confusion in interpreting the role of religion in American schools and society. By class background, attitudes toward the dominant culture, and theological content, nineteenth-century evangelicals were very different from those who use the term—or about whom it is used—at the beginning of the twenty-first century. It is important to remember William G. McLoughlin's helpful distinction:

> The history of Evangelicalism in America must be told on three levels; first as philosophy, second as theology, and third as social history. As philosophy it is the story of the permeation of nineteenth century thought with the ideas and systems of the Scottish Common Sense School. As theology it is the story of the decline of Calvinism, the Protestant Counter Reformation, against

deism, and the emergence of a new theological consensus on Arminian principles which prevailed between the Second Great Awakening and the rise of Modernism. As social history it is the story of the final triumph of voluntarism over establishmentarianism and the rise of a new revivalistic religion which was as interdenominational in its pattern as the moral reform crusades and benevolent associations which it spawned to purify the nation and redeem the world.

From William G. McLoughlin, "Introduction," *The American Evangelicals, 1800-1900* (New York, 1968), p. 2. In other words, nineteenth-century evangelicals saw themselves as much more a part of—often leaders of—the wider society and certainly not as a persecuted minority. Partly for this reason, they were also considerably more liberal in theology and especially in politics. Most were abolitionists, whether moderate or radical.

14. See Timothy L. Smith, "Protestant Schooling and American Nationality, 1800-1850," *Journal of American History,* 53 (1966-1967): 679-694, and David Tyack, "The Kingdom of God and the Common School," *Harvard Educational Review,* 36 (Fall, 1966): 454.

15. Tyack, "Kingdom of God," p. 448; see also David Tyack and Elisabeth Hansot, *Managers of Virtue: Public School Leadership in America, 1820-1980* (New York, 1982).

16. Robert W. Lynn, *Protestant Strategies in Education* (New York, 1964), p. 57.

17. Smith, "Protestant Schooling and American Nationality," p. 679.

18. Tyack, "Kingdom of God," p. 453.

19. Smith, "Protestant Schooling and American Nationality," p. 687.

20. Calvin Stowe, "The Religious Element in Education," (Boston, 1844), p. 26.

21. Smith, "Protestant Schooling and American Nationality," pp. 679-694.

22. Tyack, "Kingdom of God," p. 448.

23. Tyack, "Kingdom of God," p. 450.

24. Lyman Beecher, *A Plea for the West* (Cincinnati, 1835), p. 50.

25. Calvin Stowe, "On the Education of Emigrants," *Transactions of the Fifth Annual Meeting of the Western Literary Institute and College of Professional Teachers,* (October 1835) (Cincinnati, 1836), pp. 68-69.

26. Tyack, "Kingdom of God," p. 454.

27. Smith, "Protestant Schooling and American Nationality," pp. 679-80.

28. Stowe, "On the Education of Emigrants," pp. 69-70.

29. Daniel Drake, response to statements by Calvin Stowe, *Transactions,* p. 81.

30. See Daniel Aaron, *Cincinnati, 1818-1838: A Study of Attitudes in the Urban West,* Ph.D. dissertation, Harvard University, 1942, p. 329.

31. Stowe, "The Religious Element in Education," pp. 8 and 21.

32. Stowe, "The Religious Element in Education," p. 25, see also Mann, "Twelfth Report."

33. Calvin E. Stowe, *Report on Elementary Public Instruction in Europe* (Columbus, 1838). Page numbers in this study are from the Pennsylvania edition (Harrisburg: 1838).

34. Stowe, *Report on Elementary Public Instruction in Europe,* p. 17; *Journal of the Senate of the State of Ohio,* 24 (December 7, 1835) (Columbus, 1836): 976.

35. See "L.B. to Catharine, Boston, July 8, 1830," in Lyman Beecher, *Autobiography,* 2 vols. (New York, 1864; edited by Barbara Cross, Cambridge, MA, 1961), 2: 167, and "Catharine to Harriet, Cincinnati, April 17, 1832," in *Autobiography,* 2: 199-201.

36. Kathryn Kish Sklar, *Catharine Beecher: A Study in American Domesticity* (New Haven, 1973), pp. 110-111.

37. Sklar, p. 112, citing *American Annals of Education and Instruction*, William Woodbridge, ed., 3 (August: 1833): 380.

38. Sklar, *Catharine Beecher*, p. 113.

39. Catharine E. Beecher, "An Essay on the Education of Female Teachers" (New York, 1835), p. 5.

40. See Lawrence A. Cremin, *American Education: The National Experience, 1783-1876* (New York, 1980), pp. 142-147.

41. "Harriet E. Bishop to the Secretary, American Baptist Home Mission Society, St. Paul, Minnesota, November 25, 1848," ABHMS, *Sixteenth Report* (1848), pp. 65-66, quoted in Colin Brummitt Goodykoontz, *Home Missions on the American Frontier*, (Caldwell, ID: 1939), p. 372.

42. William G. Lewis, *Biography of Samuel Lewis* (Cincinnati, 1857), pp. 118-121; and William T. Coggeshall, "Samuel Lewis," *American Journal of Education* 5 (1858): 729.

43. Samuel Lewis, "First Annual Report" (January 1838), in Lewis, *Biography of Samuel Lewis*, p. 132.

44. Samuel Lewis, "Third Annual Report" (December 1839), in Lewis, *Biography of Samuel Lewis*, p. 245.

45. For a thoughtful study of the changing nature and growing secularization of school leadership, see Tyack and Hansot, *Managers of Virtue.*

46. *Historical Sketches of Public Schools in Cities, Villages and Townships of the State of Ohio* (n.p.: 1876), no page.

47. Tyack, "Kingdom of God," p. 451.

48. See review of Lyman Beecher, *A Plea for the West* in *Western Monthly Magazine* (May 1833), pp. 320-327.

49. Mann, "Twelfth Report."

50. Smith, "Protestant Schooling and American Nationality," p. 695.

51. Walter Havighurst, *The Miami Years, 1809-1969* (New York, 1969), p. 65; Harvey C. Minnich, *William Holmes McGuffey and his Readers* (Cincinnati, 1936), pp. 31-32; Robert Lynn, "Civil Catechetics in Mid-Victorian America: Some Notes About American Civil Religion, Past and Present," *Religious Education* (January-February 1972), p. 12, raises questions about the authenticity of the tradition.

52. Havighurst, *Miami Years*, p. 65; see also John H. Westerhoff, III, *McGuffey and His Readers: Piety, Morality, and Education in Nineteenth-Century America* (Nashville, 1978).

53. Henry Steele Commager, foreword to *McGuffey's Fifth Eclectic Reader*, 1879 edition (New York, 1962), p. i.

54. Commager, p. xii.

55. William H. McGuffey, *McGuffey's New Fourth Eclectic Reader* (Cincinnati, IL, 1857), pp. 34-36, 39-43.

56. Lynn, "Civil Catechetics," p. 15.

57. William H. McGuffey, "Characters of the Puritan Fathers of New England," *McGuffey's New Fifth Eclectic Reader* (Cincinnati, IL, 1857), p. 251.

58. See Richard D. Mosier, *Making the American Mind: Social and Moral Ideals in the McGuffey Readers* (New York: 1965), p. 17.

59. McGuffey, *New Fifth Eclectic Reader*, p. 109.

60. Lyman Beecher, in an advertisement in *McGuffey's Newly Revised Eclectic Fourth Reader* (Cincinnati: 1848), p. 6.

61. William H. McGuffey, *New First Eclectic Reader* (Cincinnati, IL, 1857), p. 50.

62. McGuffey, *New Fifth Eclectic Reader,* p. 84, see also William H. McGuffey, *McGuffey's New Eclectic Speaker* (Cincinnati, IL, 1858), p. 141.

63. McGuffey, *New Fifth Reader,* pp. 150-51; reference from Beecher, *A Plea for the West.*

64. Westerhoff, *McGuffey and His Readers,* p. 19.

65. I disagree with many who have assumed that the Sunday school was designed to teach the specifics of denominational theology while the common school carried the basics. Anyone familiar with much Sunday school curricula from the nineteenth or twentieth century knows that very little attention is given to denominational uniqueness. What is stressed is the need for salvation and a personal relationship with Jesus. See my *Pedagogue for God's Kingdom.*

66. *Minutes of the General Assembly, Presbyterian Church, U.S.A.* (Old School) (Philadelphia, 1844), p. 376, quoted in Lewis Joseph Sherrill, *Presbyterian Parochial Schools, 1846-1870* (New Haven, 1932; reprinted New York, 1969), p. 20.

67. See William B. Kennedy, *The Shaping of Protestant Education* (New York, 1966), pp. 34-38.

68. Sherrill, paraphrasing the Minutes of the General Assembly (1846), pp. 227-232, in Sherrill, *Presbyterian Parochial Schools,* p. 22.

69. Sherrill, *Presbyterian Parochial Schools,* pp. 180-81.

70. Winthrop S. Hudson, *The Great Tradition of the American Churches* (New York, 1963), p. 108.

71. Beecher, *A Plea for the West,* pp. 63-64.

72. Mann, "Twelfth Report."

73. Kennedy, *Shaping of Protestant Education,* p. 35.

74. H. H. Barney, Ohio Commissioner of Common Schools, *Introduction to A Manual of the Ohio School System,* by James W. Taylor (Cincinnati, 1857), p. v.

75. Robert T. Handy, *A Christian America: Protestant Hopes and Historical Realities* (New York, 1971), p. 113.

CHAPTER THREE

1. Neil G. McCluskey, S.J., "America and the Catholic School," in Neil G. McCluskey, ed., *Catholic Education in America: A Documentary History* (New York, 1964), pp. 2-4.

2. McCluskey, *Catholic Education,* p. 3.

3. "Pastoral Letter of Bishop Carroll" (1792) in McCluskey, *Catholic Education,* p. 46.

4. McCluskey, *Catholic Education,* p. 15.

5. For different versions of this story, see: Vincent P. Lannie, *Public Money and Parochial Education: Bishop Hughes, Governor Seward and the New York School Controversy* (Cleveland, 1968); John W. Pratt, *Religion, Politics and Diversity: The Church-State Theme in New York History* (Ithaca, NY, 1967); Diane Ravitch, *The Great School Wars, New York City, 1805-1973* (New York, 1974); and Carl. F. Kaestle, *The Evolution of an Urban School System: New York City, 1750-1850* (Cambridge, MA, 1973). Of these, I find Kaestle the most helpful. For primary material from a Protestant perspective, see William O. Bourne, *History of the Public School Society of the City of New York* (New York, 1870); for the Catholic

perspective, see Lawrence Kehoe, ed., *Complete Works of the Most Rev. John Hughes*, 2 vols. (New York, 1866).

6. For a careful description of the development of New York's unique postrevolutionary system of schooling, see Lawrence A. Cremin, *American Education: The National Experience, 1783-1876* (New York, 1980).

7. Kaestle, *Evolution of an Urban School System*, pp. 145-146.

8. Free School Society, *Annual Report* (1825), p. 7, cited in Kaestle, *The Evolution of an Urban School System*, p. 85.

9. For a detailed analysis of the changing attitude of the Free School Society, and Catholic responses, see Ravitch, *The Great School Wars*.

10. Free School Society, *Annual Report*, 1825, p. 7, cited in Kaestle, *The Evolution of an Urban School System*, p. 86.

11. "DeWitt Clinton to Isaac Collins, December 27, 1823," DeWitt Clinton Papers, Columbia University, 20: 525, in Kaestle, *Evolution of an Urban school System*, p. 86.

12. "Report of the Committee on Arts and Sciences," Document No. 80, Board of Assistant Aldermen, April 27, 1840; cited in Ravitch, *The Great School Wars*, p. 43.

13. "Petition of the Catholics of New York for a Portion of the Common School Fund," from Kehoe, ed., *Complete Works of the Most Rev. John Hughes*.

14. For a thoughtful discussion of this dilemma, see McCluskey, *Catholic Education*, p. 18.

15. "Petition of the Catholics of New York."

16. "Petition of the Catholics of New York."

17. Freeman's Journal, May 7, 1842, cited in Ravitch, *The Great School Wars*, p. 79.

18. The story of the school battle of 1840-1842 is told here primarily from the perspective of Carl Kaestle. For a thorough understanding, Kaestle, Ravitch, Lannie, and of course the original documents are all essential.

19. McCluskey, *Catholic Education*, p. 1 and 25.

20. Kaestle, *Evolution of an Urban School System*, p. 146.

21. James W. Sanders, *The Education of an Urban Minority: Catholics in Chicago, 1833-1965* (New York, 1977), pp. 3-5.

22. James W. Sanders, "Boston Catholics and the School Question, 1825-1907," in James W. Fraser, Henry Allen, and Sam Barnes, eds., *From Common School to Magnet School: Selected Essays in the History of Boston's Schools* (Boston, 1979).

23. "The Plenary Councils of Baltimore," in McCluskey, *Catholic Education*, pp. 78-94, see specifically pp. 80 and 94; see also Sanders, *Education of An Urban Minority*, pp. 12-14.

24. John Ireland, "State Schools and Parish Schools," address to the National Education Association (1890) in McCluskey, *Catholic Education*, pp. 127-140, see specifically pp. 128, 129, 131.

25. Ireland, "State Schools and Parish Schools," pp. 135.

26. Ireland, "State Schools and Parish Schools," pp. 132-133.

27. Ireland, "State Schools and Parish Schools," pp. 138.

28. Ireland, "State Schools and Parish Schools," pp. 127-140.

29. "Bernard McQuaid to Leo XIII, Rochester, December 13, 1892," in McCluskey, *Catholic Education*, pp. 161-165.

30. "Archbishop Ireland's Letter to Cardinal Gibbons Explaining in Detail His Address on State Schools at St. Paul in July, 1890," in McCluskey, *Catholic Education*, pp. 141-150, see specifically pp. 146, 147 and also 164.

31. "Archbishop Francis Satolli's Fourteen Propositions Presented November 17, 1892, to the Archbishops of the United States for Settling the School Question," in McCluskey, *Catholic Education*, pp. 151-160.

32. Sanders, *Education of an Urban Minority*, pp. 4 and 14.

33. McCluskey, *Catholic Education*, p. 25

CHAPTER FOUR

1. W. E. B. DuBois, *Black Reconstruction in America* (1935, reprinted Cleveland, 1962), pp. 641-649.

2. Carl F. Kaestle, *The Evolution of an Urban School System: New York City, 1750-1850* (Cambridge, MA, 1973), pp. 49-55.

3. For a very thoughtful and detailed study of "Black Schools in White Boston," see Stanley K. Schultz, *The Culture Factory: Boston Public Schools, 1789-1860* (New York, 1973) and Byron Rushing, "Black Schools in White Boston, 1800-1860," chapter two, pp. 15-27 in James W. Fraser, Henry Allen, and Sam Barnes, *From Common School to Magnet School* (Boston, 1979), pp.

4. Both Schultz and Rushing tell the story of the campaign against segregated schools in Boston resulting in the 1855 state legislation outlawing segregation in the public schools of Massachusetts.

5. James D. Anderson, *The Education of Blacks in the South, 1860-1935* (Chapel Hill, NC, 1988), p. 2.

6. The material on African American Sunday schools is drawn primarily from Anne M. Boylan, *Sunday School: The Formation of An American Institution, 1790-1889* (New Haven, 1988), pp. 22-29.

7. John Hope Franklin and Alfred A. Moss, Jr., *From Slavery to Freedom: A History of African Americans*, 7th ed. (New York, 1994), pp. 124-126.

8. Jamie Parker, *Jamie Parker, the Fugitive, Related to Mrs.. Emily Pierson* (Hartford, 1851), pp. 20-22.

9. Anderson, *Education of Blacks in the South*, p. 5, see also Franklin and Moss, *From Slavery to Freedom*, p. 137.

10. All quotations are from Thomas L. Webber, *Deep Like the Rivers: Education in the Slave Quarter Community, 1831-1865* (New York, 1978), pp. 80-81.

11. Webber, *Deep Like the Rivers*, pp. 43-58.

12. Webber, *Deep Like the Rivers*, pp. 43-58 and Franklin and Moss, *From Slavery to Freedom*, pp. 133-136

13. Webber, *Deep Like the Rivers*, p. 206.

14. "The Clandestine Congregation," chapter 15, pp. 191-206 in Webber.

15. Anderson, *Education of Blacks in the South*, pp. 4-17.

16. Anderson, *Education of Blacks in the South*, pp. 4-17.

17. Anderson, *Education of Blacks in the South*, pp. 4-17.

18. Anderson, *Education of Blacks in the South*, p. 17.

19. Anderson, *Education of Blacks in the South*, p. 7.

20. Anderson, *Education of Blacks in the South*, pp. 11-13.

21. David Tyack and Robert Lowe, "The Constitutional Moment: Reconstruction and Black Education in the South," *American Journal of Education* 94 (February 1986): 236-256, cited in Anderson, *Education of Blacks in the South*, pp. 18-19.

22. See Wayne Urban and Jennings Wagoner, Jr., *American Education: A History* (New York, 1996), pp. 140-151.

23. Carl Schurz reporting on comments made to him by white planters in late 1865, cited in Anderson, *Education of Blacks in the South*, pp. 20-21.

24. Urban and Wagoner, *American Education*, pp. 148-150.

25. See Urban and Wagoner, American Education; and Anderson, *Education of Blacks in the South*, pp. 18-32.

26. Anderson, *Education of Blacks in the South*, pp. 13-14.

27. Asbury P. Jones, Jr., "Public Education and the Black Church," unpublished paper, Harvard Divinity School, January, 1998

28. Evelyn Brooks Higginbotham, *Righteous Discontent: The Women's Movement in the Black Baptist Church* (Cambridge, MA, 1993), p. 55.

29. Jones, "Public Education and the Black Church."

30. Lester F. Russell, *Black Baptist Secondary Schools in Virginia, 1887-1957* (London, 1981), p. 41, cited in Jones, "Public Education and the Black Church."

31. Russell, *Black Baptist Secondary Schools*, pp. 23-24.

32. Higginbotham, *Righteous Discontent*, p. 19.

CHAPTER FIVE

1. Joel Spring, *The American School, 1642-1996* (New York, 1997), p. 46.

2. All quotations are from Ronald Takaki, *A Different Mirror: A History of Multicultural America* (Boston, 1993), pp. 101-105.

3. Cited in Lawrence A. Cremin, *American Education: The Colonial Experience, 1607-1783* (New York, 1970), p. 12.

4. Spring, *American School*, p. 39; Cremin, *The Colonial Experience*, pp. 158-161.

5. E. Jennifer Monaghan, "'She loved to read in good Books': Literacy and the Indians of Martha's Vineyard, 1643-1725," *History of Education Quarterly* 30:4 (Winter 1990): 493-521.

6. Takaki, *A Different Mirror*, pp. 24-50.

7. Lawrence A. Cremin, *American Education: The National Experience, 1783-1876* (New York: 1980), pp. 230-234; Spring, *American School*, pp. 40-41.

8. Cremin, *The National Experience*, pp. 234-235; Spring, *American School*, pp. 42-43.

9. Cremin, *The National Experience*, pp. 234-236.

10. David Wallace Adams, *Education for Extinction: American Indians and the Boarding School Experience, 1875-1928* (Lawrence, KS, 1995), p. 6; see also Cremin, *The National Experience*, pp. 234-236.

11. Herman Viola, *Thomas L. McKinney: Architect of America's Early Indian Policy: 1816-1830* (Chicago: 1974); Cremin, *The National Experience*, pp. 236-237; Spring, *American School*, pp. 42-44.

12. Takaki, *A Different Mirror*, pp. 84-105; Spring, *American School*, pp. 34-49.

13. Takaki, *A Different Mirror*, pp. 88, 93-97.

14. For a good description of the removal tragedy, see Takaki, *A Different Mirror*, pp. 84-105. For Protestant missionary issues, see Robert F. Berkhofer, Jr., *Salvation and the Savage: An Analysis of Protestant Missions and American Indian Response, 1787-1862* (Louisville, KY, 1965).

15. See Adams, *Education for Extinction*, pp. 6-9

16. Adams, *Education for Extinction*, pp. 14-15.

17. The material on the Indian boarding school experience, in this and subsequent paragraphs, including direct quotations, is drawn from Adams, *Education for Extinction;* in addition, see Richard Henry Pratt, *Battlefield and Classroom: Four Decades with the American Indian, 1867-1904*, ed. Robert M. Utley (New Haven, 1964); and Francis Paul Prucha, *The Great Father: The United States Government and the American Indians*, 2 vols. (Lincoln, NB, 1984), esp. 2: 687-715.

18. See Adams, pp. 28-59.

19. Prucha, *The Great Father*, 2: 700-715.

20. Takaki, *A Different Mirror*, pp. 228-231.

21. Adams, *Education for Extinction*, p. 32.

22. Francis La Flesche, *The Middle Five: Indian Boys at School* (1900), cited in Michael C. Coleman, "The Responses of American Indian Children to Presbyterian Schooling in the Nineteenth Century: An Analysis through Missionary Sources," *History of Education Quarterly* 27:4 (Winter 1987): 473-497.

23. Lewis Meriam, *The Problem of Indian Administration* (Baltimore, 1928), cited in Spring, *American School*, pp. 162-163; see also R. Pierce Beaver, *Church, State, and the American Indians* (St. Louis, MO, 1966), pp. 207-212.

24. John Collier, Commissioner of Indian Affairs, *Annual Report of 1934*, in Francis Paul Prucha, *Documents of United States Indian Policy* (Lincoln, NB, 1990), pp., 225-228; see also Takaki, *A Different Mirror*, pp. 238-240, Beaver, *Church State and the American Indian*, pp. 210-211; and Prucha, *The Great Father*, 2: 1100-1106.

25. American Indian Religious Freedom Act, August 11, 1978, a joint resolution of Congress, in Prucha, *Documents*, pp. 288-289.

26. Edward Everett is cited in Stanley K. Schultz, *The Culture Factory: Boston Public Schools, 1789-1860* (New York, 1973), p. 260; see Jon Reyhner and Jeanne Eder, *A History of Indian Education* (Billings, MT, 1989).

27. Carl F. Kaestle, "Ideology and American Educational History," *History of Education Quarterly* 22 (Summer 1982): 127-128; John Higham, "Hanging Together: Divergent Unities in American History," *Journal of American History* 61 (June 1974): 12-18; Adams, *Education for Extinction*, pp. 9-12.

28. Mary Crow Dog and Richard Erdoes, *Lakota Woman* (New York, 1990), p. 30.

29. Spring, *American School*, p. 33.

CHAPTER SIX

1. *Congressional Record*, 44th Congress, 1st ses., pp. 5453-5456, 5595.

2. Carl F. Kaestle, "Ideology and American Educational History," *History of Education Quarterly* 22 (Summer 1982): 127-128; John Higham, "Hanging Together: Divergent Unities in American History," *Journal of American History* 61 (June 1974): 12-18.

3. Ward M. McAfee, *Religion, Race, and Reconstruction: The Public School in the Politics of the 1870s* (Albany, NY, 1998).

4. Wayne Urban and Jennings Wagoner, Jr., *American Education: A History* (New York, 1996), pp. 144-146.

5. McAfee, *Religion, Race, and Reconstruction*, pp. 151-161.

6. McAfee, *Religion, Race, and Reconstruction*, pp. 90-96, Urban and Wagoner, *American Education*, pp. 144-146.

7. Correspondence and sermon by Bishop Bernard McQuaid in H. Shelton Smith, Robert T. Handy, and Lefferts A. Loetscher, *American Christianity*, 2 vols. (New York, 1963), 2: 317-320.

8. See Vincent P. Lannie, *Public Money and Parochial Education: Bishop Hughes, Governor Seward, and the New York School Controversy* (Cleveland, 1968); and Karl F. Kaestle, *The Evolution of an Urban School System: New York City, 1750-1850* (Cambridge, MA, 1973).

9. McAfee, *Religion, Race, and Reconstruction*, pp. 27-41.

10. McAfee, *Religion, Race, and Reconstruction*, pp. 57-75.

11. McAfee, *Religion, Race, and Reconstruction*, p. 41.

12. See McAfee, *Religion, Race, and Reconstruction*, pp. 220-222; See chapter 7 of this book, and also Albert J. Menendez, *John F. Kennedy: Catholic and Humanist* (Buffalo, n.d.).

13. Ronald Takaki, *A Different Mirror: A History of Multicultural America* (Boston, 1993), pp. 191-221.

14. Takaki, *A Different Mirror*, pp. 246-276.

15. Mary Antin, *The Promised Land* (Boston, 1912), p. 202, see also pp. 7-8.

16. Mary Antin, *The Promised Land*, pp. 8, 202, 242-244.

17. Edward J. Larson, *Summer for the Gods: The Scopes Trial and America's Continuing Debate Over Science and Religion* (New York, 1997), pp. 16-21.

18. Larson, *Summer for the Gods*, pp. 16-23.

19. See also Edward J. Larson, *Trial and Error: The American Controversy Over Creation and Evolution* (New York, 1985), pp. 7-27.

20. Material in this chapter is drawn primarily from George M. Marsden, *Fundamentalism and American Culture: The Shaping of Twentieth-Century Evangelicalism: 1870-1925* (New York, 1980), see p. 119. Ernest R. Sandeen, *The Roots of Fundamentalism: British and American Millenarianism, 1800-1930* (Chicago, 1970), gives greatest weight to fundamentalism's theological roots. Earlier historians tended to focus on the social origins, including H. Richard Niebuhr, *The Social Sources of Denominationalism* (New York, 1929); Richard Hofstadter, *Anti-Intellectualism in American Life* (New York, 1962); and William McLoughlin, "Is There a third Force in Christendom?" *Daedalus* 96 (Winter 1967).

21. Marsden, *Fundamentalism and American Culture*, pp. 38, 43-44, 66, 118-9, 153, 188.

22. See Marsden, *Fundamentalism and American Culture*, pp. 38-188.

23. Larson, *Trial and Error*, pp. 19-27; Larson, *Summer for the Gods*, p. 16-24.

24. Larson, *Trial and Error*, pp. 26-27; Larson, *Summer for the Gods*, 24-25.

25. Larson, *Summer for the Gods*, p. 24.

26. Larson, *Trial and Error*, pp. 45-48; Larson, *Summer for the Gods*, p. 43.

27. Larson, *Trial and Error*, pp. 48-57.

28. Larson, *Trial and Error*, pp. 48-57.

29. Larson, *Summer for the Gods*, p. 83.

30. Larson, *Summer for the Gods*, pp. 89-90.

31. The story and quotes from the trial here are drawn primarily from Larson, *Summer for the Gods;* see also Larson, *Trial and Error;* and Ray Ginger, *Six Days or Forever: Tennessee v. John Thomas Scopes* (New York, 1958).

32. Larson, *Trial and Error,* pp. 84-92; for the caution of textbook publishers, see Frances FitzGerald, *American Revised* (New York, 1979); Philip G. Altbach, Gail P. Kelly, Hugh G. Petrie, and Lois Weis, eds., *Textbooks in American Society: Politics, Policy, and Pedagogy* (Albany, NY, 1991); and Herbert M. Kliebard, *The*

Struggle for the American Curriculum (New York, 1987) and *Forging the American Curriculum* (New York, 1992).

CHAPTER SEVEN

1. Pierce v. Society of Sisters, 268 U.S. 512 (1925); *Meyers v. Nebraska*, 260 U.S. 390 (1923); Lawrence A. Cremin, *American Education: The Metropolitan Experience, 1876-1980* (New York, 1988), pp. 552-553; Gary L. McDowell, "The Explosion and Erosion of Rights," in David J. Bodenhamer and James W. Ely, Jr., *The Bill of Rights in Modern America After 200 Years* (Bloomington, IN, 1993), p. 31.

2. Robert T. Handy, *A Christian America: Protestant Hopes and Historical Realities* (New York, 1971), p. 213.

3. Handy, *Christian America*, pp. 199-207.

4. All quotations from Handy, *Christian America*, pp. 199-207.

5. Edwin S. Gaustad, "Consensus in America: The Churches' Changing Role," *Journal of the American Academy of Religion*, 36 (March 1968): 35-36, cited in Handy, *Christian America*, p. 209.

6. Timothy L. Smith, "Protestant Schooling and American Nationality, 1800-1850," *Journal of American History*, 53 (1966-1967): p. 687.

7. David Tyack and Elisabeth Hansot, *Managers of Virtue: Public School Leadership in America, 1820-1980* (New York, 1982), pp. 6-7, 106.

8. John Dewey, *A Common Faith* (New Haven, 1934), see esp. pp. 2, 31-32, and 86.

9. Wayne Urban and Jennings Wagoner, Jr., *American Education: A History* (New York, 1996), pp. 209-210.

10. Gilman Ostrander, *The Rights of Man in America, 1606-1861* (Columbia, MO, 1960), pp. 314-315, cited in Handy, *Christian America*, p. 209.

11. John Collier, "Annual Report of the Commissioner of Indian Affairs," (1934) in Francis Paul Prucha, *Documents of United States Indian Policy* (Lincoln, NB 1975/1990), pp. 225-228. See chapter five of this book for more detail.

12. Cited in Mark E. Dudley, *Engle v. Vitale (1962): Religion in the Schools* (New York, 1995), pp. 38-39.

13. *Minersville School District v. Gobitis* 310 U.S. 586 (1940) Note: The family name is Gobitas. A spelling error in the initial documents has been retained as the case is known as the Gobitis case. Dudley, *Engel v. Vitale*, pp. 37-52.

14. *West Virginia State Board of Education v. Barnette* 319 U.S. 624 (1943). See Dudley, *Engle v. Vitale*, pp. 48-51; David Fellman, ed., *The Supreme Court and Education*, 3rd. ed. (New York, 1976), pp. 32-47.

15. *West Virginia State Board of Education v. Barnette* in Fellman, ed., *Supreme Court and Education*. Jackson's opinion also reflects another a little noticed but far reaching Supreme Court decision, *Cantwell v. Connecticut* 310 U.S. 296 (1940), which for the first time clearly affirmed that the First Amendment guarantee of freedom of religion is covered by the Fourteenth Amendment and therefore applies to state and local jurisdictions.

16. Robert W. Lynn and Eliott Wright, *The Big Little School: Two Hundred Years of the Sunday School*, rev. and enlarged 2nd ed. (Birmingham, AL, 1980), pp. 3-4; Cremin, *The Metropolitan Experience*, pp. 236-7; Randolph S. Bourne, *The Gary Schools* (Boston, 1916).

17. Fellman, ed., *Supreme Court and Education*, pp. 48-61; see also Dudley, *Engle v. Vitale*, pp. 55-60.

18. Illinois ex rel. *McCollum v. Board of Education* 333 U.S. 203 (1948), in Fellman, pp. 48-61; see also Dudley, pp. 55-60.

19. *Zorach v. Clauson* 343 U.S. 306 (1952), cited in Fellman, pp. 62-73 and discussed in Dudley, pp. 59-60. As a side note, the author remembers attending release-time instruction in the public schools of Alhambra, California, during the 1950s. He and other Protestants, and also Jewish students, attended classes in trailers brought to the school once a week while the Catholic children walked to the nearby Catholic church. Other, presumably more secular students stayed behind for study hall.

20. Harry S. Truman, "Message to the Congress on the State of the Union," January 21, 1946, *Public Papers of the Presidents* (Washington, D.C., 1946), p. 65; *Congressional Record*, Luther Patrick, July 17, 1945; Estes Kefauver, November 27, 1945; Clifford R. Hope, March 13, 1945.

21. *New York Times*, April 26, 1946, 15:1.

22. *Everson v. Board of Education* 330 U.S. 1 (1947), in Fellman, ed., *Supreme Court and Education*, pp. 6-15.

23. *Everson v. Board of Education*, in Fellman, ed., *Supreme Court and Education*, pp. 15-20.

24. *Everson v. Board of Education*, in Fellman, ed., *Supreme Court and Education*, pp. 6-31.

25. Press Release from the Office of Senator John F. Kennedy, April 21, 1960, included in the appendix of Albert J. Menendez, *John F. Kennedy: Catholic and Humanist* (Buffalo, NY, n.d.), pp. 114-115.

26. Howard M. Squadron, testimony on behalf of American Jewish Congress at House subcommittee hearing held in New York, July 10, 1995, cited in Tricia Andryszewski, *School Prayer: A History of the Debate* (Springfield, NJ, 1997), pp. 17-18.

27. *Engel v. Vitale* 370 U.S. 421 (1962).

28. The material on the Roths and the debate around the case is from Dudley, *Engel v. Vitale.*

29. Engel v. Vitale 370 U.S. 421 (1962); see also Dudley, *Engel v. Vitale.*

30. *Abington School District v. Schempp* 374 U.S. 203 (1963); for detail, see also Andryszewski, *School Prayer:.*

31. *Abington School District v. Schempp.*

32. *Abington School District v. Schempp.*

33. Dudley, ed., *Engle v. Vitale*, pp. 79-80.

34. John F. Kennedy, *Public Papers of the Presidents*, (Washington, D.C., 1962), pp. 510-511.

35. William O. Douglas, *The Bible and the Schools* (Boston, 1966), pp. 60-61.

36. Andryszewski, *School Prayer*, pp. 7, 48-53.

37. Lyndon B. Johnson, "Special Message to the Congress, January 12, 1965," "Remarks in Johnson City, Texas, upon Signing the Elementary and Secondary Education Bill, April 11, 1965," *Public Papers of the Presidents*, (Washington, D.C., 1965), pp. 25-33 and 413-414.

38. Barbara C. Jordan and Elispeth D. Rostow, *The Great Society: A Twenty Year Critique* (Austin, TX, 1986), p. 106

39. *Board of Education v. Allen* 392 U.S. 236 (1968); *Lemon v. Kurtzman*, 403 U.S. 602 (1971); both cases are discussed in Melvin I. Urofsky, "Church and State: the Religion Clauses" in David J. Bodenhamer and James W. Ely, Jr., eds., *The Bill of Rights in Modern America After 200 Years* (Bloomington, 1993), pp. 65-66.

CHAPTER EIGHT

1. Martin Luther King, Jr., "A Time to Break Silence," address at Riverside Church, New York City, April 4, 1967, "The Trumpet of Conscience," November-December, 1967 on the Canadian Broadcasting Corporation, in James M. Washington, ed., *A Testament of Hope: The Essential Writings and Speeches of Martin Luther King, Jr.* (San Francisco, 1986).

2. For a very thoughtful analysis of the links between the politics of the post-Great Society years and schools, see Ira Shore, *Culture Wars: School and Society in the Conservative Restoration, 1969-1984* (Boston, 1986).

3. Leon Friedman and William F. Levantrosser, *Richard M. Nixon: Politician, President, Administrator* (New York, 1991), provides a very thoughtful analysis of the Nixon campaigns and administration. See especially chaps. 9, 15, and 16. Balzano is author of chap. 15, see pp. 260-261, Colson is cited on pp. 275-278; see esp. Kevin P. Phillips, *The Emerging Republican Majority* (New Rochelle, NY, 1969).

4. *Epperson v. Arkansas* 393 U.S. 97 (1968)

5. Herbert M. Kliebard, *The Struggle for the American Curriculum, 1893-1958* (Boston, 1986), p. 268.

6. *Epperson v. Arkansas.*

7. John T. Scopes, *The Center of the Storm: Memoirs of John T. Scopes* (New York, 1967).

8. *Epperson v. Arkansas;* much of the discussion of the case is taken from Edward J. Larson, *Summer for the Gods* (New York, 1997), pp. 247-266.

9. Wendell R. Bird, "Freedom from Establishment and Unneutrality in Public School Instruction and Religious School Regulation," *Harvard Journal of Law and Public Policy* 2 (1979): 179, cited in the discussion of the Epperson case in Larson, *Summer for the Gods*, 257-9.

10. *Edwards v. Aguillard* 482 U.S. 578 (1987); see also Larson, *Summer For the Gods*, pp. 260.

11. Lily Eng, "Anti-Evolutionist Teacher Sues School District," *Los Angeles Times*, October 1, 1991, cited in Stephen L. Carter, *The Culture of Disbelief: How American Law and Politics Trivialize Religious Devotion* (New York, 1993), p. 158.

12. John W. Whitehead, *The Rights of Religious Persons in Public Education* (Wheaton, IL, 1994) pp. 19-20.

13. Warren A. Nord, *Religion & American Education: Rethinking a National Dilemma* (Chapel Hill, NC, 1995), pp. 289-291.

14. Donald Kennedy, "Helping Schools to Teach Evolution," *Chronicle of Higher Education* 44 (August 7, 1998): 48.

15. Carter, *Culture of Disbelief*, p. 169; see Michael Apple, *Official Knowledge: Democratic Education in a Conservative Age* (New York, 1993).

16. The National Academy of Science, *Teaching About Evolution and the Nature of Science* (Washington, D.C., 1998), p. 1, available from the National Academy of Science

    http://www.nap.edu/readingroom/books/evolution98.

17. National Academy of Science, *Teaching About Evolution and the Nature of Science*, p. 3.

18. Donald Kennedy, "Helping Schools to Teach Evolution," 48; Leakey is cited in Carter, *Culture of Disbelief*, p. 159; The National Academy of Science, *Teaching About Evolution and the Nature of Science.*

19. National Academy of Science, *Teaching About Evolution and the Nature of Science*, pp. 7-8.

20. Nord, *Religion and American Education*, p. 291.

21. Nel Noddings, *Educating for Intelligent Belief or Unbelief* (New York, 1993), pp. 133-134.

22. Americans United for Separation of Church and State, "God and the Pubic Schools: Religion, Education & Your Rights," pamphlet.

23. Citations and description are from Eugene F. Provenzo, Jr., *Religious Fundamentalism and American Education: The Battle for the Public Schools* (Albany, NY, 1990), pp. 20-24.

24. Michael W. Apple, *Official Knowledge: Democratic Education in a Conservative Age* (New York, 1993), pp. 30 and 48-49; see also James Moffett, *Storm in the Mountains* (Carbondale, IL, 1988).

25. Provenzo, *Religious Fundamentalism*, pp. 23-24.

26. See Apple, *Official Knowledge*, chaps. 1 and 2, and Carter, *Culture of Disbelief*, pp. 168-176.

27. One point of disagreement centers on even what the movement should be called. I am mindful of Stephen Carter's warning that secular America tends to run many different groups together: "Christian fundamentalists . . . the evangelicals . . . the folks who want classroom prayer in public schools . . . John Cardinal O'Connor . . . and the 'scientific' creationists." (*Culture of Disbelief*, p. 24). The definition of who was an evangelical has changed dramatically from the nineteenth century—when it included most Protestants—to the twentieth, when it includes only a small minority. Most evangelicals are not fundamentalists, and some fundamentalists and many evangelicals do not believe in "creation science." Some level of sophisticated analysis and respect is necessary to wend one's way through the various groups and definitions. In general, I have used "conservative Christians" or "conservative religious groups," yet I remain well aware that these groups disagree with each other as much as those who call themselves liberals, progressives, or secular people.

28. Catherine A. Lugg, *For God and Country: Conservatism and American School Policy* (New York, 1996), p. 22

29. Lugg, *For God and Country*, p. 22.

30. Ralph Reed, *Active Faith* (New York, 1996), p. 105; Richard A. Viguerie, *The New Right: We're Ready to Lead* (Falls Church, VA, 1981), p. 124; both cited in Justin Watson, *The Christian Coalition: Dreams of Restoration, Demands for Recognition* (New York, 1997), p. 20.

31. *Conservative Digest*, (October 1980) pp. 11, 17, cited in Robert C. Liebman and Robert Wuthnow, *The New Christian Right: Mobilization and Legitimation* (New York, 1983), p. 27.

32. Mark E. Dudley, *Engel v. Vitale (1962): Religion and the Schools* (New York, 1995), pp. 63 and 71 (quotations from Spellman and Chandler are from this source); Edwin Scott Gaustad, *A Religious History of America, New Revised Edition* (New York, 1990), pp. 319-320.

33. "Preachers in Politics," *U.S. News & World Report*, September 24, 1979 p. 37, cited in Justin Watson, *The Christian Coalition: Dreams of Restoration, Demands for Recognition* (New York, 1997), p. 34.

34. Robert C. Liebman and Robert Wuthnow, *The New Christian Right: Mobilization and Legitimation* (New York, 1983), esp. chaps 1 and 5.

35. Ronald Reagan, *An American Life* (New York, 1990), pp. 196-197, cited in Lugg, *For God and Country*, p. 8.
36. Lugg, *For God and Country*, pp. 71 and 84-89.
37. Lugg, *For God and Country*, p. 97.
38. Lugg, *For God and Country*, p. 101.
39. Tricia Andryszewski, *School Prayer: A History of the Debate* (Springfield, NJ, 1997), pp. 59-60.
40. Andryszewski, *School Prayer*, pp. 59-69, see esp. p. 62.
41. *Board of Education of the Westside Community Schools v. Mergens* 496 U.S. 226 (1990); see Andryszewski, *School Prayer*, pp. 59-69, esp. p. 66.
42. Whitehead, *The Rights of Religious Persons in Public Education*.
43. The material and citations on the Reagan educational agenda is from Lugg's exhaustive account, *For God and Country*.
44. Liebman and Wuthnow, *The New Christian Right*, p. 36.

CHAPTER NINE

1. *Congressional Record*, June 4, 1998, pp. H4078-H4112.
2. Justin Watson, *The Christian Coalition: Dreams of Restoration, Demands for Recognition* (New York, 1997), p. 30; see Sean Wilentz, "God and Man at Lynchburg," *The New Republic*, April 25, 1988, p. 30, cited in Watson.
3. Watson, *Christian Coalition*, pp. 29-37.
4. Watson, *Christian Coalition*, p. 39.
5. Watson, *Christian Coalition*, pp. 42-52.
6. Watson, *Christian Coalition*, pp. 51-87.
7. Watson, *Christian Coalition*, p. 170-171; Stephen L. Carter, *The Culture of Disbelief: How American Law and Politics Trivialize Religious Devotion*, (New York: 1993), p. 264.
8. Watson, *Christian Coalition*, pp. 170-174.
9. Watson, *Christian Coalition*, pp. 170-174; see also the Christian Coalition web site
       http://www.cc.org
       I am grateful to Peter Niemeyer for further research on the Christian Coalition.
10. Watson, *Christian Coalition*, pp. 3 and 175.
11. See Ralph Reed, *Active Faith* (New York, 1996), pp. 238-9.
12. I am indebted to Cathleen Dennison, Delia Gerraughty, J. Oliver Lee, Jr., and Christine Sandoval for research on the Eagle Forum, the "Education Reporter," and the "Phyllis Schafly Report."
13. Bob Rosio, *The Culture War in America* (Lafayette, LA, 1995).
14. The information on the two organizations is drawn from their mailings and pamphlets. For Americans United, see:
       http://www.au.org
       for People for the American Way:
       www.pfaw.org.
15. http://www.au.org.
16. http://www.pfaw.org.
17. The material in the preceding paragraphs is taken from Scott DeNicola, "The Defamation of Two Cities," *Focus on the Family Citizen*, (October 16, 1995), pp. 10-12; the September 19, 1994 issue of *Focus on the Family Citizen;* People for

the American Way fundraising letter, May, 1997; People for the American Way, *The San Diego Model: A Community Battles the Religious Right* (April, 1993); and Eugene F. Provenzo, Jr., *Religious Fundamentalism and American Education: The Battle for the Public Schools* (Albany, NY, 1990), pp. 54-57.

18. David C. Berliner, "Educational Psychology Meets the Christian Right: Differing Views of Children, Schooling, Teaching, and Learning," *Teachers College Record* 98:3 (Spring, 1997), pp. 381-416.

19. Berliner, "Educational Psychology," pp. 384-385.

20. Pat Robertson, *The Turning Tide: The End of Liberalism and the Rise of Common Sense* (Dallas, 1993), p. 229, cited in Berliner, "Educational Psychology," p. 386.

21. Berliner, "Educational Psychology," pp. 387-391.

22. Berliner, "Educational Psychology," p. 391; see also National Council of Teachers of Mathematics, *Curriculum and Evaluation Standards for School Mathematics* (Reston, VA, 1989), p. 15.

23. Berliner, "Educational Psychology," pp. 412-413.

24. Stephen L. Carter, *The Culture of Disbelief* (New York, 1993), pp. 267-8.

25. *Employment Division v. Smith* 110 U.S. 1595 (1990); *Congressional Record*, May 11, 1993, pp. H2356-H2363; National School Board Association, *Religion, Education, and the U.S. Constitution* (Alexandria, VA,. 1994), p. 155, cited in Tricia Andryszewski, *School Prayer: A History of the Debate* (Springfield, NJ, 1997), p. 70; *Boerne v. Flores* 117 U.S. 2157 (1997); Americans United for Separation of Church and State, "Analysis of City of Boerne v. Flores,"
    http://www.au.org

26. Edwin Scott Gaustad, *A Religious History of America, New Revised Edition* (New York, 1990), pp. 324-327.

27. *Wallace v. Jaffree* 472 U.S. 38 (1985); Andryszewski, *School Prayer*, pp. 7, 55-58 and Mark E. Dudley, *Engel v. Vitale (1962): Religion and the Schools* (New York, 1995), pp. 82-86, both provide a good overview of the moment of silence debate, including all of the court cases cited here.

28. *Lee v. Weisman* 112 U.S. 2649 (1992); Andryszewski, *School Prayer*, pp. 71-75; see also *Congressional Record*, June 4, 1998, p. H4080.

29. Andryszewski, *School Prayer*, pp. 75-83.

30. *Congressional Record*, April 11, 1994, pp. S4061-S4063.

31. *Congressional Record*, October 3, 1994, pp. S13899-S13901.

32. Andryszewski, *School Prayer*, pp. 87-95.

33. "Text of President Clinton's Memorandum on Religion in Schools," *New York Times*, July 13, 1995, cited and discussed in Andryszewski, *School Prayer*, pp. 87-95; U. S. Department of Education, "Religious Expression in Public Schools, August, 1995, rev. May, 1998
    www.ed.gov/Speeches/08-1995/religion.html
    see also the discussion of prayer in chapter ten.

34. *New York Times*, November 8, 1997, p. 1; *Education Week*, November 5, 1997, pp. 1 and 16.

35. *Education Week*, December 10, 1997, pp. 1 and 12.

36. Christian Coalition web site
    http://www.cc.org

37. The reporting of the debate, in this and subsequent paragraphs, including all quotations, is from the *Congressional Record*, June 4, 1998, pp. H4078-H4112.

38. *Congressional Record*, June 4, 1998, pp. H4078-H4112.

CHAPTER TEN

1. *Congressional Record,* June 4, 1998, pp. H4078-H4112. The amendment is discussed in detail in the previous chapter.
2. "Religious Expression in Public Schools," U. S. Department of Education Document, May 1998.
3. "Radio Address of the President to the Nation, May 30, 1998."
4. *Congressional Record,* June 4, 1998, pp. H4088 and H4091.
5. Starhawk, "Witchcraft as Goddess Religion," in C. Spretnak, ed., *The Politics of Women's Spirituality* (Garden City, NY, 1982), p. 51.
6. Martin Buber, "Martin Buber, Autobiographical Fragments," in P. Schilpp and M. Friedman, eds., *The Philosophy of Martin Buber* (LaSalle, IL, 1967), p. 8; Starhawk and Buber are both cited and discussed in Nel Noddings, *Education for Intelligent Belief or Unbelief* (New York, 1993), pp. 72, 140.
7. See Noddings, *Education for Intelligent Belief or Unbelief,* p. 140; *Congressional Record,* June 4, 1998, pp. H4078-H4079.
8. *Agostini v. Felton* 117 U.S. 759 (1997); *Aguilar v. Felton* 473 U.S. 402 (1985), *New York Times,* June 24, 1997; Alvin Schiff, *The Jewish Day School in America;* Rabbi Abramson is quoted in Jeff Archer, "Breaking for Tradition," *Education Week,* March 18, 1998, pp. 36-42
9. *Agostini v. Felton; Aguilar v. Felton; New York Times,* June 24, 1997, p. 1; Mark Walsh, "Religious Schools Welcome Back On-Site Title I Services," *Education Week,* June 24, 1998, p. 8; Americans United for Separation of Church and State, "Analysis of Agostini v. Felton."
10. *Education Week,* February 19, 1997, November 5, 1997, June 24, 1998, pp. 1, 14-15, August 5, 1998, p. 19; People for the American Way, Press Release, September 4, 1997.
11. Robert Lowe and Barbara Miner, eds., *Selling Out Our Schools: Vouchers, Markets, and the Future of Public Education* (Milwaukee, 1998); see also Barbara Miner, "Vouchers: Where's the Public Accountability? or Public Dollars and Private Schools: A Bad Mix," email distributed by Rethinking Schools.
12. *Education Week,* February 19, 1997, November 5, 1997, June 24, 1998, pp. 1, 14-15, August 5, 1998, p. 19.
13. John E. Chubb and Terry M. Moe, *Politics, Markets, and America's Schools* (New York, 1989); Michael W. McConnell, "Commentary," in James T. Sears with James C. Carper, *Curriculum, Religion, and Public Education: Conversations for an Enlarging Public Square* (New York, 1998), pp. 33-35.
14. *Education Week,* February 19, 1997, November 5, 1997, June 24, 1998, pp. 1, 14-15, August 5, 1998, p. 19; Barbara Miner, "Vouchers: Where's the Public Accountability?"; People for the American Way, Press Release, September 4, 1997.
15. Donald Kennedy, "Helping Schools to Teach Evolution," *Chronicle of Higher Education,* August 7, 1998, p. A48.
16. Carl Sagan, *The Demon-Haunted World: Science As a Candle in the Dark* (New York, 1996), pp. 30, 171-172; Kennedy, "Helping Schools to Teach Evolution"; Hebrews 11:1, Revised Standard Version; David Baltimore, Letter to the Editor, *The New Yorker* (1997).
17. Noddings, *Education for Intelligent Belief or Unbelief,* pp. 143-144.
18. Thomas C. Hunt and James C. Carper, *Religion and Schooling in Contemporary America: Confronting Our Cultural Pluralism* (New York, 1997), p. xi.

19. *Abington School District v. Schempp* 374 U.S. 203 (1963); *Epperson v. Arkansas* 393 U.S. 97 (1968).

20. Warren A. Nord, *Religion & American Education: Rethinking a National Dilemma* (Chapel Hill, NC, 1995), pp. xiii-xiv, 1.

21. Noddings, *Education for Intelligent Belief or Unbelief,* pp. 78-79.

22. Noddings, *Education for Intelligent Belief or Unbelief,* p. 11, see also p. 1.

23. Harvey Cox, "The Secular City-Twenty-five Years Later," *The Secular City: Secularization and Urbanization in Theological Perspective, Twenty-Fifth Anniversary Edition* (New York, 1990), pp. xi-xii.

24. *Congressional Record,* June 4, 1998, p. H4086.

25. William O. Douglas, *The Bible and the Schools* (Boston, 1966), p. 45

26. Shirley Brice Heath and Milbrey W. McLaughlin, eds., *Identity and Inner-City Youth: Beyond Ethnicity and Gender* (New York, 1993), pp. 6, 214, 222; I reviewed this book in Book Review in *Teachers College Record* 96:2 (Winter 1994), pp. 347-352.

27. Heath and McLaughlin, *Identity and Inner-City Youth,* p. 59.

28. Justin Watson, *The Christian Coalition: Dreams of Restoration, Demands for Recognition* (New York, 1997).

29. Stephen L. Carter, *The Culture of Disbelief: How American Law and Politics Trivialize Religious Devotion* (New York, 1993), p. 52.

30. Martin Luther King, Jr., "Where Do We Go from Here: Chaos or Community?" (1967), reprinted in James M. Washington, ed., *A Testament of Hope: The Essential Writings and Speeches of Martin Luther King, Jr.* (San Francisco, 1986), pp. 555-633.

31. Stephen Arons, *Compelling Belief: The Culture of American Schooling* (New York, 1983), pp. viii-ix.

32. Michael W. Apple, "Are Markets and Standards Democratic?" Book review of Geoff Whitty, Sally Power, and David Halpin, *Devolution and Choice in Education: The School, the State and the Market* (Bristol, PA, 1998), *Educational Researcher* 27:6 (August-September, 1998): 27.

FOR FURTHER READING

CHAPTER ONE: FROM HOLY COMMONWEALTH TO THE STRANGE COMPROMISE OF 1789

Sidney E. Mead, *The Lively Experiment: The Shaping of Christianity in America*. New York: Harper & Row, 1963. Still the definitive source on the mix of social and political forces leading to America's "lively experiment" in separating church and state.

OTHER SOURCES INCLUDE:

John Calam, *Parsons & Pedagogues: The Society for the Propagation of the Gospel Adventure in American Education*. New York: Columbia University Press, 1971.

Henry Steele Commager, *Noah Webster's American Spelling Book*. New York: Teachers College Press, 1962.

Paul Leicester Ford, editor, *The New-England Primer*. New York: Teachers College Press, 1962.

Gordon C. Lee, *Crusade Against Ignorance: Thomas Jefferson on Education*. New York: Teachers College Press, 1961.

CHAPTER TWO: CREATING AN AMERICAN COMMON SCHOOL AND A COMMON FAITH—HORACE MANN AND THE PROTESTANT PUBLIC SCHOOLS, 1789-1860

Lawrence A. Cremin, editor, *The Republic and the School: Horace Mann on the Education of Free Men*. New York: Teachers College Press, 1957. An easily accessible collection of Mann's major reports.

James W. Fraser, *Pedagogue for God's Kingdom: Lyman Beecher and the Second Great Awakening*. Lanham, MD: University Press of America, 1985. Its primary focus is the particular role of Lyman Beecher in building an evangelical movement in the United States in the first half of the twentieth century, but it also includes a detailed analysis of the development of public education in the Midwest.

Jonathan Messerli, *Horace Mann: A Biography*. New York: Alfred A. Knopf, 1972. The definitive biography of Mann.

OTHER SOURCES INCLUDE:

American Book Company, *McGuffey's Fifth Eclectic Reader*. Cincinnati: American Book Company, 1836, 1920.

American Book Company, *McGuffey's Sixth Eclectic Reader*. Cincinnati: American Book Company, 1836, 1920.

Charles Leslie Glenn, Jr., *The Myth of the Common School*. Amherst: University of Massachusetts Press, 1988.

Polly Welts Kaufman, *Women Teachers on the Frontier*. New Haven, CT: Yale University Press, 1984.

Stanley K. Schultz, *The Culture Factory: Boston Public Schools, 1789-1860*. New York: Oxford University Press, 1973.

Kathryn Kish Sklar, *Catharine Beecher: A Study in American Domesticity*. New Haven, CT: Yale University Press, 1973.

CHAPTER THREE: WHO DEFINES WHAT IS COMMON? ROMAN CATHOLICS AND THE COMMON SCHOOL MOVEMENT, 1801-1892

As a number of historians have noted, the comprehensive history of Catholic parochial schools remains to be written.

Carl F. Kaestle, *The Evolution of an Urban School System: New York City, 1750, 1850*. Cambridge, MA: Harvard University Press, 1973. Probably the best source on Bishop Hughes' battle for state aid for parochial schools.

Vincent P. Lannie, *Public Money and Parochial Education: Bishop Hughes, Governor Seward, and the New York School Controversy*. Cleveland: Case Western Reserve University Press, 1968. The most thorough overview of this controversy.

Neil G. McCluskey, S.J., *Catholic Education in America: A Documentary History*. New York: Teachers College Press, 1964. A most useful collection of documents on nineteenth century Catholic education.

OTHER SOURCES INCLUDE:

J. A. Burns, *The Catholic School System in the United States: Its Principles, Origin, and Establishment* (New York: 1908).

Robert D. Cross, "Origins of the Catholic Parochial Schools in America," *American Benedictine Review* 16 (1965): 194-209.

Diane Ravitch, *The Great School Wars: New York City, 1805-1973*. New York: Basic Books, 1974.

James W. Sanders, *The Education of an Urban Minority: Catholics in Chicago, 1833-1965*. New York: Oxford University Press, 1977.

————, "Boston Catholics and the School Question, 1825-1907," in James W. Fraser, Henry L. Allen, and Sam Barnes, *From Common School to*

Magnet School: Selected Essays in the History of Boston's Schools. Boston: Boston Public Library, 1979.

CHAPTER FOUR: LITERACY IN THE AFRICAN AMERICAN COMMUNITY: CHURCH AND SCHOOL IN SLAVE AND FREE COMMUNITIES, 1802-1902

James D. Anderson, *The Education of Blacks in the South, 1860-1935.* Chapel Hill: University of North Carolina Press, 1988. The most helpful source for understanding the growth and emergence of African American schooling in the Reconstruction and post-Reconstruction eras.

John Hope Franklin and Alfred A. Moss, Jr., *From Slavery to Freedom: A History of African Americans,* 7th edition. New York: Alfred A. Knopf, 1994. Franklin frames the entire conversation.

OTHER SOURCES INCLUDE:

Anne M. Boylan, *Sunday School: The Formation of an American Institution, 1790-1880.* New Haven, CT: Yale University Press, 1988.

W. E. B. DuBois, *The Souls of Black Folk.* Greenwich, CT: Fawcett Publications, 1953, 1964.

Albert J. Raboteau, *Slave Religion: The "Invisible Institution" in the Antebellum South.* New York: Oxford University Press, 1978.

Thomas L. Webber, *Deep Like the Rivers: Education in the Slave Quarter Community, 1831-1865.* New York: W. W. Norton, 1978.

CHAPTER FIVE: NATIVE AMERICAN RELIGION, CHRISTIAN MISSIONARIES, AND GOVERNMENT SCHOOLS, 1819-1926

David Wallace Adams, *Education for Extinction: American Indians and the Boarding School Experience, 1875-1928.* Lawrence: University Press of Kansas, 1995. Tells the later stages of Indian education with detail and passion.

OTHER SOURCES INCLUDE:

James Axtell, *The European and the Indian: Essays in the Ethnohistory of Colonial North America.* New York: Oxford University Press, 1981.

R. Pierce Beaver, *Church, State, and the American Indian.* St. Louis: Concordia Publishing House, 1966.

Robert F. Berkhofer, Jr., *Salvation and the Savage: An Analysis of Protestant Missions and American Indian Response, 1787-1862.* University of Kentucky Press, 1965.

Michael C. Coleman, "The Responses of American Indian Children to Presbyterian Schooling in the Nineteenth Century: An Analysis through Missionary Sources," *History of Education Quarterly* 27: 4 (Winter, 1987): 473-497.

Mary Crow Dog, with Richard Erdoes, *Lakota Woman*. New York: Harper, 1990.

E. Jennifer Monaghan, "'She loved to read in good Books': Literacy and the Indians of Martha's Vineyard, 1643-1725, *History of Education Quarterly* 30:4 (Winter, 1990): 493-521.

Francis Paul Prucha, editor, *Documents of United States Indian Policy*, 2nd edition, expanded. Lincoln: University of Nebraska Press, 1990.

———, *The Great Father: The United States Government and the American Indians*, 2 vols. Lincoln: University of Nebraska Press, 1984.

CHAPTER SIX: PROTESTANT, CATHOLIC, JEW: IMMIGRATION AND NATIVISM FROM THE BLAINE AMENDMENT TO THE SCOPES TRIAL, 1875-1925.

Two first-rate new studies provide a careful introduction to the first and the last years of this era:

Edward J. Larson, *Summer for the Gods: The Scopes Trial and America's Continuing Debate Over Science and Religion* (New York: Basic Books, 1997). Now the definitive work on the Scopes trial.

George M. Marsden, *Fundamentalism and American Culture: The Shaping of Twentieth-Century Evangelicalism: 1870-1925*. New York: Oxford University Press, 1980. The most helpful book for a general understanding of the growth of fundamentalism as a religious movement within American Protestantism.

Ward M. McAfee, *Religion, Race, and Reconstruction: The Public School in The Politics of the 1870s*. Albany: State University of New York Press, 1998. A brilliant and detailed study of the relationship of anti-Catholicism, the ending of Reconstruction, and the renewal of the Republican public school agenda.

OTHER SOURCES INCLUDE:

Mary Antin, *The Promised Land*. Boston: Houghton Mifflin, 1911.

Ray A. Billington, *The Protestant Crusade, 1800-1860: A Study of the Origins of American Nativism*. New York: Macmillan Company, 1938.

Kathleen M. Blee, *Women of the Klan: Racism and Gender in the 1920s*. Berkeley: University of California Press, 1991.

Ray Ginger, *Six Days or Forever? Tennessee v. John Thomas Scopes*. New York: Oxford University Press, 1958.

Robert T. Handy, *A Christian America: Protestant Hopes and Historical Realities*. New York: Oxford University Press, 1971.

David F. Labaree, *The Making of an American High School*. New Haven, CT: Yale University Press, 1988.

Edward J. Larson, *Trial and Error: The American Controversy Over Creation and Evolution*. New York: Oxford University Press, 1985.

George M. Marsden, *Religion and American Culture*. Fort Worth, TX: Harcourt Brace Jovanovich, 1990.

William G. McLoughlin, *Billy Sunday Was His Real Name*. Chicago: University of Chicago Press, 1955.

William J. Reese, *The Origins of the American High School*. New Haven, CT: Yale University Press, 1995.

Ernest R. Sandeen, *The Roots of Fundamentalism: British and American Millenarianism, 1800-1930*. Chicago: University of Chicago Press, 1970.

CHAPTER SEVEN: PRAYER, BIBLE READING, AND FEDERAL MONEY: THE EXPANDING ROLE OF CONGRESS AND THE SUPREME COURT, 1925-1968

Appropriately, perhaps, two recent publications for use in school discussion of the issues represent the most thoughtful and comprehensive analysis of the great prayer and Bible reading debates of the 1960s. They are:

Tricia Andryszewski, *School Prayer: A History of the Debate*, Springfield, NJ: Enslow Publishers, 1997.

Mack E. Dudley, *Engel v. Vitale (1962): Religion and the Schools*, New York: Twenty-First Century Books/Henry Holt, 1995.

FOR FURTHER READING, SEE:

Joel S. Berke and Michael W. Kirst, *Federal Aid to Education: Who Benefits? Who Governs?* Lexington, MA: D. C. Heath and Company, 1972.

David J. Bodenhamer and James W. Ely, Jr., editors, *The Bill of Rights in Modern America After 200 Years*, Bloomington: Indiana University Press, 1993.

John Dewey, *A Common Faith*. New Haven, CT: Yale University Press, 1934.

William O. Douglas, *The Bible and the Schools*. Boston: Little, Brown, 1966.

David Fellman, *The Supreme Court and Education*, 3rd edition, New York: Teachers College Press, 1976.

Frances FitzGerald, *America Revised: History Schoolbooks in the Twentieth Century*. New York: Vintage Books, 1979.

Barbara C. Jordan and Elispeth D. Rostow, *The Great Society: A Twenty Year Critique*, Austin, TX: Lyndon Baines Johnson Library, 1986.

Herbert M. Kliebard, *The Struggle for the American Curriculum, 1893-1958*. Boston: Routledge & Kegan Paul, 1986.

Robert W. Lynn and Elliott Wright, *The Big Little School: Two Hundred Years of the Sunday School*, 2nd edition. Nashville: Abingdon, 1971.

Albert J. Menenedez, *John F. Kennedy: Catholic and Humanist*, Buffalo, NY: Prometheus Books, n.d. (approximately 1980).

David Tyack and Elisabeth Hansot, *Managers of Virtue: Public School Leadership in America, 1820-1980*. New York: Basic Books, 1982.

CHAPTER EIGHT: CULTURE WARS, CREATIONISM, AND THE REAGAN REVOLUTION, 1968-1990

Catherine A. Lugg, *For God and Country: Conservatism and American School Policy*. New York: Peter Lang, 1996. A very clearly focused and detailed study of the interplay of right-wing politics and Reagan administration policy from the perspective of a critic.

The National Academy of Sciences, *Teaching About Evolution and the Nature of Science*. Washington, D.C.: National Academy Press, 1998. A very helpful and respectful report on the importance of the study of evolution and on ways to teach the subject with respect for all students.

Eugene F. Provenzo, Jr., *Religious Fundamentalism and American Education: The Battle for the Public Schools*. Albany, NY: State University of New York Press, 1990. A goldmine of material on the emergence of fundamentalism as a force for change regarding school curriculum, especially in the arena of evolution, prayer, and family issues.

OTHER SOURCES INCLUDE:

Stephen Arons, *Compelling Belief: The Culture of American Schooling*. New York: McGraw-Hill, 1983.

Tim M. Berra, *Evolution and the Myth of Creationism: A Basic Guide to the Facts in the Evolution Debate*. Stanford, CA: Stanford University Press, 1990.

Leon Friedman and William F. Levantrosser, editors, *Richard M. Nixon: Politician, President, Administrator*. New York: Greenwood Press, 1991.

Robert C. Liebman and Robert Wuthnow, *The New Christian Right: Mobilization and Legitimation*. New York: Aldine, 1983.

James Moffett, *Storm in the Mountains: A Case of Censorship, Conflict, and Consciousness*. Carbondale: Southern Illinois University Press, 1988.

Kevin P. Phillips, *The Emerging Republican Majority*. New Rochelle, NY: Arlington House, 1969.

Susan D. Rose, *Keeping Them Out of the Hands of Satan: Evangelical Schooling in America*. New York: Routledge, 1988.

Michael Ruse, editor, *But Is It Science? The Philosophical Question in the Creation/Evolution Controversy*. Amherst, NY: Prometheus Books, 1996.

Ira Shor, *Culture Wars: School and Society in the Conservative Restoration, 1969-1984.* Boston: Routledge & Kegan Paul, 1986.

James M. Washington, editor, *A Testiment of Hope: The Essential Writings and Speeches of Martin Luther King, Jr.* San Francisco: Harper Collins, 1986.

Ann E. Weiss, *God and Government.* Boston: Houghton Mifflin, 1982.

CHAPTER NINE: CHANGING SCHOOL BOARDS, CURRICULUM, AND THE CONSTITUTION, 1990-

Melvin I. Urofsky and Martha May, *The New Christian Right: Political and Social Issues.* New York: Garland Publishing, 1996. A valuable collection of a very wide range of literature debating the role and value of the religious right in the 1990s.

Justin Watson, *The Christian Coalition: Dreams of Restoration, Demands for Recognition.* New York: St. Martin's Press, 1997. The clearest and best discussion of the Christian Coalition and of many of the religious right movements leading up to the current moment. Watson combines a thoughtful review of the issues and respect for the emerging religious right with incisive political judgments.

OTHER SOURCES INCLUDE:

David C. Berliner, "Educational Psychology Meets the Christian Right: Differing Views of Children, Schooling, Teaching, and Learning," *Teachers College Record* 98:3 (Spring, 1997), 381-416.

David C. Berliner and Bruce J. Biddle, *The Manufactured Crisis: Myths, Fraud, and the Attack on America's Schools.* Reading, MA: Addison-Wesley, 1995.

Robert Boston, *The Most Dangerous Man in America? Pat Robertson and the Rise of the Christian Coalition.* Amherst, NY: Prometheus Books, 1996.

———. *Why the Religious Right Is Wrong: About Separation of Church & State.* Buffalo, NY: Prometheus Books, 1993.

J. Chubb and T. Moe, *Politics, Markets, and America's Schools.* Washington, DC: Brookings Institution, 1990.

James Moffett, *Storm in the Mountains.* Carbondale: Southern Illinois University Press, 1988.

Ralph Reed, *Active Faith.* New York: Free Press, 1996

Pat Robertson, *America's Date with Destiny.* Nashville: Thomas Nelson, 1986

Bob Rosio, *The Culture War in America: A Society in Chaos.* Lafayette, LA: Huntington House, 1995.

John W. Whitehead, *The Rights of Religious Persons in Public Education.* Wheaton, IL: Crossway Books, 1994.

Raymond Williams, *The Long Revolution.* London: Chatto and Windus, 1961.

CHAPTER TEN: WHAT'S NEXT? PRAYERS, VOUCHERS, AND CREATIONISM: THE BATTLE FOR THE SCHOOLS OF THE TWENTY-FIRST CENTURY

Nel Noddings, *Educating for Intelligent Belief or Unbelief.* New York: Teachers College Press, 1993. In my mind this is the most helpful book in framing the conversation about the appropriate ways to approach the issues of religion and public education today.

A number of thoughtful books have emerged in the last few years seeking a new approach to the issue of religion and the schools. I have found three especially helpful. While I have disagreements with all of them, I recommend them to anyone seeking a better understanding of contemporary debates.

Stephen L. Carter, *The Culture of Disbelief: How American Law and Politics Trivialize Religious Devotion.* New York: Basic Books, 1993.

Warren A. Nord, *Religion & American Education: Rethinking a National Dilemma.* Chapel Hill: University of North Carolina Press, 1995.

James T. Sears with James C. Carper, *Curriculum, Religion and Public Education: Conversations for an Enlarging Public Square.* New York: Teachers College Press, 1998.

This chapter's approach to the issues that have emerged around the relationship between conservative religion and public school policy is significantly informed by the work of Michael Apple, although he may not agree with all aspects of my interpretation. Apple's most recent work is Cultural Politics and Education, *New York: Teachers College Press, 1996. Others include:*

Michael Apple, *Ideology and the Curriculum.* Boston and London: Routledge & Kegan Paul, 1979

———, *Teachers and Texts.* New York: Routledge, 1988.

———, *Official Knowledge: Democratic Education in a Conservative Age.* New York: Routledge, 1993.

SEE ALSO:

Harvey Cox, *The Secular City: Secularization and Urbanization in Theological Perspective, Twenty-fifth Anniversary Edition.* New York: Collier Books, 1965, 1990.

Barbara B. Gaddy, T. William Hall, and Robert J. Marzano, *School Wars: Resolving Our Conflicts Over Religion & Values.* San Francisco: Jossey-Bass, 1996.

John I. Goodlad, Roger Soder, and Kenneth A. Sirotnik, editors, *The Moral Dimensions of Teaching.* San Francisco: Jossey-Bass, 1990.

Thomas C. Hunt and James C. Carper, *Religion and Schooling in Contemporary America: Confronting Our Cultural Pluralism.* New York: Garland Publishing, 1997.

Philip W. Jackson, Robert E. Boostrom, and David T. Hansen, *The Moral Life of Schools*. San Francisco: Jossey-Bass, 1993.

George Johnson, *Fire in the Mind: Science, Faith, and the Search for Order.* New York: Vintage Books, 1995.

Warren A. Nord and Charles C. Haynes, *Taking Religion Seriously Across the Curriculum*. Alexandria, VA: Association for Supervision and Curriculum Development, 1998.

David E. Purpel, *The Moral and Spiritual Crisis in Education: A Curriculum for Justice & Compassion in Education*. New York: Bergin & Garvey, 1989.

Carl Sagan, *The Demon-Haunted World: Science as a Candle in the Dark*. New York: Ballantine, 1996.

UNDERSTANDING THE CONTEXT: GENERAL WORKS IN THE HISTORY OF EDUCATION

Lawrence A. Cremin, *American Education: The Colonial Experience, 1607-1783*. New York: Harper & Row, 1970.

———, *American Education: The National Experience, 1783-1876*. New York: Harper & Row, 1980.

———, *American Education: The Metropolitan Experience, 1876-1980*. New York: Harper & Row, 1988.

Joel Spring, *American Education*. New York: McGraw-Hill, 1994.

———, *The American School, 1642-1996*. New York: McGraw-Hill, 1997.

Ronald Takaki, *A Different Mirror: A History of Multicultural America*. Boston: Little, Brown, 1993.

Wayne Urban and Jennings Wagoner, Jr., *American Education: A History*. New York: McGraw-Hill, 1996.

FOR MORE INFORMATION ON THE MAJOR CONTEMPORARY ORGANIZATIONS, CONTACT THEIR WEB SITES

Americans United for Separation of Church and State: www.au.org

The Christian Coalition: www.cc.org

Education Week: www.edweek.org

People for the American Way: www.pfaw.org

U.S. Department of Education: www.ed.gov

INDEX